Transformational Grammar and the Teacher of English

Theory and Practice
Second Edition

OWEN THOMAS *and*
EUGENE R. KINTGEN
Indiana University

Holt, Rinehart and Winston, Inc.

New York   Chicago   San Francisco
Atlanta   Dallas   Montreal   Toronto

The stumbling way in which even the ablest of the scientists in every generation have had to fight through thickets of erroneous observations, misleading generalizations, inadequate formulations, and unconscious prejudice is rarely appreciated by those who obtain their scientific knowledge from textbooks.

James Bryant Conant, *Science and Common Sense*

Library of Congress Cataloging in Publication Data

Thomas, Owen Paul.
    Transformational grammar and the teacher of English.

    1.   English language—Grammar, generative.
I. Kintgen, Eugene R, joint author.   II. Title.
PE1112.T47   1974   425   73-16033

ISBN: 0-03-079605-9

Printed in the United States of America
4   5   6   7   8   090   9   8   7   6   5   4   3   2

Preface

This book is not only a complete revision of the first edition, it is also a somewhat different kind of book. Specifically, it has two major parts: the first—"Theory"—places transformational-generative grammar into the context of earlier forms of language study and then traces the history of transformational studies, covering the fifteen years that followed the initial publications in this new field; the second—"Practice"—presents a relatively detailed "grammar of English" that is based on the most fully developed form of the theory.

We believe that both these parts present material which is important for teachers and prospective teachers to consider. The general introduction that precedes them provides a starting point for a detailed discussion of the history of language study. Why have people studied language? What forms has this study taken? How has such study affected the writing of textbooks used in the schools? The introduction and Chapter 2 provide some answers to these questions; the exercises following Chapter 2 present additional questions; and the bibliography lists works that readers may wish to consult when searching for more comprehensive answers.

The chapters in the section on theory—which trace the history of transformational theory—grew out of our experience in working with teachers. We discovered that most teachers treated grammar—any grammar—as a kind of *fait accompli*. Traditional school-grammar had remained constant for more than two hundred years, and the so-called American structural grammar apparently consisted of a body of knowledge that most linguists accepted without question. (At least this was the impression left by many textbooks.) The earliest books devoted to transformational grammar seemed to be (and in some cases were) similar to traditional and structural books. They said, in effect, here is a description of English; you don't need to be particularly concerned with the source of the description; your job, as a teacher, is to present the description to children so they will learn to write and speak "Better English." At best, such claims represent an oversimplification; at worst, they are false. There is not now, and there probably never will be, a complete grammar of English. Additionally, the philosophies which underlie various statements about language are not universally accepted by all linguists. And, further, it is obviously becoming more and more important for teachers to know—and to discuss—*why* they are teaching a given subject, particularly when this subject is so vitally important as language is. The best way to overcome the simplifications, correct the false claims, and lay a foundation for a discussion of teaching philosophies is, in our opinion, to provide the kind of historical context that indicates why transformational grammarians reject earlier forms of study, how and why transformational theory has changed since 1957, and what additional changes teachers can expect as the theory continues to evolve. The section on theory seeks to do these things.

The second major part—"Practice"—is frankly eclectic. We include it because we believe that a knowledge of theory alone is insufficient for teachers; that is, we believe that a theory cannot be fully understood unless it is applied in practical situations. The section, in brief, provides considerable opportunity for a teacher or prospective teacher to work with a linguistic model. The model is based on the "standard theory" of transformational grammar (which is discussed in the section on theory), but it also incorporates—partially for illustration—more recent proposals. We chose the "standard theory" for our model because this theory occupies a unique position as the point of departure for most current research, and is thus an indispensable prerequisite for advanced study in language. In sum, we feel that teachers familiar with the "standard theory" will be better able to evaluate current research as well as current textbooks used in the schools.

A word about the exercises and discussion questions. The questions which follow Chapter 2 are, in most cases, open-ended. Consideration of these questions will provide a context for a reading of the rest of the book. The other chapters in the section on theory all conclude with questions and exercises which should help readers evaluate how well they have assimilated the material presented in each chapter. In the section on practice, the exercises have a somewhat different form, chiefly because the chapters in this section are considerably shorter than in the section on theory. (These shorter chapters permit readers to assimilate the mechanics of a working grammar more easily.) Thus, in the section on practice the exercises are arranged in four groups, covering: (1) the introductory material, particularly the base component, (2) the transformations which apply to simple sentences, (3) the transformations which produce restrictive relative clauses, adjectival and adverbial modifiers, appositives, and infinitive and participial phrases, and (4) the transformations which apply to conjunction, nonrestrictive relative clauses, and pronominalization.

Readers familiar with the first edition of this book will note that the *aim* of the two editions is the same; namely, we hope "that teachers will learn something valuable about the nature of English from this text and that this knowledge will improve their teaching and help their students." But the method of achieving this aim is somewhat different. While the present edition has both a section on theory and a section on practice, the first edition focused almost exclusively on a single "practical" model. Additionally, the final chapter of the first edition was "frankly polemical": an argument in favor of introducing transformational grammar into the schools and also in favor of utilizing transformational insights in the analysis of literary form. Such an argument is no longer necessary since both these tasks have begun to be realized. (We list, in the bibliography of the present edition, some of the important work that has been performed in applying the theory to related fields.)

As with most books having more than one author, there has been a division of labor in the writing. Owen Thomas is chiefly responsible for the section on theory; Eugene Kintgen is chiefly responsible for the section on practice and also for the exercises. Nonetheless, the book as a whole is finally the result of close collaboration. Also as with most books, the authors have benefited from helpful criticism by colleagues and students. Their suggestions have helped to make this a better book. Errors that remain are—as Samuel Johnson said—the result of "ignorance . . . sheer ignorance."

O.T.
E.R.K.

Bloomington, Indiana
December, 1973

Contents

CHAPTER 1

Introduction

The best part of human language, properly so called, is derived from reflection on the acts of the mind itself.
COLERIDGE, *Biographia Literaria*

This is a book about the English language. Equally important, it is a book about the attitudes that scholars hold toward language as well as toward the linguistic knowledge possessed by speakers of a language. The context of the book is that of transformational-generative grammar.

Hopefully, readers of this book will learn some important facts about two sets of topics: first, about language acquisition, the nature of language, the purpose of linguistic research, and the value of this research to school teachers and literary scholars; and second, about the details of one recent form of the grammar. Thus, following this introductory chapter there are two major parts. The first part is concerned with the history of transformational studies between 1956 and the early 1970s and with the relation of these studies to other types of grammar, the intent being to provide a philosophical perspective that may permit a reader to understand the nature of linguistic research into language in general and English in particular. The second part has a practical rather than a theoretical emphasis; it presents, in some detail, a grammar of contemporary English that should be useful for teachers and literary scholars.

The philosophical perspective of the first part can provide at least partial answers to questions such as the following:

1. How is transformational grammar related to earlier grammatical studies, particularly to the so-called "traditional grammars" of the seventeenth and eighteenth centuries?
2. What prompted linguists to abandon the older and established ways of studying language?
3. Has the *theory* of transformational grammar changed in the last 15 years?

4. What is the meaning of the current debate among linguists, and how does this relate to the usefulness of transformational grammar in the classroom?
5. How can teachers evaluate those school texts that incorporate research from transformational linguistics?
6. What do linguists hope to learn from their research, and how does this relate to teaching school children about their language?
7. What can teachers expect from future research in linguistics?
8. How can teachers with little formal training in linguistics apply what knowledge they do have in practical ways?

These and similar questions can be combined into a single broad question:

What does recent research into the nature of language actually mean for teachers of English?

There are two types of answers to this question, practical and theoretical, and this fact governs the structure of this book. Ten or even five years ago, there were few transformationally oriented textbooks available for use in the schools, and the only sources from which prospective teachers could conveniently learn the details of generative grammar were books such as the first edition of this book. Now, however, books incorporating material from linguistic research are being used in many elementary and secondary schools; what prospective teachers presently need, in addition to an acquaintance with the details of a contemporary grammar, is a broader understanding of the philosophy that guides linguistic research and that informs the writing of school texts.

In brief, developments in linguistics and in textbook publishing during the last ten years now make it possible—and perhaps necessary—to change the focus of the typical "language for teachers" course from one concerned exclusively with details to one that examines the philosophical as well as the practical importance of linguistic research. We can begin such an examination by looking briefly at each word in the phrase: transformational-generative grammar.

1.1 Grammar

The definitions of **grammar** are almost legion. A nine-year-old child once said that grammar is "talk about talking." Somewhat more metaphorically, a teacher said that a grammar is "a place to stand to look at language." While these definitions are informal, they are also perceptive. And they are quite in accord with the traditional use of the term.

In the traditional sense, a "grammar of a language" provides us with a vocabulary for discussing that language. When teachers use the term in this way, they are generally referring to a traditional textbook—a compilation of definitions, paradigms, declensions, so-called rules, and long lists of irregularities and exceptions.

A linguist—a scholar who studies language scientifically—uses the term "grammar" in a related but somewhat different sense. For a linguist, a grammar is a model of a language. The technical meaning of "model" should not be confused with the popular meaning. In popular usage, "model" may mean "ideal"; but in the technical sense, a model is a conceptual system: an idealized representation that sometimes rounds off the rough edges of reality but that nonetheless is useful because it helps us conceive of a totality.

By way of analogy, we can consider the solar system. Astronomers have constructed an idealized mathematical representation of the system, and such a representation is a "model" that permits them to make generalizations about the system. The model provides a vocabulary for discussing the elements of the system (the sun, the planets, and so on) and also for discussing the laws that define the motion of these elements.

In a similar way, a linguistic model also provides a vocabulary, one we can use in discussing the elements of language (sounds, words, phrases, clauses, and so on) as well as in discussing the linguistic rules—the "laws"—that define our use of these elements.

As scientists, astronomers and linguists both use models in their attempts to learn more about their subjects.[1] In a classroom, a teacher can use simplified versions of these models in explaining these subjects to students.

Both a solar model and a grammatical model are *representations*. Thus, the solar system is a physical reality, while a solar model is a scientific representation of what that reality *is*. Similarly, the knowledge that a native speaker possesses—knowledge that enables him to use language—is also a reality. Consequently, we can say that a grammatical model is a representation of what a native speaker *knows*.

As our first formal definition, then, we can say that a grammar is "a model—a scientific representation—of the linguistic knowledge possessed by a native speaker." And with this definition as a formal starting place, we can turn to other, related definitions.

Sometimes linguists also use the word "grammar" to refer to the actual linguistic knowledge that a native speaker possesses (rather than to the scientific repre-

---

[1] For example, more than 2000 years ago, Ptolemy (the Greek astronomer) used an "earth-centered" model to predict the existence of two planets that had never been observed. More than 1500 years later, Copernicus used a more accurate model to predict the existence of yet another planet. Such a change from one model to another is typical of most "scientific revolutions." An extremely valuable and readable discussion of such changes is presented by Thomas Kuhn in *The Structure of Scientific Revolutions,* 2nd ed. (Chicago: University of Chicago Press, 1970). In discussing the framework of assumptions and beliefs within which a scientist works, Kuhn uses the term "paradigm" (a term also used in traditional grammar). So long as the beliefs and assumptions remain constant, then this work is "normal science"—that is, the gradual acquisition of new knowledge through the application of widely accepted techniques and methods. A change in beliefs and assumptions can lead to a revolutionary change in a science. As we shall see, such a change has occurred in the study of language.

sentation of this knowledge). In this sense, every speaker has a grammar—a knowledge of language—in his head.[2]

As we shall see more fully below, linguists have not always been concerned with internalized knowledge (that is, with developing generative grammars to describe intuitive grammar). In particular, during the first half of this century most American linguists deliberately ignored internalized knowledge and focused, instead, on speech (that is, on the *product* of internalized knowledge). Thus, they made recordings of speech, or else they carefully transcribed speech in a special and highly detailed phonetic alphabet; then they attempted to describe—in a grammar—exactly those things that they could observe. The linguists who focused on speech are generally referred to as "the American structuralists." Because they focused on classifying the elements of spoken language and did not attempt to characterize internalized knowledge, the grammars that the American structuralists wrote are quite different from those we have designated as generative grammars. We shall use the term "taxonomic grammar" to refer to the structuralists' descriptions and classifications of physical language (that is, actual speech).

In addition to these three meanings of the word *grammar*, there are two popular meanings that we can also label. First, there are the so-called traditional school-grammars, that is, the textbooks based on the eighteenth-century prescriptive grammars used in Great Britain. These are the books we referred to when we mentioned the "compilation of definitions, paradigms, declensions," and so on. We can label these "traditional school-grammars" (and we shall also return to them below). These school-grammars are not formal descriptions of internalized knowledge, nor are they descriptions of actual speech; generally, they are informal attempts to describe some idealized form of written English.

Finally, there is the most common (and least scientific) meaning of all, the one people generally intend when they say such things as, "You better watch your grammar!" Technically, such people generally mean "usage" (of a type that derives from traditional school-grammars). Nonetheless (but with some qualms), we can refer to this popular meaning as "usage grammar."[3] Figure 1.1 may help in distinguishing among the various types of grammar we have been describing.

---

[2] To facilitate further discussion (and to avoid confusion as our definitions multiply), we can distinguish the various uses of the term "grammar" by the consistent use of two-word terms to refer to particular meanings. Thus, we can use the following terms for the two meanings already discussed:

Intuitive grammar: the internalized knowledge that every native speaker possesses.

Generative grammar: a model—a scientific representation—of the knowledge that a native speaker possesses. Thus, a generative grammar is a description of intuitive grammar.

[3] The word *grammar* has still other meanings, which some teachers and students might wish to discuss. There are the philosophical grammars written in Europe during the seventeenth century; these are similar to generative grammars in their concern with internalized knowledge, but they lack scientific precision. There are the historical and comparative grammars written, for the most part, during the nineteenth and early twentieth centuries; these were generally written by men who were extremely sensitive to the beauty and variety of lan-

Figure 1.1   Types of grammar

1.2 Generative

The adjective **generative** derives from the verb *generate*. And like the noun *grammar*, the words *generate* and *generative* each have more than one meaning. In the popular sense, *generate* means:

1. to bring into existence; cause to be. 2. to reproduce; to procreate.

There are, however, several technical meanings of the word, and these concern us directly:

6. *Math* a. to trace (a figure) by the motion of another: *A point generates a line.* b. to act as a base for all the elements of a given set: *The number 2 generates the set 2, 4, 8, 16.*
     —*The Random House Dictionary of the English Language*

In addition to mathematicians, logicians and linguists also use the word in the sense of 6.b. Unfortunately, many linguists also use both *generate* and *generative* in the more popular ways, even in their scholarly writing.

In the technical sense, a linguistic rule (like a mathematical or logical rule) is

---

guage; they provide a wealth of practical examples; and they raise valuable theoretical questions about the nature of language as well as about change in language. Additionally, there are various ancient grammars (for example, of Greek and Latin), which have influenced the writing of later grammars; we shall return to some of these in Section 1.5.

generative if it characterizes some part of the knowledge a speaker must have *to be able to produce* sentences. That is, the generative rule—in itself—does not produce; rather, the speaker is able to produce sentences if (among other things) he knows the rule, or more precisely, if he has the knowledge that the formulaic rule attempts to represent.

To belabor the point: A linguist assumes that, in an intuitive grammar, a speaker has an internalized knowledge of language, which includes (among other things) various "rules"; these rules (presumably) enable the speaker to produce and understand sentences. The linguist tries to characterize—to describe—this "internalized knowledge" by constructing a generative grammar. In the strictest sense, the rules of a generative grammar represent knowledge. Or in still other words: Because our understanding of the mind is extremely limited, we have no way of determining the precise form that linguistic rules assume *in the mind*; thus, a rule in a generative grammar attempts to represent the substance—and not necessarily the form—of the presumed rules of an intuitive grammar.[4]

In sum, the grammar on which we shall focus is generative because, among other things, it defines a set of the elements that comprise a language and also a set of rules that specify the permissible relationships that exist among the elements.

1.3 Transformational

As we have already noted, a model is a representation of some thing; it is not the thing itself. In general, given a particular thing that we wish to describe, we can construct more than one model of the thing. Moreover, given any two models of the same thing, it is sometimes possible—on independent grounds—to say that one model is "better than" the other. Conversely, it is sometimes impossible to choose between different models, in most cases because there is insufficient evidence for making a decision. Our astronomical analogy can provide examples of each situation.

As we have already mentioned, the astronomer Ptolemy developed an "earth-centered" model of the solar system which, for more than a thousand years, provided scientists with a vocabulary for discussing planetary motion. The Ptolemaic system was eventually replaced by the Copernican system, a "solar model" in which the planets move around the sun in ellipses. The Copernican system was accepted by scientists (although not without considerable argument) chiefly because it was simpler, more complete, and had "greater explanatory power"

---

[4] Teachers and students of English probably have more difficulty understanding the technical meanings of the terms *generate* and *generative* than they do in understanding any other part of the grammar. In particular, many persons need to "experience" the meaning in several contexts before they feel completely comfortable with the terms. For this reason, we shall return to the terms on several different occasions in the chapters that follow.

than Ptolemy's system. (For example, it predicted the existence of two planets —Uranus and Pluto—which were not included in Ptolemy's system.)

In contrast to the clear choice between these models, astronomers are not, at present, able to choose between two other theories—two models—that aim to describe the origin of the solar system. The reason is simple: They do not currently have sufficient evidence for making a clear choice. In technical terms, the choice is an empirical one, that is, one that can be decided when sufficient evidence is available and understood.

Returning to our subject: language. In our case, the reality—the fact—is that speakers possess a knowledge of language. In theory, we could construct various generative models of such knowledge, each of which would attempt to characterize, in some explicit way, a speaker's understanding of various grammatical relationships. In considering possible models, linguists have established two broad classes. One class, favored by most American structuralists a generation ago, contains rules of only one kind, namely, phrase-structure rules. The other class of grammar contains two kinds of rules, namely, phrase-structure rules and **transformations**.

In later chapters, we shall examine both kinds of rules in considerable detail. Here, we can note briefly that a phrase-structure rule can be used to define basic grammatical relationships such as, for example, "subject of a sentence." In contrast, a transformation (in effect) arranges the elements of a sentence into a form that is acceptable to a native speaker of the particular language.

To cite only one example here (many more will be given later in the text), consider the placement of polysyllabic adjectives in English and French. In English, such adjectives normally precede the nouns they modify; in French, they generally follow the noun[5]:

Sentence 1.1 Invisible God created the visible world.
Sentence 1.2 Le Dieu invisible a crée le monde visible.

The position of an adjective relative to a noun is more or less accidental, and the position does not necessarily affect the relationship of "modification" that exists between adjectives and nouns. Thus, suppose that a Frenchman spoke the following sentence in English:

Sentence 1.3 *God invisible created the world visible.

While a native speaker of English would recognize that this sentence is ungrammatical, such a speaker would probably have little difficulty in determining the meaning of the sentence. Clearly, the Frenchman understands the relationship of "modification" that exists between nouns and adjectives. But also clearly, the

[5]We shall return to this example in Chapter 3. To facilitate discussion, all illustrative sentences are numbered consecutively through each chapter, that is, Sentence 1.1, Sentence 1.2, Sentence 1.3, and so on. In addition, we shall sometimes use the linguistic convention of placing an asterisk (*) in front of a sentence that is not fully grammatical.

Frenchman does not know the rule governing the placement of adjectives in an English sentence.

This kind of rule—for example, one that positions an adjective before a noun in English and (sometimes) after a noun in French—is known as a *transformation*.

At this point in our discussion, the precise meaning of the term *transformation* is not particularly important (although it will become quite important later in the text). Rather, what is important is that some generative models of language contain transformations, and some do not. The choice between the two kinds of models (one with transformations and one without) is an empirical question—as was the choice between the Ptolemaic and Copernican models. We shall return to the question in Chapter 6. Here we are concerned with the term only because it designates one kind of generative grammar, a kind that contrasts with any generative grammar that does not incorporate transformations in a description of language.

To summarize our discussion of the phrase *transformational-generative grammar*: One kind of grammar (a generative grammar) is a model, a conceptual system, an idealized representation of the knowledge possessed by a native speaker of a language. Such a model is generative since it defines a list of the elements of the system as well as a list of the rules that govern the operations of these elements. And one such generative model is transformational since it contains a particular type of rule, the function of which is to "arrange" the elements of a sentence into a form that is acceptable as grammatical in a particular language.[6]

In the years since 1955, when linguists first began to use the term transformational-generative grammar, there have been several modifications of the theory. But the basic meaning of the terms has not changed. Thomas Kuhn, in the book mentioned in footnote 1, has used the term *paradigm* to refer to a framework within which scientists conduct research. In the field of physics, Isaac Newton provided one paradigm within which other physicists could conduct investigations. In what Kuhn calls a "scientific revolution," the Newtonian paradigm was replaced by another developed by Albert Einstein. The history of science is, in part, a history of such scientific revolutions. The modern theory of transformational-generative grammar is a new paradigm. Once we have considered the nature of this paradigm in some detail (in Chapters 2 and 3), we shall compare it with preceding paradigms that linguists have used, most particularly with that of the American structural grammarians who dominated linguistic research in this country for 25 years, beginning in 1933.

At this point, we are concerned only with the general shape of the paradigm

---

[6] While the phrase *transformational-generative grammar* is both descriptive and accurate, it is also extremely long! For this reason, it is frequently shortened, sometimes to TG (which some people—including the authors—find slightly barbarous), and sometimes to *transformational grammar* (which assumes that "transformational" implies "generative"). With some exceptions, we shall adopt the two-word form throughout the rest of the text.

and with the fact that this general shape has not changed significantly during the last 15 years.

1.4   Some Additional Terms

We can now define, briefly, some additional terms that will be useful in our discussion, after which we can place the theory of transformational grammar within the context of other grammatical studies.

Linguistics. The term *linguistics* refers to the scientific study of language. Things scientific were formerly anathema to teachers who were by disposition more concerned with the humanistic values of literature and writing. But most teachers now realize that the arts and sciences are interdependent, both in the academic world and in life itself.

Like most fields of study, linguistics can be divided into many areas. Some linguists, for example, are interested in cataloguing and describing various features of languages, just as some botanists prefer to catalogue and describe plants. Other linguists are interested in the history of various languages and language families, just as some anthropologists are interested primarily in tracing the history of various families of mankind. Still other linguists are concerned with the interrelationships between language and society, or language and learning, or language and intelligence, just as sociologists, educational theorists, and psychologists are interested in similar questions. And finally, some few linguists are interested in general theories of language, just as some physicists are interested in theories that explain the operations of the universe. No single linguist is trained in all these fields, and, quite obviously, no teacher of English need become expert in any one of them.

Transformational linguists are interested primarily in the theory of language. More particularly, they want to describe a general theory of grammar itself: What form should a grammar take? How can we evaluate two or more grammars to determine which offers the best description of a language? How does a speaker acquire linguistic knowledge? This book is also concerned with these questions.

Scientific Grammar and Pedagogical Grammar. Transformationalists hope to specify a *scientific grammar* (that is, a comprehensive generative grammar) that offers a logical, complete, and self-consistent explanation for the linguistic knowledge that a native speaker possesses. We may get some idea of what this means by looking at two sentences that generative grammarians have frequently used for illustrative purposes:

Sentence 1.4 John is easy to please.
Sentence 1.5 John is eager to please.

All mature native speakers of English recognize that the underlying forms of these two sentences are different. The difference becomes more obvious when we try to rearrange the sentences. Thus, we can say *It was easy for us to please John*, but we cannot say **It was eager for us to please John.*[7] On the other hand, we can say *He was eager to please us*, but not **He was easy to please us*. In English, there are many such cases. A scientific grammar, among other things, aims at providing a generalized explanation for all these cases. Moreover, it also aims at showing the relationship between these kinds of constructions and hundreds of others that are similar but not identical in form. In brief, a scientific grammar is concerned with logical generalizations about the internal structure of language.

By its very nature, a scientific grammar is quite different from a *pedagogical grammar* such as a teacher will use in a classroom with students. In particular, scientific and pedagogical grammars have different goals.

As we have already suggested, a scientific grammar provides a framework—a paradigm—within which a linguist can conduct research. In contrast, pedagogical grammars have a variety of uses, and they can take a variety of forms. For example, one type of pedagogical grammar might be intended to teach English to a speaker of another language. Another type might be used to teach school children certain facts about their language. A third type, to which we referred earlier, might provide teachers with a detailed exposition of the rules proposed by a particular group of linguists. Pedagogical grammars such as these are normally concerned with presenting very specific data as well as with providing a vocabulary for discussing such data.

This book is pedagogical in another sense. Although we shall make considerable use of linguistic data, particularly in Part Two, our concern is not exclusively with detailed rules. Rather, we shall also be concerned with the implications that linguistic research has for teachers. And this distinction suggests why the title of the book refers to the "teacher" rather than to the "teaching" of English. All teachers need to have some knowledge of current scientific descriptions of language; they need, in short, to know something about the theory. But they will not all use the theory and the descriptions in the same way when it comes to teaching English.

Infinite System. Technically, all human languages are *infinite systems*; that is, the number of sentences in any language is "unbounded." We can easily illustrate the unbounded nature of English through the following examples:

Sentence 1.6 I ate one peanut.
Sentence 1.7 I ate two peanuts.
Sentence 1.8 I ate three peanuts.
Sentence 1.9 I ate four peanuts.

and so on.

---

[7] This sentence is grammatical for some speakers of English. But even so, it is no longer semantically equivalent to *John was eager to please*. In a transformational grammar, if two sentences are not semantically equivalent, they must have different underlying forms.

Sentence 1.10 There's a hole in the bottom of the sea.
Sentence 1.11 There's a log in the hole in the bottom of the sea.
Sentence 1.12 There's a bump on the log in the hole in the bottom of the sea.
Sentence 1.13 There's a frog on the bump on the log in the hole in the bottom of the sea.

and so on.

Since there is no (theoretical) limit to the number of peanuts a person can eat, there is also no limit on how long the sequence of Sentences 1.6-1.9 can be extended. Similarly, there is no theoretical limit to the number of words, phrases, and clauses that can be added to Sentence 1.10. In other words, there is no limit to the number of possible sentences in English, and there is no "longest sentence."

Thus, the number of sentences in English is potentially infinite (and we shall return to this point in later chapters). Obviously, no speaker could possibly *produce* this infinite number of sentences, but all speakers have some method of *understanding* completely novel sentences, ones that they have never heard before. In other words, the generative rules of language (in a speaker's intuitive grammar) permit each speaker, among other things, to evaluate the acceptability of novel sentences.

We can illustrate this fact with relative ease. Most, if not all, of the following sentences are novel; that is, they have never been spoken or written before:

Sentence 1.14 My sister, an eminent orthodontist, is inordinately fond of pickled marshmallows.
Sentence 1.15 Gertrude, why are you throwing those party hats into the well?
Sentence 1.16 Every college in New Zealand should offer a course in how to prepare peanut butter.

As any native speaker recognizes, the examples are all perfectly good English sentences, and we can "understand" what they mean even though they are probably unique. In sum, the fact of infiniteness is an important aspect of language, which an adequate grammar must describe.

Later in the text, we shall introduce other technical terms. Now, however, we can return to the earlier historical context and define the earlier paradigms in greater detail.

1.5   A Brief History

As we have already noted in discussing the various meanings of the word *grammar*, the history of English grammatical studies divides into several periods. Each of these periods is characterized by widely held assumptions about the nature of language as well as about the nature of language study.

The traditional English school-grammars have their origins in the Greek grammar of Dionysius Thrax (c. 200 B.C.) and in the Latin grammars of Donatus (c. 400 A.D.) and Priscian (c. 600 A.D.). Basically, all these grammarians worked within the framework of Aristotelian logic. Their methodology was adopted, almost in toto, by several British grammarians who published textbooks—pedagogical grammars—in the eighteenth century. The best known of these grammarians are Joseph Priestley, Robert Lowth, George Campbell, and Lindley Murray. The grammars of these men were all based on an Aristotelian assumption that "the structure of various languages, and especially that of Latin, embodies universally valid canons of logic." [8]

Briefly, the British grammarians of the eighteenth century sought to discover logical rules of syntax and usage. They generally assumed that Latin was the most logical of languages, and they consequently based their rules for English on Latin models. These rules were almost invariably prescriptive; that is, they dictated precisely the usage to be followed by all speakers and writers. The early British grammarians either overlooked the fact that all languages change, or else they considered such change as corruption. Yet for all their appeals to "classical logic" in language, they also displayed a heavy reliance on "intuition" in discovering the rules. In other words, they based their rules for English partly on the rules for Latin, but partly also on their intuition about what was correct in their own language. Consequently, we must recognize that many of their "rules" are actually explanations of intuition.

Moreover, these eighteenth-century British grammars were pedagogical. Among other things, they attempted to establish a more or less standard language as well as a set of linguistic norms for the burgeoning middle class of a newly industrialized society. For the most part, these attempts were successful. Nonetheless, their success should not cause us to overlook the fact that they contained many misleading and confusing statements, and that they were based on assumptions about languages that we now know are false. As an example of a confusing statement, consider the definition of "preposition" found in most of these grammars:

A preposition is a word that expresses a relationship between its object and some other word in the sentence.

Aside from assuming that a reader knows what an "object" is in this sense (and this is nowhere defined in most school-grammars), the definition is far too comprehensive since it also applies to every transitive verb in English. Thus, given the sentence *Cats like milk*, the word *like* has an object, *milk*, and, moreover, the word *like* expresses a relationship between *milk* and *cats*. In brief, while the statement may be true, it is certainly not a precise definition.

And as an example of false assumptions about language, we can cite the widely held belief that English is unusually crude when compared with Latin or Greek. In *A Short Introduction to English Grammar* (1762), Lowth asks the following rhetorical question about charges brought against the English language: "Does it mean, that the *English* Language as it is spoken by the politest part of the nation, and as it stands in the writings of our most approved authors, oftentimes

---

[8] Leonard Bloomfield, *Language* (New York: Holt, Rinehart and Winston, 1933), p. 6.

offends against every part of Grammar?" And he answers his question by saying: "I am afraid, the charge is true."

Such statements may seem amusing to us now, but only because we have acquired, during the last 200 years, a considerable body of knowledge about the nature of language, knowledge that was unavailable to the well-intentioned grammarians of the eighteenth century. What is less than amusing is the fact that many contemporary school-grammars currently in wide use in elementary and secondary schools are based almost exclusively on the models of the eighteenth-century British grammarians. The school-grammars totally ignore many of the important facts that we have learned about language in the last 150 years.

Comparative and Historical Grammars. On the European continent, at the end of the eighteenth century, many grammarians were looking at language more speculatively, and their grammars were written for fellow scholars rather than for school children. These scholars rediscovered Panini's magnificent grammar of Sanskrit (the ancient literary dialect of India), which was probably written late in the fourth century, B.C. Sanskrit bore a strong resemblance not only to Latin and Greek, but also to German and English and even to Russian. This led many grammarians to suggest, at first tentatively but then with increasing conviction, that most modern European languages, as well as Sanskrit and classical Latin and Greek, derive historically from some common source. Briefly, these grammarians noted one apparently universal linguistic fact: All languages change.

This observation led to two kinds of study: comparative and historical. Many grammarians began a wide investigation of various languages, looking for similarities, or as they are called, cognate forms. They discovered some striking facts. For example, the English word *mother* has cognates in Greek (*meter*), Latin (*mater*), Russian (*mat'*), and German (*Mutter*). They also discovered that within the large family of languages that includes Sanskrit, Greek, Latin, Russian, German, and English, there are several smaller families. Consider, for example, the English word *drink*[9]; as the lists in Table 1.1 indicate, there are strong similarities among the words in the three groups. (The *c* in the Polish word *pic'* is pronounced like the -*ts* ending on the English word *cats*.) English belongs to the Germanic group, and the Germanic, Romance, and Slavic groups are all part of a larger language family generally called *Indo-European.*

Table 1.1

Germanic Group	Romance Group	Slavic Group
English *drink*	French *boire*	Russian *pit'*
Dutch *drinken*	Italian *bere*	Polish *pic'*
German *trinken*	Spanish *beber*	Bohemian *piti*
Danish *drikke*		Serbian *piti*
Swedish *dricka*		

[9] Leonard Bloomfield, *Language*, p. 10.

At the same time that some grammarians were making comparative studies, others were tracing the history of particular languages as far back as written records permitted. The chief result of this study, for students of English, was an elaborate description of Old and Middle English. Like modern German, Old English had masculine, feminine, and neuter genders that were "grammatical" rather than "logical"; for example, the word *stan* ("stone") was masculine, and the word *giefu* ("gift") was feminine. Nouns could be either "strong" or "weak," depending on whether the stem ended in a vowel or consonant, and there were four distinct declensions for the strong nouns. Each declension had separate singular and plural forms for each of four cases: nominative, genitive, dative, and accusative. In addition, adjectives also had strong and weak, and masculine, feminine, and neuter forms. The strong declension of adjectives even had a fifth case: the instrumental. The definite article was also fully inflected; Old English had eleven separate forms for the word *the*. There were six major classes of strong verbs, each with distinctive endings, as well as a large class of weak verbs and a special class of "reduplicating verbs." In short, Old English was a highly inflected language.

Middle English, the language of Chaucer, had far fewer inflections. As a consequence, word order became increasingly important. And this trend away from inflections and toward a more rigid word order has continued into modern English. We can, therefore, speak of a contrast between *inflected* and *positional* languages. And with this distinction in mind, we can look back at the works of the eighteenth-century British grammarians. In particular, we need to note that their descriptions of English, a positional language, were based on models of Greek and Latin, which are inflected languages. Their descriptions, therefore, were almost certain to be misleading and even at variance with their own intuition.

The scholarly grammarians, as we have already noted, compiled enormous collections of data relative to English, and their discussions of their data are frequently perceptive and informative. Unfortunately, they had very little effect on the grammars being written for school children. This points up a basic fault of many school-grammars: at worst, they ignore the research findings of the last century; at best, they trivialize these findings. Any person who had, for example, a thorough knowledge of George Curme's *A Grammar of the English Language* (1931, 1935) would know a great deal about English, vastly more than he could ever learn from the typical "traditional school-grammar."

American Structural Grammar. It was not until the nineteenth century that linguists made any serious attempt to describe precisely the form of modern English. And it was not until the early part of the twentieth century that linguists began to develop relatively precise methods of description. The late nineteenth and early twentieth centuries saw some major compilations of linguistic data relating to modern English. Many of these compilations were the work of non-English scholars, perhaps the most notable of whom is the Dane, Otto

Jespersen. Jespersen did, in fact, attempt to develop a theory and to describe linguistic data in a formal way; he also coined several terms that are still useful. But Jespersen's theory lacks the detailed logical structure of a generative grammar. Moreover, a later group of grammarians—the American structuralists (also called "descriptivists")—felt that his and similar theories were overly intuitive; that is, most structural grammarians wanted to make linguistics a completely objective science. (Today many persons, including the authors of this text, believe that the American structuralists had an erroneous notion of what constitutes scientific objectivity.)

In America, the most notable of the early descriptivists was Leonard Bloomfield. Briefly, Bloomfield sought to describe present-day English not as people think it "should be" but as it actually is. We must note that he was not concerned primarily with generative rules; he was not attempting to explain intuition. Rather, he (and even more particularly his followers) was looking for methods of describing language that were free of human error and subjective judgments. He sought to make the study of language as objective as the study of physics and chemistry. In brief, Bloomfield and his followers sought to bring rigor to linguistics.

The achievements of the structuralists are many, and they compiled some excellent grammars (see the Bibliography). We shall have frequent occasion to comment on their work in the following chapters since, in part, transformational grammar developed in reaction to the theories of the structuralist grammars. Most particularly, the early structuralists believed (and their followers still believe) that the proper object of linguistic research is the spoken language; in contrast, the transformational grammarians believe that the proper object of research is the linguistic knowledge that a native speaker possesses.

1.6   The Old and the New

The various distinctions we have noted thus far suggest an important question: What is the function of grammar? The answer, of course, is that different kinds of grammars have different functions. This is true historically, and it is also true of contemporary grammars.

Most probably, the earliest grammars—those of classical Greece, Rome, and India—had a partly religious and even moral purpose. Many sacred and important secular writings of these civilizations were written hundreds of years before scholars compiled grammars of these writings. These grammars helped later generations of scholars to read and understand the early writings.

The traditional school-grammars of the eighteenth century had a partly social purpose. As society became more industrialized, it was necessary (in the opinion of those who governed society) to train people in some standard form of English so that these people, in turn, could help society operate. In particular, it was necessary for a great many people to learn to read and write in some standard way that would be mutually intelligible throughout the society. The school-grammars were a major force in the attempt to achieve universal literacy in both the United States and Great Britain.

But these school-grammars, as we have seen, were—and are—imperfect. We now know vastly more about language than the eighteenth-century grammarians did when they were writing. Even if the reasons for teaching grammar are the same now as they were in the eighteenth century, we have no reason for continuing to use the same grammars that our predecessors used 200 years ago. In many ways, the aim of these early school-grammars was commendable, but the means by which the eighteenth-century grammarians sought to achieve these aims are certainly out of date.

Many teachers are surprised to learn that the transformationalists are quite traditional in some of their aims. In fact, however, the transformationalists share many of the goals of the early philosophical grammarians, but they also have the advantage of 200 years of scholarship which the eighteenth-century grammarians did not have. They can, and do, draw freely on the findings of the historical, comparative, and descriptive grammarians. They also have the developments of modern logic to draw upon, particularly those that relate to symbolic operations. They recognize, as many of their predecessors did not, that every language has its own logic and that Latin and Greek are neither more nor less logical than any other language.

In one very important sense, then, transformational grammar is a new way of looking at some old and traditional ideas concerning language. It is neither esoteric nor forbidding in its aims. And if it seems so in its methods, it is only because we—that is, teachers and prospective teachers of English—have not made use of all the devices that modern scholarship offers us. We have not recognized that Huxley's statement in defense of the theory of evolution—"Irrationally held truths may be more harmful than reasoned errors"—may apply to our attitudes toward grammar.

To the writers of this book, it seems that many teachers have not kept pace with modern scholarship. They have been content merely to preserve the traditional; they have not nurtured it and helped it grow. They have failed to continue what the eighteenth-century grammarians began. They have provided a window to the past rather than a bridge from the past to the future. They—and we—must now reassess our obligations.

These obligations, of course, are continuous. Transformational grammar is not complete. The details of the grammar are changing now and will continue to change. This means, among other things, that Part Two is not a definitive "grammar of English." Some of the details are undoubtedly wrong; others are needlessly complicated. Future grammarians will correct the former and improve the latter. But that is not our present concern. We have much to learn from our colleagues in the sciences. In particular, we must recognize that all theories are merely that: theories. They are subject to replacement by more comprehensive and powerful theories. But this fact does not prevent scientists from working out theories in detail. Nor does it prevent school teachers from discussing these theories.

In Part One, we shall examine this "working-out" process, beginning with the first major statements in transformational theory (Chapter 2), then looking at some of the factors in the development of the early theory (Chapter 3), continuing with a fairly detailed examination of the most comprehensive presentation of the theory, namely, Noam Chomsky's *Aspects of the Theory of Syntax* (Chapters 4 and 5), and concluding the survey with a brief look at more recent research, including some that challenges the standard form of the theory (Chapter 6). In Part Two, we shall present some relatively specific details of a grammar that teachers and scholars may find useful in their work.

THEORY

1

CHAPTER 2

The Early Theory: I

. . . these elaboratedly constructed forms, so different from each other, and dependent on each other in so complex a manner, have all been produced by laws acting around us.
DARWIN, *The Origin of the Species*

From 1957 through 1964, the transformational-generative theory of language focused primarily on syntax rather than on semantics. (Less technically, we can say that the early theory was concerned more with form than with meaning.) Although this focus has changed considerably in the years since 1965, an understanding of later developments generally presupposes some familiarity with the original theory, and for this reason we can best begin with an outline of the main characteristics of the theory as it was commonly defined in the early 1960s.

A generative grammar is a theory of language—one that seeks to relate sound and meaning—and the core of the theory is the concept of **sentence**. More completely, we can note that English, like every other natural language, is complex, flexible, changing, and systematic, and that the basis of this system is the sentence. To see why this is so, we can look briefly at the nature of language itself.

First, then, language is complex. We got some notion of the complexity of language previously when we examined the sentences:

Sentence 1.4 John is easy to please.
Sentence 1.5 John is eager to please.

But the complexity is actually much deeper than these rather simple examples suggest. Consider two more sentences that Chomsky has frequently used for illustration:

Sentence 2.1 I expected the doctor to examine John.
Sentence 2.2 I persuaded the doctor to examine John.

Superficially (that is, on the face or surface of language), these latter two sentences are quite similar. But note how they behave when we change the infinitive from the active to the passive voice:

Sentence 2.1a I expected John to be examined by the doctor.
Sentence 2.2a I persuaded John to be examined by the doctor.

In Sentence 2.1, the speaker expects that an event will happen, namely, that *the doctor will examine John*. When this sentence is changed from the active to the passive voice, the expectation remains much the same, for if *the doctor will examine John*, it is also true that *John will be examined by the doctor*. But a very different situation prevails with Sentence 2.2. In the case of the active voice, the speaker is persuading the *doctor*. And this is obviously quite different from the case of the corresponding sentence in the passive voice (Sentence 2.2a), in which the speaker is persuading *John*.

In other words, although at first glance the original sentences appear—and actually are on the surface—similar, every mature native speaker of English knows that they are somehow different. This fact has led linguists, and should lead us, to suspect that in addition to the **surface structure** of language, there is also a **deep structure**. We shall return to this important distinction frequently in the following chapters.[1]

Language is also extremely flexible. Consider, for example, the difference between declarative and interrogative sentences. If we set out to design a language, we would certainly want to be able to ask questions in that language. But would we recognize the wide variety of possibilities available to us in asking questions? Suppose we have the sentence:

Sentence 2.3 My roommate was quietly eating sunflower seeds in class today.

We can interrogate the subject, object, or verb:

Sentence 2.3a Who was eating sunflower seeds? (subject)
Sentence 2.3b What was my roommate eating? (object)
Sentence 2.3c What was my roommate doing in class today? (verb)

We can also interrogate the adverbs of time, location, and manner:

Sentence 2.3d When was my roommate eating sunflower seeds? (time)
Sentence 2.3e Where was my roommate eating sunflower seeds? (location)
Sentence 2.3f How was my roommate eating sunflower seeds? (manner)

These kinds of questions, as we shall note later, can be called *wh-* questions,

[1] We could perhaps say that the difference between the sentences is purely semantic, and as we shall see in a later chapter, such a statement is partly true. At this point, however, we should attempt to maintain the distinction between syntax and semantics that existed in the early form of transformational theory. Thus, in this chapter we shall accept the statement that "form underlies meaning"; that is, we shall try to see if differences in semantics conceal differences in syntax. The so-called first generation of transformational grammarians assumed that differences in syntax would help us understand differences in semantics.

since (with the obvious exception of the irregular form *how*) they all begin with one of the *wh-* words: *who, what, when, where.*

But we can also ask a variety of questions that can be answered with a "yes" or "no." Sentence 2.3g is the so-called regular yes/no question. Sentences 2.3h and 2.3i are known as tag questions. And Sentence 2.3j, which has a rising inflection, as if the person speaking were incredulous, is called an echo question.

Sentence 2.3g Was my roommate quietly eating sunflower seeds in class today? (regular yes/no)

Sentence 2.3h My roommate was quietly eating sunflower seeds in class today, wasn't she? (negative tag)

Sentence 2.3i My roommate wasn't quietly eating sunflower seeds in class today, was she? (positive tag)

Sentence 2.3j My roommate was quietly eating sunflower seeds in class today? (echo)

At this point, such flexibility is probably confusing, but we shall see in later chapters that it is quite systematic.

Language is constantly changing. We have already seen in Chapter 1 that Old English was primarily an inflected language. During the past 1500 years English has been changing—and developing—in the direction of fewer inflections and more rigid word order. But there are also other obvious changes. As the more than 200 million people who speak and read English as either a native or foreign language know all too well, the spelling system of English certainly appears to be chaotic, at least on the surface. George Bernard Shaw was fond of illustrating this chaos by citing the word *ghoti* which, he claimed, was a perfectly reasonable way to spell the English word *fish.* The *gh-* has the pronunciation found in the word *enough*; the *-o-* has the pronunciation of *women*; and the *-ti* has the pronunciation of *action.* Several hundred years ago, when the spelling of words became fixed because of the demands of the newly invented printing press, Shaw's example would not have had much meaning, because most English words were pronounced exactly as we spell them (rather than pronounce them) today. In short, the pronunciation of English, as every student of Chaucer knows, has changed radically throughout the centuries.

Word meanings have also changed. The word *anon*, which now means "in a little while," originally meant "immediately," "at this very instant." And there is certainly no reason to suspect that language has stopped changing. Languages are changed by people, generally because of the changing patterns of the societies in which they live.

Above all, however, and almost in spite of the flexibility, complexity, and changing nature of language, it remains rigidly systematic. Language has rules. A grammar is, among other things, a collection of these rules, and it is our knowledge of these rules that permits us to understand and produce sentences.

Finally, we can note again that the English language is, in logical terms, an infinite system. That is, as we saw in the Chapter 1, there are more sentences in the language than can be counted, and there is no "longest sentence." In this respect, we can compare English and mathematics. Both have elements (for example, words and numbers), and both have rules that operate on these elements. Thus, there are rules that relate to sentence structure, just as there are rules of multiplication. In studying arithmetic, we learn one set of rules for multiplying all the numbers from one to ten by each other; we also learn a set of rules for applying the rules of the first set to numbers larger than ten. With these two sets of rules, we are able to multiply an infinite number of numbers.

Mathematicians study the properties of numbers and the nature of the rules that operate on these numbers. Linguists study the properties of linguistic elements (for example, words), and attempt to define the rules that operate on these elements to generate sentences.

2.1 Language

In *Syntactic Structures*, the first major publication relating to transformational grammar, Noam Chomsky gives the following definition:

> A language is a set (finite or infinite) of sentences, each finite in length and constructed out of a finite set of elements.[2]

This important definition, which sums up much of what we have said to this point, requires some comment.

Chomsky is here talking about all languages, both natural and man-made (man-made languages would include, for example, those that are used in computing machines; they are vastly simpler than human—or natural—languages). Many man-made languages are finite; that is, the number of sentences in the language can be counted, and it is possible to "point to" the longest sentence. English and all other natural languages are *infinite*.

The word *set* is used in a technical sense. For our purposes, we can consider a set as a collection of anything. A set may contain an infinite number of things (such as, for example, the set of all possible integers in mathematics), or it may contain only one thing (such as the Eiffel Tower). When adapted to our purposes, then, the first part of the definition says that the English language is a set (or collection) of the infinite number of possible English sentences.

The second part of the definition says that there is no "infinitely long sentence." This is a very different thing from saying that there is no "longest sentence." If sentences were infinitely long, we could not possibly understand them. In other words, every sentence, by definition, must be finite in length, but it is always possible to make any one of these finite sentences at least one word longer.

Finally, the definition says that every sentence is made up of *elements,* that we can collect these elements into a set, and that the number of elements can be counted. Some of these elements, for example, might be the letters of the

[2] Noam Chomsky, *Syntactic Structures* (The Hague: Mouton, 1957), p. 13.

alphabet (or somewhat more precisely, the sounds represented by the letters of some kind of phonetic alphabet); obviously, we need only a very limited number of these letters. Other elements will be words, and it is certainly possible to count all the words in an English dictionary. And all of these various things constitute a set of elements.

We can now rephrase the definition:

> The English language is made up of an infinite number of sentences. Every individual sentence, however, is finite in length. And every sentence is constructed from a relatively limited number of elements.

This definition is worth noting for another reason. It defines "language" in terms of "sentences"; that is, it assumes that the reader knows, perhaps intuitively, what a sentence is. Moreover, in *Syntactic Structures*, Chomsky proposes a grammar that "generates all of the grammatical sequences of [a language] and none of the ungrammatical ones" (p. 13). This definition makes an assumption similar to that given in the definition of "language," since sentences are obviously "grammatical sequences." Most of our later definitions will also assume a knowledge of sentences. This fact is undoubtedly disconcerting to many readers, particularly those who have come to rely on the "definitions" of traditional grammar. We should, therefore, pause to consider the theoretical questions that such usage raises.

Again, we can usefully draw an analogy. As Robert B. Lees pointed out in discussing this same problem, the "working biologist" very rarely, "if ever," attempts to define the notion of "cell," although this notion "underlies all of biology." He goes on to point out that there is no procedure whereby a biologist can determine whether a given object "is a cell or is not a cell."

> This requirement is not necessary in order to use intelligently the notion *cell* or for that matter in order to intelligently explicate the notion *cell*, and similarly to explicate notions on the *basis* of the *cell*, for example tissue, or bone.

And Lees concludes by noting that if we "already knew how to define 'grammatical sentence of English,' there would be no earthly reason for trying to formulate a theory of English sentences, i.e., an English grammar."[3]

Lees is saying, in effect, that the only valid definition of "grammatical sentence in English" is a complete grammar of English. He is also saying that no other discipline, including mathematics, physics, and chemistry, even makes a pretense of defining its basic elements *except in terms of each other*. Thus, we cannot define the axioms of Euclidean geometry, but we can use these axioms to develop theorems. Using Einstein's theory, we can define space and time in terms of each other, but we cannot define them outside the system the physicist uses to investigate the universe.

---

[3] Robert B. Lees, "Discussion," in *Report on the Eleventh Annual Round Table Meeting on Linguistics and Language Studies*, Bernard Choseed, Ed. (Washington, D.C.: Georgetown University Press, 1962), pp. 52, 181-182.

A decade ago, most teachers of English found statements such as these disconcerting; they were reluctant to abandon the centuries-old "definitions" of traditional school-grammar. Part of the problem lay in the lack of communication between teachers and linguists, who frequently used the same words, but who failed to recognize that these words did not have identical meanings. One word that caused problems was *definition*. The linguists used this word as a logician might; in this sense, true definition is possible only within a closed system. In contrast, English teachers used the word as a lexicographer might; in this sense, complete definition is impossible. Even the massive *Oxford English Dictionary* does not provide complete definitions of words. Rather, a lexicographer attempts to make one or more true and significant statements about the meaning of a word. In a day-to-day world, a dictionary "definition" has practical value even though it might be inadequate within a logical framework. And the key word here is *inadequate* (rather than *incorrect*). Thus, it may be both true and significant that, as many school grammarians say, "a sentence consists of a group of words containing a subject and predicate and expressing a complete thought." Such a statement may, at times, have a practical value. Yet no logician (or linguist) would consider it as a full and complete definition of a sentence. For one thing, it assumes that we know what "a complete thought" is, although this notion has defied philosophers for thousands of years. Plato wrote an entire book, *The Republic*, trying to define not a complete thought but a single word: *justice*. Even that attempt was not successful. The conclusion is inescapable, and school children have known it for years. Many of the so-called definitions offered by school grammarians are inadequate *as definitions* even though they may have practical value when we talk informally about language. In brief, there is no complete definition of *sentence* outside a fully developed generative grammar—and we may never have such a grammar.

Actually, the lack of notional definition of sentence will not in any way hinder our discussion of English grammar. We shall, in fact, find the discussion simpler, more meaningful, and more revealing because we are no longer "hot for certainties" that, at this stage of our understanding, are beyond our grasp.

2.2   Basic English Sentences

The simplest place to begin our discussion of English grammar is with the pedagogically useful notion of **basic English sentences**. And the most elemental description of a basic sentence divides the sentence into two parts: a **subject** and a **predicate**. This fact, of course, was also obvious to the older traditional grammarians and indicates again the close tie between traditional and transformational grammar.

For purposes of elaboration, particularly later in the text when we discuss such things as subordination, it is convenient to represent some of these descriptions symbolically. Such representation also helps to ensure accuracy, since it frequently makes errors in description more obvious. Consequently, we shall adopt the following symbols[4]:

Sentence: S
Noun phrase: NP
Verb phrase: VP

Each of these symbols represents a **constituent** of language. The primary constituent of any language is the sentence, which we symbolize by S. The first rule of language says that the constituent **sentence** consists of two other constituents, namely, a **noun phrase** (symbolized by NP) and a **verb phrase** (symbolized by VP). The entire rule can be represented symbolically as follows:

PS 2.1 S → NP + VP

Technically, a rule that indicates that one constituent "consists of" one or more other constituents is called a **phrase-structure rule**.[5]

The earliest transformational grammars of English contained a great many phrase-structure rules. As we shall see, many linguists now believe that there are very few such rules and that these few may well be common to all languages. For this reason we shall consider only the most important of the early rules; that is, we shall emphasize the concepts—rather than the details—inherent in the design.

In addition to phrase-structure rules, transformational grammarians developed another kind of symbolism, the so-called **branching-tree diagram**, which is a graphic representation of the syntactic structure underlying a given sentence. Superficially, these "trees" seem to be similar to the base-line diagrams of traditional school-grammar, but there is actually an extremely important difference, namely, the trees are especially useful in representing the *deep-structure relationships* that underlie a spoken or written sentence. (The concept of deep structure was mentioned on p. 22. We shall return to this concept frequently in the following chapters.) The branching tree in Figure 2.1 is, obviously, inordinately simple. In addition, we have introduced words into the tree (for illustrative

---

[4] A reminder may be in order at this point. We are concerned here with the early form of transformational theory, when the symbols shown above were universally accepted by generative linguists; later we shall see that some linguists have proposed alternatives to the early form of the theory and have, consequently, modified the symbolism.

[5] As indicated in the text, the arrow in the rule means "consists of." The arrow has direction because "S consists of an NP and a VP" (while "NP and VP do *not* consist of S"). Some linguists, borrowing a term from mathematics, say that the arrow means "rewrite as," and for this reason, phrase-structure rules are sometimes called rewriting rules. As we shall see within a few pages, this usage refers only to the process of constructing a so-called "derivation"; it bears no relation to the actual process of producing—or comprehending—sentences.

To facilitate discussion, each phrase-structure rule is identified with a PS number. Thus, PS 2.1 refers to the first phrase-structure rule given in Chapter 2, PS 2.2 refers to the second rule given in Chapter 2, and so on. If a rule is revised or expanded later in the chapter, then the later rule is marked with an identifying letter, for example, PS 2.1a.

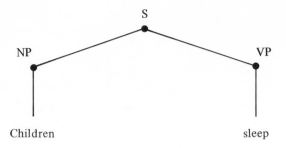

Figure 2.1 $S \rightarrow NP + VP$

purposes) without specifying how these words were chosen; we shall continue this informal practice throughout this subsection. But as the sentences we are using for examples become more complicated, so too will the trees that represent the structures underlying these sentences. At this point in our discussion, however, it is probably wisest to begin simply, since—as we shall see in a few pages—even the simplest trees incorporate a considerable amount of structural information.

The dots on the tree are called **nodes**; the lines connecting the nodes are, quite naturally, called **branches**. One node above another on a tree is said to **dominate** the lower node. Thus, in Figure 2.1, the S node dominates both the NP node and the VP node.

We run into complexity at the very next step in elaborating early transformational theory. In particular, we must decide how to handle the various forms of be that occur in English sentences. Even a brief consideration will show that the forms of be are significantly different from those words we traditionally call $verbs$. For example, if we look at all the so-called $regular\ verbs$ in English, we find that—excluding auxiliaries—each one has only four distinct spelling forms:

> call, calls, called, calling
> walk, walks, walked, walking

None of the so-called $irregular$ (or "strong") $verbs$ has more than five distinct spelling forms, while a few of them (such as hit) have only three:

> sing, sings, sang, sung, singing
> hit, hits, hitting

Yet there are $eight$ separate forms of be:

> be, is, am, are, was, were, been, being

There are sound historical reasons for this variety, just as there are also historical reasons for the fact that, in some ways, the forms of be do not behave, in sentences, like other words that grammarians call verbs (for example, $call$ and $sing$). For these reasons, among others, generative grammarians (like many historical grammarians) separate be from all other types of verbs.

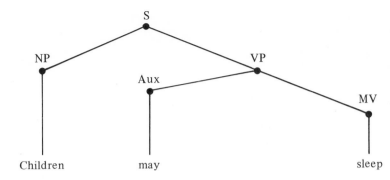

Figure 2.2 *NP + Aux + MV*

Yet all "main verbs"—including *be*—can be preceded by auxiliaries, and we can illustrate this fact in a phrase-structure rule. Thus, our next symbolic presentation says that a **verb phrase** (*VP*) may consist of one or more **auxiliaries** (*Aux*) followed by a **main verb** (*MV*):

PS 2.2 VP → Aux + MV

Now we can also enlarge the basic branching-tree diagram, as in Figure 2.2. And we can make the notion of "dominate" more specific. In particular, we may say that *VP* "immediately dominates" *Aux* and *MV*; *S* "immediately dominates" *NP* and *VP*; and *S* simply "dominates" *Aux* and *MV*. In other words, one node "immediately dominates" the next node down a branch and only "dominates" any node farther down the branch.

These terms permit us to define some basic relationships in sentences. Although these definitions will be qualified in a later section, the system given here will remain constant. Thus, we can define the *subject of a sentence* as a noun phrase that is immediately dominated by an *S* node; similarly, the *predicate of a sentence* is a verb phrase that is immediately dominated by an *S* node.

Turning again to the verb phrase, we can now treat the distinction between *be* and all other verbs. In particular, we say that a main verb consists of either (1) *be* followed by a **predicate complement,**[6] or (2) any other verb. Symbolically, we may state this as follows:

PS 2.3 $MV \rightarrow \left\{ \begin{matrix} be + \text{Pred} \\ V \end{matrix} \right\}$

The braces, { }, indicate a choice. That is, when we come to the *MV* node in a branching tree, we may choose either *be + Pred* or else *V*. Thus, the simple rules

---

[6] Readers should note that we are using the term **predicate** (*Pred*) in two different senses, just as the early generative grammarians did: first, to refer to the entire "predicate of a sentence" (that is, a *VP* immediately dominated by *S*), and second, to refer to certain kinds of structures that can follow a form of *be* when that form occurs as a main verb. This double usage has historical precedents.

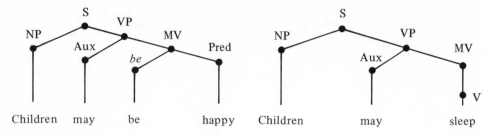

Figure 2.3   Expanding *MV*

we have given thus far permit us to derive two branching trees, as shown in Figure 2.3.

At this point, it is useful to oversimplify somewhat in order to clarify the presentation. The oversimplification is not serious, and we shall correct it later before developing this aspect of transformational theory further. In particular, we want to say now that there are three primary types of verb (V) in English: **intransitive** (V_i), **transitive** (V_t), and **copulative** (V_c).[7] Any verb in English may be followed by an adverb of location or time (or both). With intransitive verbs, however, nothing intervenes between the verb and the adverb. With transitive verbs, a direct object (and sometimes an indirect object) intervenes between the verb and the adverb. With copulative verbs, the so-called **subjective complement** *(Comp)* intervenes; as we shall note more fully later, the kinds of words that can occur as subjective complements are sometimes different from those than can occur as predicates following a form of *be.*

Again, all this can be shown symbolically:

$$\textbf{PS 2.4}\quad V \rightarrow \left\{ \begin{array}{l} V_i \\ V_t + NP \\ V_c + Comp \end{array} \right\}$$

This phrase-structure rule says that the symbol V consists of any one of three other symbols, or sequences of symbols. Specifically, V may consist of (1) V_i, which is the symbol for all intransitive verbs; or (2) $V_t + NP$, where the V_t is the symbol for all transitive verbs and the *NP* indicates that every transitive verb is followed by a noun phrase that is, by definition, the direct object of the verb; or (3) $V_c + Comp$, where V_c is the symbol for all copulative verbs—except *be*—and the *Comp* indicates the subjective complement that follows copulative verbs.

Obviously, we could also give a branching tree for each of the alternatives indicated in this formula. One possible tree is shown in Figure 2.4; the reader may wish to draw his own trees for the other possibilities. We should notice,

---

[7] In this presentation, the copulative verb (V_c) excludes *be*, but includes most of the verbs traditionally called **linking** verbs, for example, *seem, become, taste,* and so on.

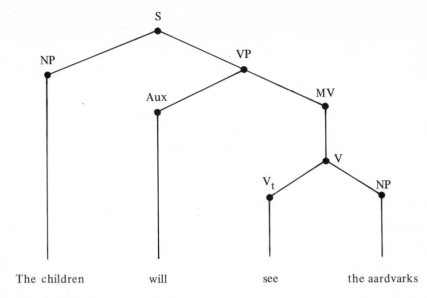

Figure 2.4 $NP + Aux + V_t + NP$

here, that a second *NP* has been introduced into our branching tree. This *NP* is not a "subject" because it is not immediately dominated by *S*. Rather, as noted above, we may define this *NP* as the **direct object** because it is immediately dominated by a *V* node, which also dominates a V_t node. This description is therefore a specification of the intimate connection between transitive verbs and direct objects; it also indicates that other kinds of verbs cannot have direct objects.

Before developing additional facts about the language, it is profitable to pause at this elementary stage and sum up the information presented thus far. At the same time, we can introduce another important pedagogical notion, which we have tacitly assumed in the earlier part of this chapter: *sentence positions.* Table 2.1 defines four basic sentence types in English, and arranges the elements in these sentences according to positions. As Table 2.1 indicates, we can define four basic positions in simple English sentences. The parentheses in the fourth, or adverbial, position indicate that adverbs are optional. The ϕ in position 3 of sentence type I is called a *null*; it indicates that this position is empty in sentences containing intransitive verbs.

Table 2.1 illustrates a number of facts, some of them obvious and some a bit obscure. We may take the obvious ones first. Each of the basic sentences contains an identical element, a noun phrase (*NP*), in the first position. Noun phrases, however, may vary enormously in their complexity. They may be quite simple:

Table 2.1 Basic Sentence Positions

Type	Position			
	1	2	3	4
be	NP	be	Pred	(Adv)
I	NP	V_i	ϕ	(Adv)
II	NP	V_t	NP	(Adv)
III	NP	V_c	Comp	(Adv)

Sentence 2.4a The buildings [are factories].

Or they may be expanded and elaborated to a considerable degree:

Sentence 2.4b All of the five quite old buildings there at the bend of the county's most famous river [are factories].

Expansions such as this will be investigated in later chapters.

Each of the second positions contains either a verb or some form of *be*, but the verb obviously differs according to the type of sentence. Traditionally (as well as in most dictionaries), each verb of English is assigned to one of three major categories: transitive, intransitive, or copulative. (We shall later suggest modifications for this system.) For purposes of discussion, the particular kind of verb is a good indicator of sentence type, and consequently, we may say that the nature of the verb defines the sentence type.

The third position contains the greatest variety. Following a form of *be* we have an element known as a **predicate** (*Pred*). Among other things, the predicate can be a noun phrase (as in *The boy is my brother*), an **adjective** (as in *The boy is tall*), or an adverb of location (as in *The boy is here*). Symbolically, this is shown as follows:

PS 2.5 Pred → $\begin{Bmatrix} NP \\ Adj \\ Loc \end{Bmatrix}$

Following intransitive verbs, the third position is empty. This description may seem artificial at this point, but in a pedagogical analysis of English, the description is useful since it makes the comments on the fourth—or adverbial—position more inclusive and general. As we have seen, the *NP* that follows transitive verbs in the basic sentence patterns is also known as the direct object. We have also already seen that the subjective complement that follows copulative verbs is different in significant ways from the predicate (*Pred*) that follows a form of *be*.

As already noted, the parentheses in Table 2.1 indicate that the fourth position is optional. Yet adverbs are so basic to the language, and occur with such frequency, that the simplest pedagogical description of English is one that includes them as part of the structure of basic sentences. We should note, however, that the symbol for **adverb** (*Adv*) is generalized at this point; certain restrictions on the use of adverbs will be discussed in later chapters. By way of preview, we may note that *be* can be followed in the fourth position by **adverbs of location** (*Loc*) and **adverbs of time** (*Tm*) but—in general—not by **adverbs of manner** (*Man*). That is, we can say *John is happy here* and *John is happy today*, but we cannot say **John is happy furiously.*[8]

There are many sentences in English that apparently do not conform to these basic patterns. For example, the sentence *Come here!* appears not to contain a noun phrase in position 1, and the sentence *We elected John president today* appears to contain two noun phrases in position 3. These irregularities are apparent rather than real, however, and can be dealt with quite logically in our pedagogical grammar once we have established the notion of basic sentence types.

The sentence types given in Table 2.1 were originally called **kernel** sentences. (Optionally, kernel sentences may also incorporate auxiliary verbs.) All other types of sentences were called **nonkernel**, or to use a more descriptive term, **derived** sentences. Pedagogically, these terms are still useful even though, as we shall see, their scientific "validity" is open to question.

We need to define one more concept before we observe the operation of a generative grammar. In discussing the phrase-structure rules, we observed that the symbols in these rules represent constituents of language. We noted that the primary constituent of any language is the sentence. The five rules presented thus far have included the following additional constituents:

NP, VP, Aux, MV, *be*, Pred, V, V_i, V_t, V_c, Comp, Adj, Loc

The phrase-structure rules permit us to specify how one constituent relates to one or more other constituents, and this relation may be shown graphically in a branching tree. After we have applied the phrase-structure rules—after we have derived a tree—we have produced a series of related constituents that can be arranged linearly. Any linear arrangement of constituents is called a **string**. Thus, in a transformational grammar there are strings of constituents that "underlie" every sentence.

Now we can clarify the distinction between kernel sentences and derived sentences. Given a string of constituents that underlies a kernel (that is, a "basic") sentence, if we modify this string in various well-defined ways (if, for example, we introduce a negative element, or we add a subordinate clause, or we transpose elements into an order that relates to passive voice structures), then the resultant string will be one that underlies a nonkernel (that is, a "derived") sentence.

The following are examples of the "basic sentence types" given in Table 2.1.

---

[8] As we shall note in Chapter 4, adverbs are a "relatively unexplored" part of English grammar. Readers whose knowledge of English is derived chiefly from traditional school-grammars should note that the typical definition of adverb, "a word that modifies a verb, an adjective, or another adverb," is partly circular, too narrow, and insufficiently precise.

(As noted above, and discussed more fully below, basic sentences may contain auxiliary verbs.)

be	Sentence 2.5	The animal is an aardvark.
	Sentence 2.6	The aardvark may be happy.
	Sentence 2.7	The aardvark has been there.
Type I:	Sentence 2.8	The forest is sleeping.
	Sentence 2.9	The dew has fallen.
	Sentence 2.10	The parachutist may jump tomorrow.
Type II:	Sentence 2.11	The Frenchman drank the wine yesterday.
	Sentence 2.12	The draftsman may have bought an elephant.
	Sentence 2.13	The aardvark is eating his supper.
Type III:	Sentence 2.14	The professor has become angry.
	Sentence 2.15	The team looks terrible today.
	Sentence 2.16	The steak tastes good.

The structural relationships underlying these basic sentences may be represented by branching trees, as shown in Figures 2.5 and 2.6 (the trees are somewhat simplified).

2.3   A Simple Grammatical Model

We can now give a vastly simplified **grammatical model** that will generate simple English sentences (that is, it will specify the relationships that exist within various sentences). The grammar will be modified considerably as we work through a more realistic presentation of English; particularly, we must also introduce the notion of *transformations*. But this simplified model can serve to illustrate some fundamental properties of any generative grammar.

For the present discussion, we shall restrict the model in the following ways. We shall not use *be* as a main verb. All of the "noun-phrase subjects" will be animate and plural; all verbs will be in the present tense. We shall use only modal auxiliaries (that is, *shall, will, can, may,* and so on). And we shall use only adverbs of time in the fourth position. Even with these restrictions, however, this "grammar" generates 120 sentences; furthermore, it will *not* generate any ungrammatical strings of words (that is, nonsentences).

The grammar is divided into two parts: (1) phrase-structure rules, and (2) a **lexicon**. In constructing a **derivation** that will represent the grammatical relationships of a sentence, we can proceed as follows: First, we begin with the phrase-structure rule that says: $S \rightarrow NP + VP$. Then we select the rules in any order, rewriting each element on the right of the arrow until the element cannot be rewritten again. Then we turn to the lexicon and substitute words for the symbols. The result, in each case, will represent the structure of a grammatical sentence in English. Obviously, this vastly simplified grammar will generate derivations for only an insignificant number of sentences, but each sentence will be

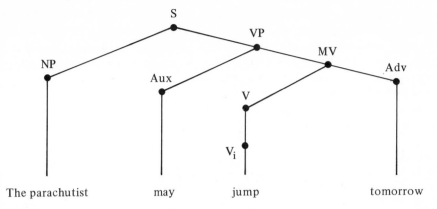

Figure 2.5   Sentence 2.10

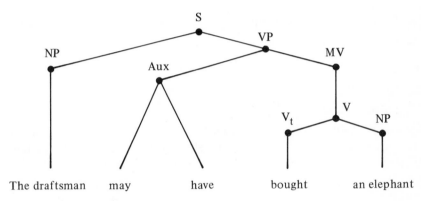

Figure 2.6   Sentence 2.12

grammatical, and the structure of each sentence can also be represented by a unique branching-tree diagram.

A. Phrase-Structure Rules[9]

PS 2.1   S → NP + VP

PS 2.2   VP → Aux + MV

PS 2.3a   MV → V (+Adv)

PS 2.4a   V → $\left\{ \begin{array}{l} V_i \\ V_t + NP \\ V_c + Adj \end{array} \right\}$

B. Lexicon

NP: the aardvarks, the pterodactyls

Aux: may, will V_c: seem, appear

V_i: dance, run   Adj: lonesome, hungry

V_t: see, devour   Adv: today, tomorrow

[9] Notice that rules PS 2.3a and PS 2.4a are simplified forms of rules presented earlier in the chapter.

The symbols have the following meanings: the arrow, $\rightarrow$, means "consists of"; the braces, $\{\ \}$, indicate that one complete line, and only one line, of the elements included within the braces must be chosen; the parentheses (around the *Adv* in PS 2.3a) indicate that the element contained within the parentheses is optional—a grammatical sentence will result whether or not the element is chosen.

As we noted earlier, the process of defining a sentence structure with this type of grammar is called a *derivation*. The following is a typical derivation:

1. S
2. NP + VP   (using PS 2.1)
3. NP + Aux + MV   (PS 2.2)
4. NP + Aux + V + Adv   (PS 2.3a)
5. NP + Aux + V_t + NP + Adv   (PS 2.4a)

Then we attach appropriate words from the lexicon to produce, for example:

Sentence 2.17 The aardvarks may see the pterodactyls today.

Or perhaps:

Sentence 2.18 The pterodactyls will devour the aardvarks tomorrow.

Notice that we "rewrite" only one item at a time. Thus, in going from step 2 to step 3 of the derivation, we rewrote *VP* as *Aux + MV*, and in going from step 4 to step 5, we rewrote *V* as $V_t + NP$. The restriction—that in constructing a derivation we may rewrite only one element at a time—is an important part of early transformational grammars. It is this restriction that gives us a unique branching-tree diagram for every derivation, as in Figure 2.7.

Another derivation from this simple set of rules might look quite different:

1. S
2. NP + VP   (PS 2.1)
3. NP + Aux + MV   (PS 2.2)
4. NP + Aux + V   (PS 2.3a)
5. NP + Aux + V_i (PS 2.4a)

This is as far as the phrase-structure rules will take us. The final line of this derivation (that is, $NP + Aux + V_i$) is known as a **terminal string**; we might say that the elements are "strung together" by the plus signs. But we also use the term *string* even if there are no plus signs in the line. Thus, the S is called the **initial string**. Lines 2, 3, and 4 are called **intermediate strings**.

When we come to the terminal string of the phrase-structure derivation, we attach words from the lexicon for the symbols in the string:

Sentence 2.19 The aardvarks may dance.

Or perhaps:

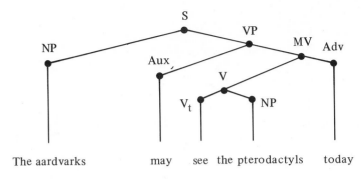

Figure 2.7   Sentence 2.17

Sentence 2.20   The pterodactyls will run.

Since both of these sentences have the same underlying derivation, they both have the same unique branching-tree diagram. In other words, a branching-tree diagram is merely a graphic means of representing a derivation.[10]

At the risk of redundancy, we can note that a derivation is *not* some kind of recipe for producing sentences. Rather, the steps in a derivation represent, in an increasingly detailed fashion, the structural relationships that underlie a given sentence. We might, therefore, "read" a derivation as follows (using the derivation on p. 36):

> The first line states, in effect, that a given sentence is—in fact—a sentence.
> The second line states that the sentence consists of a noun phrase and a verb phrase.
> The third line states that, moreover, the verb phrase of the sentence consists of an auxiliary and a main verb.
> The fourth line states that, moreover, the main verb of the sentence is a *V* (and not a form of *be*).
> The fifth line states that, moreover, the *V* of the sentence is intransitive.

Thus, the derivation represents the kind of knowledge that a speaker must have *before* he can produce or understand a sentence successfully; it does *not* represent either the act of production or the act of understanding. Two sentences can be represented with the same branching-tree diagram if, and only if, their derivations in terms of phrase-structure rules are equivalent, that is, if their initial and terminal strings are identical.

---

[10]Because the branching-tree diagrams do represent the derivation of a string from phrase-structure rules, transformational grammarians occasionally refer to them as phrase-structure markers, or more briefly as P markers. The term *derivation,* which refers to the steps that interconnect an initial string to a terminal string, should not be confused with the term *derived,* which refers to a sentence or word that is made from another sentence or word (as, for example, *manly* is made from—or derived from—*man*).

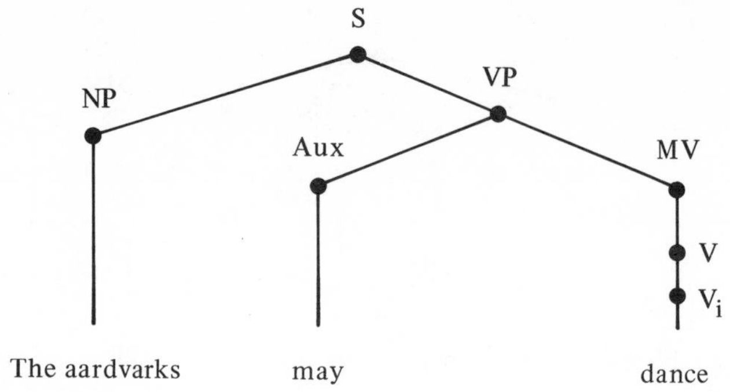

Figure 2.8   Sentence 2.19

2.4   Transformations

The first grammatical model contained two parts: a set of phrase-structure rules, and a lexicon of words. Additionally, we used an informal set of instructions for constructing a derivation. Thus, we began with the basic constituent, *Sentence*; we rewrote this constituent into two other constituents (that is, *noun phrase* and *verb phrase*); following the rules, we continued to rewrite constituents into other constituents, exercising choice where possible, until we produced a terminal string; and finally, we attached words from the lexicon to each symbol in the terminal string. We used the pedagogical term *kernel sentence* to characterize each sentence generated by the model.

In this section, we shall begin to expand the first grammatical model; in particular, we shall add a second kind of rule: a *transformation*. Transformational rules are fundamentally different from phrase-structure rules.

There is no simple and succinct way to describe the distinction between phrase-structure rules and transformations. As in many similar cases, the distinction becomes obvious when we work with the two kinds of rules. Nonetheless, we can state some broad differences. Thus, the phrase-structure rules generate a string of symbols that form the **deep structure** of a sentence; having generated such a structure, we then continue the derivation by inserting items from the lexicon; next, we apply transformational rules; and eventually, we produce the **surface structure** of the sentence.[11] In this pedagogical grammar, the surface structure is, effectively, the same as the written form of the sentence.

[11]The observant reader will note—and perhaps worry about—the qualification inherent in the word "eventually." True enough, there may sometimes be additional steps between the initial application of the transformational rules and the final representation of an English sentence. As noted earlier in the chapter, language is complex, vastly more so than scholars realized for 2000 years. To penetrate the complexity, we must proceed in simple steps, looking first at the major components and then returning to fill in details that are less major. But while honesty dictates this caveat, experience suggests that this kind of presentation is, in the long run, the simplest to follow.

Returning again to our familiar caveat, the sequence (". . . then . . . next . . . eventually . . .") given in the preceding paragraph does not relate to sentence production; rather, it relates *only* to the process of constructing a derivation— that is, a detailed representation of the structure that underlies a particular sentence. The resulting derivation is independent of direction. It states, in effect: "*Here* is a deep structure that represents certain grammatical information (for example, subject of a sentence); *here* is a surface structure that represents how a given sentence may be written (or spoken); and *here* is a set of rules that define how the surface and deep structures are interrelated." Figure 2.9 is a graphic way of representing these distinctions.

According to this form of transformational theory, the meaning of a sentence inheres completely in the deep structure. Transformations, in this view, relate "meaning" to a surface "form" that is acceptable to speakers of English.

Suppose now that we expand the first phrase-structure rule by adding an optional constituent to the right of the arrow. For illustrative purposes, we can use the **question** constituent (Q) which, we can say, represents "an internalized idea of a question." Symbolically, we can now present the first phrase-structure rule as follows:

PS 2.1a $S \rightarrow (Q) \, NP + VP$

The parentheses in this rule serve the same purpose as those in Table 2.1: They indicate that the constituent is optional.

Now suppose we apply the rules as indicated in the following derivation:

1. S
2. $Q + NP + VP$ (PS 2.1a)
3. $Q + NP + Aux + MV$ (PS 2.2)
4. $Q + NP + Aux + V + Adv$ (PS 2.3)
5. $Q + NP + Aux + V_i + Adv$ (PS 2.4a)

If we attach words from the lexicon to the symbols in the terminal string, we might get:

Q + the aardvarks + will + dance + today

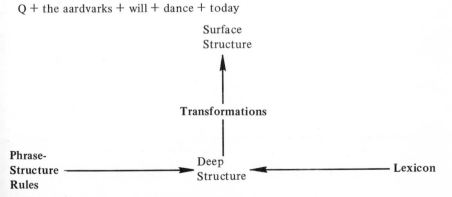

Figure 2.9   Organization of the early theory

The lexicon does not contain a word to replace the question constituent. Rather, this constituent acts as a signal to perform a transformation.[12] As a result, we reverse the order of the noun phrase and the auxiliary, and then we delete the question constituent, giving:

will + the aardvarks + dance + today

Through a series of conventional rules that apply to standard written English, we eventually define a surface structure, namely:

Sentence 2.21 Will the aardvarks dance today?

We can also use two branching trees (Figures 2.10 and 2.11) to represent, first, the deep structure (before transformations), and second, the surface structure (after transformations).

As this example indicates, transformations may serve to rearrange constituents and also to delete constituents. Additionally, we need to note a particularly important point: In this form of generative grammar, *transformations do not change meaning.* To repeat an observation made earlier in this section, the meaning of a sentence inheres completely in the deep structure, and transformations merely relate this meaning to an acceptable surface structure in English.[13]

There are, of course, a great many transformations in English; at present, no linguist would even estimate the number. A particular favorite in early publications was the so-called *passive transformation.* For our purposes, we can postulate a **passive** constituent (similar to the question constituent) which we can also

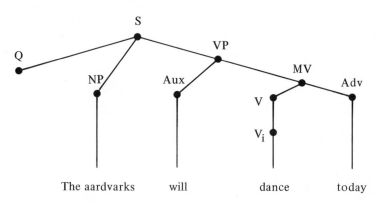

Figure 2.10 Deep structure of Sentence 2.21

[12]Some linguists prefer to say that the question constituent activates *two* transformations: the first one permutes *NP* and *Aux,* and the second deletes the constituent *Q.*

[13]In Part Two, we shall discuss a number of particular transformations in some detail.

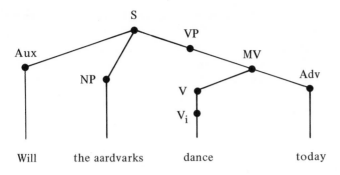

Figure 2.11 Surface structure of Sentence 2.21

introduce as an optional element in the first phrase-structure rule. If, in constructing a derivation, we choose this constituent in applying the first rule, then we must also choose the transitive-verb (V_t) constituent at a later step in the derivation. Following this procedure, we might possibly derive the following terminal string (the subscripts on the noun-phrase constituents are included simply to facilitate discussion):

Passive + NP_1 + Aux + V_t + NP_2 + Adv

As before, we attach words from the lexicon to the symbols in this string; we might get:

Passive + the aardvarks + will + devour + the pterodactyls + today

In constructing this derivation, the passive constituent acts as a signal to perform various transformations which (along with others) will eventually produce another string[14]:

The pterodactyls + will + be + devour + {-en} + by + the aardvarks + today

As before, the conventional rules for written English will define a surface structure:

Sentence 2.22 The pterodactyls will be devoured by aardvarks today.

Here again, the various transformations permuted constituents (NP_1 and NP_2) and deleted a constituent (*Passive*). Additionally, the transformations introduced some items that are *not* in the deep structure, namely, *be*, {-en}, and *by*. These items do not introduce new meanings into the sentence; rather, they serve

---

[14]The symbol {-en} is used frequently in early publications on generative grammar; it represents the past participle suffix (sometimes called the **past participle morpheme**). The term *morpheme* is a pedagogically useful one, and readers who are unfamiliar with the term may wish to consult Appendix 2, which presents an extended discussion.

to inform the reader (or listener) that the so-called **passive transformation** applies to the sentence.[15]

If human languages contained only rules such as those we have considered so far, they would still be interesting, but they would lack the single most important feature of real languages: infinite creativity. With the framework we have now established, we are ready to turn—in the next chapter—to the ways of describing this creativity.

Discussion and Exercises

1. Check some additional etymologies in the *Oxford English Dictionary* to see how words have changed in *meaning* over a period of time. In particular, check to see what relationship exists between the two words *grammar* and *glamour* and to see what changes have taken place in such words as *nice* and *fond*. Discuss the implications of the fact that all languages change.

2. Discuss some examples (similar to Lees' example of biology and the impossibility of defining *cell*) that support the claim that the other major academic disciplines have abandoned the notion of precise definition in their discussion of fundamentals. Transformationalists generally feel that, although students may have a difficult time *labeling* such things as nouns and verbs in a sentence, they nonetheless know *intuitively* what the words are because they generally use them correctly in sentences. That is, to use Plato's terms, they have a knowledge "of" their language, but not a knowledge "about" their language. Discuss some of the implications of this belief. Can you think of any other areas where many people have a knowledge "of"—but not a knowledge "about"—something? For example,

---

[15]Some persons find this confusing, and they raise an objection such as the following: "You say that transformations don't change meaning. Yet in this sentence you use a transformation to introduce *be*, a past participle suffix, and *by*. Surely these things have meaning."

The point to remember is this: the meaning of these items—*be, by,* and {-en}—already inheres in the passive constituent which is a part of the deep structure. We might say that the transformations simply change (that is, *trans form*) the way we represent this meaning in the surface structure.

This point sometimes prompts another objection. "That's very clever. But why make it so complicated? Why not start with the things you need in the deep structure?" The answer to this objection touches upon the universal aspects of generative grammar. By postulating abstract constituents such as the question constituent (and, in this case, the passive constituent), we can discuss a number of languages; for example, we can say that all languages incorporate the abstract concept of *question* although the surface structures of questions may differ widely from language to language. In brief, and we shall return to this subject later, languages differ from each other primarily in their lexicons and their transformations.

everyone knows how to tie a shoelace, but can you *explain* how to tie a shoelace using words only (no gestures, no pictures)?

3. As indicated in the text, the school-grammar definition of sentence is semantic and, for all practical purposes, meaningless if we do not know how to define "a complete thought" (something no philosopher has ever been able to define). The school-grammar definitions of *noun* and *verb* are also semantic. To use them, in most cases, we must know what "names" and "actions" are. And, of course, if we already know what these words mean, we have no need for the definitions. Students use thousands of nouns and verbs correctly every day, but many of them have a difficult time *labeling* the nouns and verbs in a sentence. Discuss the usefulness, in a pedagogical grammar, of such labeling. What, precisely, do we expect a student to do with a definition? Are definitions more important in studying one's own language or in studying a foreign language? Why?

4. Discuss the terms *inadequate* and *incorrect*, as applied to definitions. You might, for example, choose a technical term used in some field you have studied and then investigate the definitions of that term in a paperback dictionary, a "collegiate" dictionary, and an "unabridged" dictionary. Besides dictionary definitions, what other kinds of definitions are there? (Hint: How do young children come to learn the meanings of words?)

5. Refer to the list of constituents on p. 33 and give examples of each kind. Which of these constituents *cannot* occur as the constituents of a terminal string? Why? Which constituents can occur in a terminal string generated by the grammatical model on p. 35? Which constituents can be used to define the concept: *subject of a sentence*? *predicate of a sentence*? *direct object of a verb*?

6. Construct five kernel sentences for each of the basic sentence types given in Table 2.1. Use Sentences 2.5 to 2.16 as models.

7. Derive five sentences using the phrase-structure rules and the lexicon of the model grammar.

8. For each derivation in Exercise 7, give a "reading" similar to the one on p. 37.

9. Draw branching-tree diagrams for each of the derived sentences in Exercise 7.

10. Identify the phrase-structure rules that are applied in the following derivation:

   S
   a. NP + VP   (PS 2.   )
   b. NP + Aux + MV   (PS 2.   )
   c. NP + Aux + V   (PS 2.   )
   d. NP + Aux + V_c + Adj   (PS 2.   )

11. Complete the labeling of the nodes in the following branching-tree diagram:

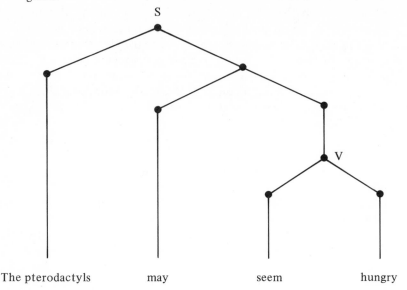

S

V

The pterodactyls   may   seem   hungry

12. Suppose we add the following phrase-structure rule to the grammatical model given on p. 35:

PS 2.5 NP → $\left\{ \begin{array}{c} \text{Name} \\ \text{Art + Noun} \end{array} \right\}$

And suppose we replace the listing for *NP* in the lexicon with the following items:

Art: the, my, our
Noun: pandas, ocelots, students
Name: Arthur, Bertha, Irving, Ms. Dufek

Using the new lexical items and the new rule, construct five new derivations from the grammatical model. (Note: If the same constituent occurs twice in a string—as, for example, *NP* might in a string that also contains V_t—then in proceeding to the next line of the derivation, you may rewrite both of the repeated constituents at the same time.)

13. For each derivation in Exercise 12, give a "reading" similar to those in Exercise 8.

14. Draw branching-tree diagrams for each of the sentences in Exercise 12.

15. What is the total number of constituents for each sentence for which you constructed a derivation in Exercise 12? (Hint: Simply count the number of nodes in the relevant branching tree.) What is the total number of *different* constituents for each of these sentences?

CHAPTER 3
The Early Theory: II

Our minds are finite, and yet even in these circumstances of finitude we are surrounded by possibilities that are infinite, and the purpose of human life is to grasp as much as we can out of that infinitude.
ALFRED NORTH WHITEHEAD, *Dialogues*

The earliest form of transformational theory did not present a formal means of representing subordination. Rather, the relationship between a main clause and a subordinate clause was defined through so-called **double-base transformations**, and the constraints on these transformations were only loosely stated. In one of the first major developments of the early theory, these informal double-base transformations were replaced by integrating, into the base rules, the logical property of **recursiveness**.

3.1 Recursiveness

Grammarians have known for thousands of years that speakers can combine two or more sentences to produce a single new sentence. The resulting sentence may be **compound** or **complex**. And it is particularly complex sentences—sentences with subordinate clauses—that distinguish human languages from the "languages" of logic. We can demonstrate part of this property of language by considering those adjectives that precede nouns in the surface structure of sentences.

Again, there is an example that the early generative grammarians frequently used, one on which we touched in Chapter 1 and which was first proposed by a group of French grammarians in the seventeenth century. We can place this example in the context of the present discussion by formulating two additional phrase-structure rules: the first is a revision of an earlier rule for rewriting the main verb (*MV*) constituent; and the second is (part of) a rule for rewriting the noun phrase (*NP*) constituent. Thus, we now want to say that:

PS 3.1 $MV \rightarrow \left\{ \begin{array}{c} V \\ be + Adj \end{array} \right\}$ (Adv)   **PS 3.2** $NP \rightarrow \left\{ \begin{array}{c} Name \\ Art + Noun \end{array} \right\}$ (S)

Both the braces and parentheses serve the same functions as before (see pp. 29 and 36). When we come to a main verb constituent in developing a derivation, we can choose either the top line within the brace (*V*) or the bottom line (*be + Adj*); similarly, when we come to a noun phrase constituent in a derivation, we must choose a name or else an article followed by a noun.[1] Additionally, in the phrase-structure rule that rewrites the noun phrase constituent, there is a sentence constituent following the braces, and this sentence constituent is enclosed within parentheses (*S*), which indicate that the selection of a sentence constituent is optional. In other words, when—in a derivation—we come to a noun phrase constituent, we always have the option of introducing a new sentence after the constituent; in technical terms, we have the option of **embedding** one sentence following a noun phrase in another sentence. In many of the early transformational grammars, this embedding process was the source of such things as adjectival modifiers and subordinate clauses.

By way of practical illustration, consider the following string (which incorporates elements from the new rule for rewriting noun phrase constituents)[2]:

Name + V_t + Art + Noun

Given this string, we might attach words from some lexicon to produce, ultimately, the sentence:

Sentence 3.1 God created the world.

Suppose, however, that we had chosen to select a sentence constituent at each possible point in the derivation of this sentence. We would then have produced a string like the following:

Name + S + V_t + Art + Noun + S

We have now a structure that permits us to embed two new sentences into the original sentence, which we can represent as follows:

God + *S* + created the world + *S*

At this point, it is useful to introduce two new terms: **matrix** and **insert**. The basic sentence—the one we would get if no sentence constituents were em-

---

[1] This is, of course, a simplification, and is introduced to facilitate the discussion. In many sentences, nouns occur without preceding articles, for example, *Cats like milk.*

[2] The auxiliary constituent is irrelevant to the present discussion and has been omitted for the sake of simplicity.

bedded—is frequently called the **matrix sentence** (or, sometimes, the **outside sentence**). An embedded sentence is frequently called an **insert sentence** (or, sometimes, an **inside sentence**).

Thus, our matrix sentence is: *God created the world*. And into this matrix sentence we elect to embed two insert sentences, one following the name constituent and the other following the article-plus-noun constituent. We can represent the result as follows:

God + *God is invisible* + created the world + *the world is visible*

(where the italicized words indicate the embedded sentences).

At this point, various transformational rules apply. They delete some words from the embedded sentences, words that—we might say—are "understood" by the reader or listener. The transformations also move the ajectives into their standard English positions.[3] The conventional rules of writing then give:

Sentence 3.2 Invisible God created the visible world.

Figures 3.1 and 3.2 are two branching trees that show the deep structure and surface structure of this sentence; a few details not relevant to the present discussion are omitted.

Now consider the following phrase-structure rules (PS 3.2 has been repeated for ease of reference):

PS 3.3 $S \rightarrow NP + VP$ **PS 3.2** $NP \rightarrow \begin{Bmatrix} \text{Name} \\ \text{Art + Noun} \end{Bmatrix} (S)$

In the first of these rules, the symbol S, which represents the sentence constituent, appears to the *left* of the arrow; in the other rule, the same symbol S appears as an optional constituent on the *right* of the arrow. When this condition exists (that is, when a symbol appears to the left of the arrow in one rule and also to the right of the arrow in a later rule), then—by definition—the rules are *recursive*. Because the rules are recursive, we can apply them again and again in constructing a derivation of a sentence. Thus, we always begin with the sentence constituent as the first line in a derivation; at some later step in the derivation we may elect to introduce another (embedded) sentence constituent as we rewrite a noun phrase constituent; if we do, then—at that point—we begin to apply the rules again. Similarly, as we work through the phrase-structure rules the second time, we may—again—elect to introduce still another (embedded) sentence constituent, and if we do, then we apply the rules yet another time. Thus,

---

[3] In French, as we noted in Chapter 1, there is a difference: The last part of this transformational operation does not apply; that is, the adjectives remain behind the name and the noun: *Le Dieu invisible a crée le monde visible*. Except for the different lexical items, the deep structures of the French and English sentences are identical; the transformations in the two languages simply order the adjectives differently.

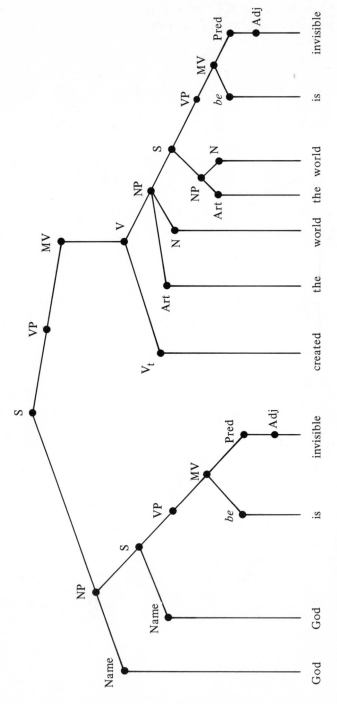

Figure 3.1 Deep structure of Sentence 3.2

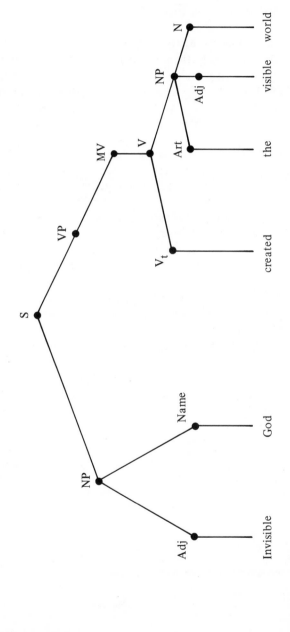

Figure 3.2 Surface structure of Sentence 3.2

the recursive property of the phrase-structure rules permits us to embed sentences into sentences an indefinite number of times.[4]

3.2   Some Pedagogical Simplifications

The rules we have examined thus far have a relatively simple structure. But as we continue to make revisions to these rules—and to the early form of transformational grammar—it will be useful to make a few pedagogical simplifications. Such simplifications incorporate the essential facts that teachers and students of English should know about this first phase of research in transformational grammar; the simplifications also facilitate discussion of the research conducted since 1963.

Briefly, then, the early transformational grammarians defined a grammar as a "device that generates all of the grammatical sequences of [a language] and none of the ungrammatical ones."[5] The early grammatical models contained three major components: a lexicon of elements; a set of phrase-structure rules; and a set of transformations. (The elements in the lexicon were sometimes referred to as **morphemes**; see Appendix 2.) In using these components to develop a derivation, we usually begin with the phrase-structure rule that rewrites the sentence constituent. We then apply additional phrase-structure rules, exercising whatever options are available, and finally produce the terminal string of the derivation. Next, we attach items from the lexicon to appropriate symbols in the terminal string. And the result constitutes the deep structure of a sentence. The entire meaning of the sentence inheres in this deep structure.

At this point, we begin to apply transformational rules to the deep structure. The particular transformational rules to be applied are completely determined by the nature of the deep structure.[6] After applying all the necessary transformations (as well as the standard rules of writing and punctuation), we have generated the surface structure—the written form—of a sentence. Alternatively,

---

[4] The very earliest transformational grammars did not incorporate recursiveness as a formal property of the phrase-structure rules. The process of embedding one sentence into another was accomplished through so-called *double-base transformations,* and this term appears widely in the research reports published between 1957 and 1963. The incorporation of recursiveness into the phrase-structure rules was the first major revision of the early transformational models.

[5] The choice of the word "device" has caused some confusion. By "device," a linguist generally means a logical model, one that can be represented in a consistent symbolism; conversely, a linguist does *not* mean some sort of physical device such as a computer. In place of the word "device," this text uses the term **model.**

[6] Before recursiveness was incorporated into the grammar as a formal property, the methods of applying some transformations were rather loose. Some transformations were considered "obligatory," while others were "optional." The revision that introduced recursiveness negated this distinction.

we could apply various rules of pronunciation to generate a spoken surface structure.[7]

Transformational linguists have adopted several symbolic conventions to facilitate presentation and discussion. As we have seen, the names of sentence constituents are generally abbreviated, particularly in presenting rules and in drawing branching trees. The two types of rules—phrase-structure and transformational—are distinguished graphically by using two types of arrows: in phrase-structure rules, the arrow has a single shaft ($\rightarrow$); in transformational rules, the arrow has a double shaft ($\Rightarrow$) and is sometimes called a "double arrow."

Branching trees generally incorporate only those details that are relevant to a particular discussion. (Nonetheless, it is always possible to draw complete trees for any deep structure.) One simplification, which has not previously been used in this chapter but will be used in subsequent chapters, consists in representing embedded sentences as simple triangles (thereby omitting all constituents lower than the sentence constituent). Using this symbolism, we could represent the deep-structure tree for Sentence 3.2 as shown in Figure 3.3.

Another simplification omits most of the formal details involved in applying a transformation. Thus, we might have presented Sentences 2.21 and 2.22 as follows:

Sentence 3.3 *Question* + the aardvarks will dance today $\Rightarrow$ Will the aardvarks dance today?
Sentence 3.4 *Passive* + the aardvarks will devour the pterodactyls today $\Rightarrow$ The pterodactyls will be devoured by the aardvarks today.

Similarly, we can present Sentence 3.2 as follows:

Sentence 3.2a God (God is invisible) created the world (the world is visible) $\Rightarrow$ Invisible God created the visible world.

In the remainder of this book, we shall employ these—and other—simplifications whenever possible. In short, we are interested in the outline and application of transformational theory rather than in minutiae.

3.3   A Few "Early" Transformations

Early works on transformational grammar generally referred to transformations by name, for example, "the passive transformation," "the question transformation," and so on. In the early 1960s, a few transformationalists formulated the hypothesis that *transformations do not change meaning.* (This is sometimes called the "meaning-preserving" hypothesis.) As a result of this hypothesis, it was no longer strictly correct to refer to transformations by name, at least not with the same implications as in earlier years. Thus, in the deep structure that

---

[7] Readers who still need to ponder the caveat against considering derivations as "sentence-producing machines" may wish to reread p. 37 in Chapter 2.

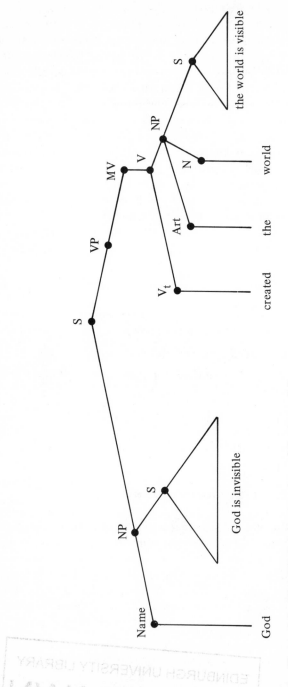

Figure 3.3 Simplified deep structure of Sentence 3.2

underlies any interrogative sentence, there is a question constituent, and this constituent activates one or more transformations. In brief, meaning inheres in the specific constituent rather than in the transformations associated with the constituent. Nonetheless, the early habit persists, particularly in informal discussions, and we shall generally follow the early custom in this book. In other words, we shall use a term such as the "question transformation" as a short way of referring to the transformation (or transformations) activated by the question constituent.

Thus far, we have looked briefly at three transformations: the question, the passive, and the restrictive-clause transformation that introduces adjectives into a matrix sentence (Sentences 3.3, 3.4, and 3.2). This last transformation also functions to embed **regular restrictive clauses** into a matrix sentence. Thus, suppose we have a matrix sentence such as

Sentence 3.5 The witches will become hungry.

In deriving this sentence, we could have embedded an insert sentence, which we might represent as follows:

Sentence 3.6 The witches (the witches dance at midnight) will become hungry.

The restrictive-clause transformation applies to a structure such as this, substituting a *relative pronoun* for the repeated nominal and ultimately giving the following surface structure:

Sentence 3.6a The witches who dance at midnight will become hungry.

Notice that this transformation is different from those that apply to Sentences 3.3 and 3.4; in those cases there are special constituents—question and passive— in the deep structure that activate the appropriate transformations. In the case of the restrictive-clause transformation, there is no special constituent in the deep structure; rather the transformational process is activated by the existence of a nominal in an insert sentence that is identical to a nominal in the matrix sentence.

Another of the early transformations is related to the restrictive-clause transformation, and in some cases they operate together. This related transformation operates on the so-called *wh-* words (for example, *who, what, when,* and so on); consequently, it is frequently referred to as "**the *wh-* transformation.**" The transformation applies not only in relative clauses but also in *wh-* questions. We shall consider the latter application first. Suppose we have a matrix sentence such as

Sentence 3.7 The baby has eaten something.

If we add a question constituent to the underlying structure of this sentence, we will have

Sentence 3.8 *Question* + The baby has eaten something ⇒ Has the baby eaten something?

In Sentences 3.7 and 3.8, the direct object of the verb is the same: the indefinite pronoun *something*. In discussing this and similar pronouns, we can usefully postulate a generalized form, called a PRO-**form**, which has two parts: a PRO *article* and a PRO-*noun*. Given this concept, we can then postulate a set of underlying PRO-forms such as: SOME + ONE, SOME + THING, SOME + TIME and so on. The usefulness of these forms will become obvious below.

Sentence 3.8 is a "yes-or-no" question; that is, the expected answer to the question is either a "yes" or a "no." But as we noted earlier in the chapter, we can also ask *wh-* questions in English, that is, questions that begin with words such as *who, what, when,* and so on. We can begin to investigate *wh-* questions by returning, first, to the structure underlying Sentence 3.8:

Sentence 3.8 *Question* + The baby has eaten something.

In place of the surface structure pronoun *something*, we can now substitute an underlying PRO-form:

Sentence 3.8a *Question* + The baby has eaten SOME + THING.

Now suppose that we replace the PRO-article in this structure with a special *wh-* element. (Since the underlying structure will have a different meaning, we must also change the sentence number.)

Sentence 3.9 *Question* + The baby has eaten *wh-* + THING.

At this point, the question transformation applies, producing

Sentence 3.9a Has the baby eaten *wh-* + THING?

Finally, the *wh-* transformation applies: in effect, it moves the constituent that contains *wh-* to the front of the sentence:

Sentence 3.9b *wh-* + THING has the baby eaten.

A spelling rule converts *wh-* + THING into the interrogative pronoun *what,* giving[8]:

Sentence 3.9c What has the baby eaten?

Like all other transformations, the *wh-* transformation always performs the same function, independent of the type of sentence to which it applies. That is, the *wh-* transformation *always* "moves" the constituent containing a *wh-* to the front of its own sentence.

Consider now a matrix sentence such as

Sentence 3.10 The box contained sunflower seeds.

---

[8] This series of rules for deriving *wh-* questions was modified after the revision of generative grammar in the mid-1960s. Nonetheless, the presentation given above is pedagogically useful, particularly when discussing language with children in middle or junior high schools.

As before, we can embed an insert sentence into this matrix, perhaps as follows:

Sentence 3.11 The box (I found the box) contained sunflower seeds.

In the insert sentence, there is a nominal (*the box*) which is identical to a nominal in the matrix sentence. This permits us to incorporate a *wh-* into the insert sentence. We can now represent the underlying structure as

Sentence 3.11a The box (I found *wh*-box) contained sunflower seeds.

Given a structure such as this, the *wh-* transformation applies to move the constituent containing the *wh-* to the front of its own sentence, giving:

Sentence 3.11b The box (*wh*-box I found) contained sunflower seeds.

The fact that *box* is inanimate affects the next step. Specifically, *wh-box* is converted to the relative pronoun *which*, and the final surface structure sentence is[9]

Sentence 3.11c The box which I found contained sunflower seeds.

Now consider a simple sentence such as

Sentence 3.12 You will go.

On p. 31, where we defined four types of basic sentences, we noted that such a sentence could incorporate an adverbial in the fourth position. We can represent a generalized adverbial of time by using a PRO-form:

Sentence 3.12a You will go SOME + TIME

Suppose, now, we add two new elements to the structure represented by Sentence 3.12a. In particular, suppose we add the question constituent to the beginning of the structure and then replace the PRO-article (SOME) with *wh-*. (Since this addition changes the meaning of the structure, we must also change the sentence number.)

Sentence 3.13 *Question* + you will go *wh-* + TIME

The question transformation applies, giving

Sentence 3.13a Will you go *wh-* + TIME

---

[9] In most dialects of English, we may use either *which* or *that* in sentences such as Sentence 3.11c. In other words, *which* and *that* are simply stylistic variants in such sentences. Additionally, there is an optional (stylistic) transformation that, in this case, permits us to delete *which* or *that* from the surface structure:

Sentence 3.11d The box I found contained sunflower seeds.

As noted, the noun *box* is inanimate. If, instead, the noun referred to a human (if it were "animate"), then the surface-structure pronoun would be *who* or, in some cases, *whom*.

and the *wh-* transformation applies, giving

Sentence 3.13b *wh-* + TIME will you go

And finally, the standard rules of spelling and punctuation apply to give the surface structure:

Sentence 3.13c When will you go?

Instead of adding a generalized adverbial of time to Sentence 3.12, we might have chosen to add one of location, giving

Sentence 3.12b You will go SOME + PLACE

If we change this structure by adding the question constituent and a *wh-*, we would then proceed through the following steps:

Sentence 3.14 *Question* + you will go *wh-* + PLACE
Sentence 3.14a Will you go *wh-* + PLACE
Sentence 3.14b *wh-* + PLACE will you go
Sentence 3.14c Where will you go?

There are still other ways to use PRO-forms and the *wh-* transformation. Consider the following two simple sentences:

Sentence 3.15 I fell asleep.
Sentence 3.16 The soprano began to sing.

Suppose we add a generalized adverbial of time to each of these sentences. We could then represent the deep structures in the following way:

Sentence 3.15a I fell asleep SOME + TIME
Sentence 3.16a The soprano began to sing SOME + TIME

The generalized adverbial in Sentence 3.15a is actually a nominal, and the second phrase-structure rule permits us to embed an insert sentence after any nominal, including this one. We can represent the structure as

Sentence 3.17 I fell asleep SOME + TIME + (*S*)

Now let us assume (without, at this point, presenting the formal details) that the PRO-forms in Sentences 3.16a and 3.17 are *coreferential,* that is, that they refer to the same moment of time. This permits us to embed Sentence 3.16a as the insert sentence in the matrix Sentence 3.17, giving

Sentence 3.17a I fell asleep SOME + TIME + (the soprano began to sing SOME + TIME)

We next replace the SOME of the insert sentence with *wh-*:

Sentence 3.17b I fell asleep SOME + TIME + (the soprano began to sing *wh-* + TIME)

The *wh-* transformation moves the constituent containing *wh-* to the front of its own sentence, giving:

Sentence 3.17c I fell asleep SOME + TIME + (*wh-* + TIME the soprano began to sing)

At this point, we can transformationally delete the PRO-form from the matrix sentence (since, in a sense, it is "understood" by a listener), and then apply the appropriate rules of spelling and punctuation to give the surface-structure sentence:

Sentence 3.17d I fell asleep when the soprano began to sing.

The following pair of sentences illustrates a slightly different case. Both sentences contain regular (rather than generalized) adverbials of location.

Sentence 3.18 I have walked on the street.
Sentence 3.19 You live on the street.

The adverbial in Sentence 3.18 contains a nominal (*the street*) which, according to the second phrase-structure rule, permits us to embed an insert sentence. We might produce the following:

Sentence 3.20 I have walked on the street (you live on the street)

We next replace the article in the insert sentence by *wh-*, giving

Sentence 3.20a I have walked on the street (you live on *wh*-street)

The *wh-* transformation applies to move the constituent containing *wh-* (that is, to move the entire adverbial) to the front of its own sentence:

Sentence 3.20b I have walked on the street (on *wh*-street you live)

Again, we shall simply state that the adverbials in the matrix and insert sentence are coreferential; we can replace the insert adverbial with a relative pronoun, eventually producing

Sentence 3.20c I have walked on the street where you live.

In the early discussion of transformational grammar, linguists paid considerable attention to the structure of auxiliary verbs, and they developed another useful transformation that applied to these auxiliaries. As we have already noted, one of the early phrase-structure rules presented the verb phrase as follows:

PS 3.4 VP → Aux + MV

A later phrase-structure rule rewrote the auxiliary constituent in this way:

PS 3.5 Aux → Tense + (Modal) + (*have* + *en*) + (*be* + *ing*)

This rule incorporates considerable information about the structure of English auxiliaries. Before discussing this information, however, we must first consider one additional phrase-structure rule:

PS 3.6 Tense → $\left\{\begin{array}{l} Present \\ Past \end{array}\right\}$

This rule indicates that there are, linguistically speaking, only two **tenses** in English.[10] And when this rule is used in conjunction with the auxiliary rule, we can generate all the structures that underlie every possible combination of auxiliary and main verb in all active, declarative sentences in English.

Returning now to the phrase-structure rule for writing auxiliaries. Briefly, the rule gives the following information:

1. We must choose the **tense**. (That is, every English sentence incorporates the element of tense.)
2. We may also choose a **modal** auxiliary. (As noted on p. 36, linguists use parentheses to indicate that an element in a rule is optional.)
3. We may also choose the so-called **perfect auxiliary**. If we do, then some form of the word *have* will appear in the surface structure of the sentence, *and* the next following verb will be in the past participle form. (The *en* associated with *have* represents the so-called *past participle morpheme*.)
4. We may also choose the so-called **progressive auxiliary**. If we do, then some form of the word *be* will appear in the surface structure of the sentence, *and* the next following verb will be in the present participle form. (The *ing* associated with *be* represents the so-called *present participle morpheme*.)
5. If we choose more than one of the optional elements (and we may choose all three if we wish), then they will invariably appear in the order shown by the rule.

The following sentences illustrate the choices available to speakers of English.

---

[10] Again, we are presenting the auxiliary rule as it was originally given in Chomsky's *Syntactic Structures*. As we shall note in Chapter 6, some linguists have prepared alternatives to this rule. At this point, however, we can note that tense is a strictly grammatical concept which refers, not to time, but to the inflectional endings that occur as suffixes on verbs; in other words, tense is an element that must be added to a verb. Consider the verb *call*. If we add *Present* to this verb, then we get *call* or *calls* (depending on the number and person of the subject); if we add *Past*, then we get *called*.

To belabor the point, a verb has no tense until it is used in a sentence, and even then the verb incorporates tense *only if* there are no preceding auxiliary verbs. If there are one or more auxiliary verbs, then the first of these incorporates tense in the surface structure.

Additionally, this early analysis assumes that a modal can also incorporate tense, although some linguists reject this assumption. If modals do incorporate tense, then the present and past forms would be as follows:

Present	Past
can	could
may	might
shall	should
will	would

The first set (Sentences 3.21 to 3.28) all incorporate *Present*; the second set (Sentences 3.29 to 3.36) all incorporate *Past*.

Sentence 3.21 The boy runs (*Tense* and *Main verb*).
Sentence 3.22 The boy may run (*Tense, Modal,* and *Main verb*).
Sentence 3.23 The boy may have run (*Tense, Modal, Perfect,* and *Main verb*).
Sentence 3.24 The boy may be running (*Tense, Modal, Progressive,* and *Main verb*).
Sentence 3.25 The boy may have been running (*Tense, Modal, Perfect, Progressive,* and *Main verb*).
Sentence 3.26 The boy has run (*Tense, Perfect,* and *Main verb*).
Sentence 3.27 The boy has been running (*Tense, Perfect, Progressive,* and *Main verb*).
Sentence 3.28 The boy is running (*Tense, Progressive,* and *Main verb*).
Sentence 3.29 The boy ran.
Sentence 3.30 The boy might run.
Sentence 3.31 The boy might have run.
Sentence 3.32 The boy might be running.
Sentence 3.33 The boy might have been running.
Sentence 3.34 The boy had run.
Sentence 3.35 The boy had been running.
Sentence 3.36 The boy was running.

We now come to one of the most celebrated of the early transformations, upon which—in the original edition—one author bestowed the name **flip-flop transformation.** (A colleague has called this "inelegant but descriptive.") Briefly, the flip-flop transformation guarantees that the "bound morphemes" (see Appendix 2) of the auxiliary rule (that is, *Tense, en,* and *ing*) will be associated with the right verbs in the surface structure. Thus, suppose we refer to the "bound morphemes" (*Tense, en, ing*) in the rule as **affixes** and use the symbol *Af* to represent them; and suppose we use the symbol v to represent any modal, *have, be,* or main verb. Thus, the *affix* (or flip-flop) transformation may be represented as: $Af + v \Rightarrow v + Af$. We can use these symbols and a "half-made" sentence to illustrate the operation of the flip-flop transformation.

Sentence 3.37 My dog (*Tense* + like) cheese.

If we choose *Present* for this sentence, then we would get

Sentence 3.37a My dog (*Present* + like) cheese

Now the flip-flop transformation applies:

$$Af \overset{\frown}{} v$$

Sentence 3.37b My dog (*Present* + like) cheese
                    v Af
                My dog (like + *Present*) cheese
                My dog likes cheese.

The rule is easy to follow in this simple example. But consider the structure tha‖ underlies Sentence 3.33, which we can represent as follows:

$$Af \overset{\frown}{}v \quad v \quad Af \overset{\frown}{}v \quad Af \overset{\frown}{}v$$

Sentence 3.33a The boy (*Past* + may + *have* + *en* + *be* + *ing*) run

As the arrows indicate, the flip-flop transformation applies three times to thi‖ structure to produce

$$v \quad Af \quad v \quad v \quad Af \quad v \quad Af$$

Sentence 3.33b The boy (may + *Past* + *have* + *be* + *en*) run + *ing*

The affixes are now in the correct position (that is, following rather than preced‖ ing the appropriate verbs), so we can apply the rules of spelling and punctuatio‖ to produce[11]

Sentence 3.33 The boy might have been running.

Before finishing this brief survey of pedagogical simplifications of transforma‖ tional grammar, we can look at one more deep-structure constituent, namely **negative**, and one more transformation, the so-called **do-insertion transforma‖ tion.** Consider a variation of Sentence 2.21:

Sentence 3.38 *Negative* + the aardvarks will dance today

The negative transformation now applies. Specifically, this transformation move‖ the negative constituent behind the *first verb* in the auxiliary structure. (In th‖ case of Sentence 3.38, there is only one verb in the auxiliary structure.)

Sentence 3.38a The aardvarks will *negative* dance today

Finally, the standard rules give

Sentence 3.38b The aardvarks will not dance today.

But suppose there is no auxiliary verb structure (that is, suppose there is n‖ modal, *have*, or *be*). In this case, the negative transformation moves the negativ‖ constituent to the position following the tense constituent—either *Present* o‖ *Past.* Consider a deep structure represented as follows:

Sentence 3.39 *Negative* + Irving (*Present*) like girls

If the negative constituent were not part of this sentence, it would lead eventu‖ ally to the surface structure: *Irving likes girls.* But the presence of the negativ‖ constituent activates the negative transformation, which moves the negative con‖ stituent behind *Present*:

Sentence 3.39a Irving (*Present* + *Negative*) like girls

[11] The reader may wish to experiment in deriving some of the other sentences in the exam‖ ples given above (Sentences 3.21-3.36). In every case, the flip-flop transformation wil‖ attach the proper affix to the proper surface verb.

The flip-flop transformation cannot apply to this structure, since there is an element (the negative constituent) that intervenes between the affix (*Present*) and the verb (*like*). When such a condition exists (when some element intervenes between an affix and a verb as defined in the flip-flop transformation), then in the standard dialect of English we *invariably* insert *do* as a carrier for the affix. This **do-insertion** transformation applies as follows:

Sentence 3.39b Irving (*Present* + do + *Negative*) like girls.

Finally, the standard rules apply to produce

Sentence 3.39c Irving does not like girls.

At this point, we apply the **contraction transformation** to produce

Sentence 3.39d Irving doesn't like girls.

Suppose now that we modify Sentence 3.39 by substituting the question constituent in place of the negative constituent. This would give a different underlying structure, which we can represent as

Sentence 3.40 *Question* + Irving (*Present*) like girls

In Chapter 2, we used the question transformation to permute the order of the subject noun phrase and the auxiliary constituent. At the time, however, we were using a grammatical model that contained only present-tense modals in the auxiliary position. We now need to modify the transformation somewhat, since we have expanded the auxiliary constituent, by introducing the auxiliary rewrite rule:

PS 3.5 Aux → Tense + (Modal) + (*have* + *en*) + (*be* + *ing*)

Specifically, we now need to say that the question transformation applies to the first *full verb* in any given auxiliary phrase (that is, to the modal, *have*, or *be*); if there is no full verb in a given auxiliary phrase, then the transformation applies to the tense morpheme.[12]

In Sentence 3.40, the auxiliary phrase contains only tense (that is, *Present*). In applying the question transformation, we must permute the order of the subject noun phrase and the tense, and then delete the question constituent, giving

Sentence 3.40a *Present* + Irving like girls

Once again, we have isolated a "bound morpheme" from the auxiliary structure; consequently, the flip-flop transformation cannot apply. Thus, as we did in the similar case involving the negative constituent, we must insert *do* as a carrier

---

[12]The question transformation is similar to the negative transformation. Both operate on the auxiliary constituent; moreover, both operate on the first full verb within a given auxiliary phrase; and finally, when there is no full verb in a given phrase, then both operate on tense. (Again, there is a different set of rules that apply when *be* is the main verb.)

of tense. As before, the transformation that accomplishes this is the do-insertion transformation, which gives

Sentence 3.40b *Present* + do + Irving like girls

Now the flip-flop transformation can apply to invert the order of the affix (*Present*) and the auxiliary verb (*do*), giving

Sentence 3.40c do + *Present* + Irving like girls

And the standard rules of writing finally produce:

Sentence 3.40d Does Irving like girls?

3.4   Looking Backward

The late 1950s were the infancy of transformational grammar; the first few years of the 1960s were the early childhood. The metaphorical child was lusty and loud during these years; like real children, he stumbled from time to time but generally managed to pick himself up and eventually grew into a healthy adolescence, which will be the subject of our next two chapters. But before examining the next stage of development, it is useful to summarize the significant accomplishments made during the first period.

The major accomplishment, of course, was the refocusing of grammatical studies. In the previous few decades, grammarians had been concerned chiefly with describing speech. They focused particularly on defining and cataloguing the sounds and morphemes of language. They also restricted themselves to those aspects of language that they could see and hear; that is, to sentences that had already *been produced.* They studiously avoided discussing the nature of the human mind; they made no attempt to characterize the rules of language that a speaker needs to know if he is to create sentences in the language. Transformational grammarians, in contrast, focused chiefly on these rules, that is, on the knowledge a speaker must have if he is *able to produce.* For the transformationalist, a grammar is more than a set of descriptions of observable elements; a grammar must also incorporate a set of generative rules.

In studying the possible nature of these generative rules, the early transformationalists concluded that there are really two kinds of rules: phrase-structure rules, which define the parts (or constituents), and transformational rules, which delete, substitute, and otherwise alter the basic constituents (among other things).

The existence of two types of rules led the transformationalists to formulate a distinction between deep and surface structures. Briefly, the phrase-structure rules combine with the lexicon to generate a deep structure for every sentence in English. (Each deep structure can be represented by a unique branching tree.) Then the transformations apply to produce a surface structure, without changing the meaning inherent in the deep structure.

The very earliest transformational grammars were not recursive; that is, they did not incorporate within the phrase-structure rules a means for combining sentences. (In these earliest grammars, sentences were combined exclusively through the operation of so-called optional transformational rules.) In the first major revision of transformational grammar, recursiveness was moved from the set of transformational rules into the set of phrase-structure rules. This shift permitted the transformationalists to formulate the hypothesis that transformations do not change meaning.

Some transformationalists used the term **competence** to refer to the internalized knowledge of language that every speaker of that language possesses. They also contrasted competence with **performance**, a term that refers to the use a speaker makes of his competence in a particular situation (that is, when he speaks or writes a sentence).

Many of the details of the earliest grammars have been modified considerably in recent years. Nonetheless, these early ideas have considerable pedagogical usefulness, particularly in discussing composition, and this fact prompted our extended examination of some important early transformations. The following examples provide a review and summary of this examination.

1. **The Restrictive Clause Transformation**
   a. The "Full" Relative Clause
   Sentence 3.41 The boy (the boy found a dime) bought a balloon ⇒ The boy who found a dime bought a balloon.
   b. The Adjective Clause
   Sentence 3,42 The man (the man is tall) bowed deeply ⇒ The tall man bowed deeply.

2. **The Question Transformation ("Yes-or-No" Questions)**
   Sentence 3.43 *Question* + I may have this dance ⇒ May I have this dance?

3. **The *wh-* Transformation**
   a. In Relative Clauses
   Sentence 3.44 The cake (you baked *wh-* + cake) was delicious ⇒ The cake which you baked was delicious.
   b. In wh- Questions
   Sentence 3.45 *Question* + You will give *wh-* + thing to the rooster ⇒ What will you give to the rooster?

4. **The Passive Transformation**
   Sentence 3.46 *Passive* + The boy ate the hamburger ⇒ The hamburger was eaten by the boy.

5. **The Negative Transformation**
   Sentence 3.47 *Negative* + I can solve this problem ⇒ I cannot solve this problem.

6. **The Contraction Transformation**
   Sentence 3.48 I cannot solve this problem. ⇒ I can't solve this problem.

7. The do-Insertion Transformation

a. In Negative Sentences

Sentence 3.49 *Negative* + I know the answer ⇒ I don't know the answer.

b. In Questions

Sentence 3.50 *Question* + John likes snails ⇒ Does John like snails?

8. The Flip-Flop Transformation

Sentence 3.51 Cecily (*Past* + shall + *have* + *en* + *be* + *ing*) try harder ⇒ Cecily should have been trying harder.

Even these simplified transformations provide strong evidence of the usefulness of transformational grammar. Had the theory not developed any further, such rules would still have had considerable practical value for teachers and students of English. But, as we shall soon see, the theory did develop. Our small metaphorical child grew to be a sometimes rambunctious, sometimes pensive adolescent.

3.5 Looking Forward

Any complex theory grows and develops in myriad ways. One part of the theory might remain unchanged for many years; a second part might undergo considerable revision; and a third part might develop in a more or less normal, linear expansion. Consequently, it is impossible to say that a single form of a theory is representative of an extended period of research. Thus, the grammatical models presented in this chapter are actually fictions. At no time was there a complete agreement among transformational linguists on all the details we have examined. Nonetheless, the fiction does present a fairly accurate and general outline of the structure of transformational theory for the period from 1957 to late 1964, particularly as presented in reports, monographs, and books published during the period.

In 1965 came the publication of *Aspects of the Theory of Syntax*, which is, perhaps, Noam Chomsky's most important statement of his linguistic interests and position. Chapters 4 and 5 will focus on this book or, more precisely, on those parts of *Aspects* (which is the widely used "short title") that have particular relevance for students and teachers of English.

But before turning to *Aspects*, we need first to examine some of the factors that prompted the writing of the book. Thus, by way of preparation, we shall look, again, at recursiveness and also at such subjects as language acquisition, classification within a grammar, and the representation of meaning. And this necessitates a brief digression into another field of scholarly research, namely, mathematics.

Many persons are surprised to learn that, in recent years, mathematicians have spent considerable time investigating the theories that underlie simple arithmetic. In fact, however, the principles underlying such apparently simple operations as addition, subtraction, multiplication, and division were only poorly understood as recently as 50 years ago. We can find an analogy with language in this fact. People can speak and write without having a conscious awareness of the rules they use in doing these things; similarly, people can learn to perform the operations of simple arithmetic without being aware of the theory that underlies these operations.

One major result of research into arithmetic theory is a better understanding of so-called "iterative processes," that is, processes that can be repeated, sometimes indefinitely. The four branches of simple arithmetic all incorporate iterative processes. Thus, in addition, we can add one number to another, and then add the resulting number to some other number, and so on. Similarly, we can multiply two numbers, and then multiply the result by still another number, and so on. Mathematicians determined that these processes were different manifestations of a single, underlying property, namely, the property of recursiveness.

In Section 3.1, we noted that recursive rules have characteristics such as the following:

PS 3.3 $\text{S} \rightarrow \text{NP} + \text{VP}$ **PS 3.2** $\text{NP} \rightarrow \left\{ \begin{array}{c} \text{Name} \\ \text{Art} + \text{Noun} \end{array} \right\} (\text{S})$

In rule PS 3.3 the sentence constituent appears on the left side of the arrow, while in PS 3.2 the sentence constituent appears on the right side of the arrow. As we noted earlier, these conditions define that form of iteration known as recursiveness.

A generative grammar also incorporates other forms of iteration. For example, rule PS 3.3 might be written to show the right-side noun phrase constituent as indefinitely repeatable, with a conjunction between each occurrence; that is,

NP and NP and NP . . . and NP

This portion of the rule can be used in deriving sentences such as

Sentence 3.52 Bob and Pat and David and Paul wore funny hats.

We can apply the **conjunction-reduction transformation** to this sentence to produce

Sentence 3.52a Bob, Pat, David, and Paul wore funny hats.

Rules whereby a constituent is rewritten as itself are not recursive, in the sense used above, since the constituents on the right-hand side of the arrow are *not* elements that appear to the left of an arrow in an earlier rule.

Facts such as these are useful in understanding the history of grammatical studies. Grammarians have known for hundreds of years that speakers possess "creative power"; that is, they are able to produce an indefinite number of unique sentences that are fully grammatical and readily comprehended by other speakers of the same language. But these grammarians had no precise way to represent this knowledge in their grammars, since logicians and mathematicians had not completely formalized a theory of iterative processes. Had such a theory been formulated earlier, it is quite possible that studies in generative linguistics could also have begun earlier. In other words, the limitations of earlier grammar frequently derive from external constraints on the ways of expressing knowledge.

With these constraints removed, linguists were finally able to consider the nature of linguistic competence (which we can redefine, informally, as what a person "knows" when he knows a language). Such competence is sometimes called an "internal or intuitive grammar," in contrast to the formal or generative grammar that a transformationalist aims to write. As noted in Chapter 1, a formal grammar is also called a "model," and we can note again, here, that such formal grammars are "models of knowledge" rather than "models of the use of knowledge." Or, to use the technical terms introduced earlier, formal grammars are models of competence rather than of performance.

In the early 1960s, it became apparent that even a *competence model* must be extraordinarily complex, and this realization led linguists to speculate about the process of acquiring linguistic competence. In other words, they became interested in the question: How does a child learn a language?

In one sense, their answer to this question was simple, although it boggled the minds of many persons who held to the old hypothesis that the mind of an infant is a *tabula rasa* (to use John Locke's famous way of describing an absolutely blank condition of the human mind). Put simply, the transformationalist concluded that the mind of a child is predisposed, by its very nature, to learn human language.

We can restate the argument as follows. Language is enormously complex. Yet all normal children learn at least one language (and sometimes two or more), and they do so without receiving formal instruction in the language. Most generative linguists believe that none of the available "theories of learning" can provide formal explanation for the fact of language acquisition. Therefore, they also believe that it is logical to formulate an empirical hypothesis that claims language acquisition is a "natural" function of the human brain. And finally, generative grammarians claim that, as with any empirical hypothesis, those who reject it have the burden of disproving it.

In brief, generative grammarians consider language acquisition to be an innate property of the human mind. And this "innateness doctrine" (as it came to be called) had a considerable effect on linguistic research. In light of the doctrine we can divide this research into two parts: one concerned with specifying *competence* itself, and the other concerned with the way in which a speaker *acquires* competence. In the first case, the linguist wants to specify the grammar of a particular language, such as English; in the second case, the linguist wants to specify so-called "linguistic universals." The subject of universals is one that we shall discuss at some length in the following chapter, but we can anticipate part of that discussion by considering the problem of classification with a formal grammar.

In transformational studies, the first major work to follow *Syntactic Structures* was *The Grammar of English Nominalizations* by Robert B. Lees, published in 1960. Our concern here is not with the insights that Lees brought to the study of such things as gerunds and infinitives, although these insights were certainly significant; rather, we are concerned with the difficulties Lees had in presenting his arguments and discussion. Specifically, Lees found it necessary to create many different subcategories for English verbs; that is, he found the traditional categories of *transitive, intransitive,* and *linking* to be far too general. Thus, in most traditional grammars, *have* is classified as a transitive verb in a sentence such as: *I have a cold.* Yet, in contrast to regular transitive verbs, *have* cannot be used in the passive voice. That is, we normally would not say: **A cold is had by me.* Lees used the term **middle verb** to apply to words such as *have.*

The problem Lees faced in classifying verbs is similar to the problem traditional grammarians faced in classifying nouns. In discussing nouns, traditional grammarians sometimes used such terms as *common, proper, mass, abstract, animate, inanimate, feminine, masculine, neuter,* and so on. Yet such terms are not mutually exclusive. Thus, some common nouns are masculine, some are feminine, and some are neuter, and the same is true of proper nouns. Some mass nouns are animate, but then again, so are some common nouns and some proper nouns. In short, some nouns—like some verbs—fit into more than one category. This fact led to the question: How are we to classify nouns and verbs?

The answer to this question, which came from the study of sounds, has also had considerable impact on linguistic research. We can understand the answer best by making another brief digression, this time into a branch of linguistics that we have so far ignored: **phonology**.

Linguists concerned with the study of sounds faced a classification problem similar to the one we have been discussing. For example, /b/ and /p/ are both "stops," while /v/ and /f/ are both "fricatives"; and yet /b/ and /v/ are also "voiced," while /p/ and /f/ are "voiceless." Here, again, there is a problem of cross classification. A solution was proposed by Roman Jakobson, who developed the system of **distinctive features**. Briefly, Jakobson postulated the existence of a few significant qualities (that is, "features") that could be present in various sounds. Thus, many sounds are "voiced," many sounds are "consonantal" (that is, the flow of air is impeded in some way), and many sounds are "continuants" (that is, the flow of air is not stopped—as it is with sounds such as /t/ or /b/—but can continue indefinitely, as in making the sounds /s/ and /f/). Jakobson then stated that every sound could be characterized by the presence or absence of these features. Thus, the sound that is indicated phonetically as /s/ could, in a "distinctive-feature" representation, be indicated as

$$\begin{bmatrix} +consonantal \\ +continuant \\ -voiced \\ \text{and so on} \end{bmatrix}$$

Such an arrangement of distinctive phonological features is sometimes called a **feature matrix**.

Linguists concerned with morphology and syntax recognized the usefulness o features as well as of the matrix system of representing sets of features, and they began to apply features to characterize various syntactic and semantic qualitie of particular nouns. Again, the linguists found that they could incorporate (with some redefinition) a number of terms from traditional grammar as a basis fo establishing the new system.[13]

We can use features to represent (partial) meanings of the words *boy, wheat love,* and *Rome* as follows:

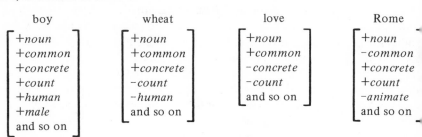

These examples illustrate some of the conventions used by linguists when they employ features. First, redundant features—those implied by the presence o other features—are generally omitted. Thus, the feature (+*human*) implies the feature (+*animate*), so this latter feature can be omitted from a matrix. The use of a "plus-or-minus" notation system also helps to simplify exposition. Thus +*common* has its traditional meaning, whereas the traditional term "abstract" can be represented by -*concrete*.

The **count** feature is used in distinguishing so-called *mass nouns* (such a *wheat*) from those nouns that signify countable things (such as *boy*).[14]

All the features we have been discussing (including the distinctive phonologica features) are probably **linguistic universals**. That is, they represent various quali ties that are available to any child learning any language, and they can be use by linguists in constructing formal grammars of any language. This suggests tha they might possibly represent part of the innate "knowledge" that a child bring to the learning of language.

[13]The line between syntax and semantics has proved to be difficult, and perhaps impossible to draw. We shall return to this question in Chapter 6 on research since 1966. We can als note that most linguists enclose individual features within "angle brackets" as follow <+*common*>. For the sake of simplicity (and to avoid higher typesetting costs), thi convention has been ignored in this book.

[14]Lexicographers use a system that shares many similarities with the linguistic system o features. Although the usual dictionary method of representing pronunciations is muc simpler than the method of using phonological features, the actual definitions employ man of the same terms used to represent syntactic and semantic features. Thus, the first featur listed under *boy, wheat, love,* and *Rome* is (+*noun*), which serves the same function as th n. used by lexicographers. Similarly, a dictionary "definition" of the word *boy* woul almost certainly refer to the fact that a boy is *human* and *male*.

In the following chapter, we shall consider this question of innateness in some
etail, particularly as it relates to the goals of linguistic research. We shall then
eturn to the subject of features when we investigate the nature of the lexicon in
he so-called *standard model* of transformational-generative grammar.

Exercises

1. For each of the sentences derived for Exercises 6 and 7 in Chapter 2, derive
   a new sentence by including an *S* (an embedded sentence) after each noun.
2. Use the relative clause transformation to derive three sentences with restrictive relative clauses and three with adjectives.
3. For each of the PRO-adverbials discussed on p. 56, derive two *wh*- questions.
4. Provide one sentence for each different combination of auxiliary elements.
5. For each sentence in Exercise 4, give the form before and after the flip-flop
   transformation has been applied.
6. In the discussion of contraction, *doesn't* was given as an example. Provide
   ten more examples.
7. What Lees called "middle verbs" were discussed on p. 67, where *have* was
   given as an example. How many other "middle verbs" can you identify?

CHAPTER 4

The *Aspects* Model: I

In our description of nature the purpose is not to disclose the real essence of
the phenomena but only to track down, so far as it is possible, relations between
the manifold aspects of our experience.
NIELS BOHR, *Atomic Theory and the Description of Nature* (1934)

In 1965, Noam Chomsky published *Aspects of the Theory of Syntax* which—
to continue our earlier metaphor—marked the end of childhood and the beginning of puberty for generative linguistics. Several purposes prompted the writing
of the book. In particular, Chomsky wanted (1) to clarify various "background"
assumptions" (particularly those that had been criticized by some other linguists); (2) to discuss some defects of the earliest forms of generative theory
(1955-1964); (3) to suggest revisions that, hopefully, would overcome some of
these defects; and (4) to point out some "residual problems" that require further
investigation.

In this and the following chapter, we shall consider each of these issues,
although the focus—as before—will be on those parts of the theory that have
particular and practical significance for teachers of English.

4.1   The Purpose of Linguistic Research

Much of the misunderstanding and confusion that followed the publication of
Syntactic Structures can be traced to questions concerning the purpose of linguistic research. And these questions are important for teachers to consider. To
bring the questions into focus, we can (again) contrast the two so-called schools
of American linguistics which have dominated research in the twentieth century,
namely: (1) the American structuralist school, and (2) the transformational-generative school.

As recently as 1955, most American linguists were structuralists, and they conducted their research within the framework established by Leonard Bloomfield in the 1930s.[1] The structuralists focused primarily on *spoken language*, which they sought to describe within a model that consisted of various "levels." In a structural description of English, the simplest of these models had three levels: the **phonemic**, which contained units of sound; the **morphemic**, which contained units of lexical meaning (for example, prefixes, suffixes, word stems, and so on); and the **syntactic**, which contained structures larger than words (for example, phrases, clauses, and so on). The syntactic level was also called the level of "phrase structure."

In describing a particular language, the structuralists generally proceeded according to the principle of levels. Thus, they generally began by making an inventory of the significant sounds—the phonemes—of the language. Some languages, such as Hawaiian, have little more than a dozen; others, such as Georgian, have more than four dozen. After cataloguing the sounds, the structuralists would then classify the minimal units of meaning—the morphemes—of the language. These units of meaning might be single words (*boy, climb*) or parts of the words; for example, prefixes (*un-, re-*, and so on) and suffixes (*-ing, -ness,* and so on). At the next stage of analysis, the structuralists considered the ways in which morphemes of the language could be arranged into grammatical phrases and clauses. Some linguists used the term **tagmeme** to refer to structures on the syntactic level.

By way of illustrating these levels, we can consider certain features of English that differ from those of other languages. Thus, English has a phoneme /č/, which appears in words such as *chair* and *peach*.[2] Slavic languages also have this phoneme, but they also have another and similar phoneme which English does not have, namely, /ć/. Thus, the first and last sounds of the Croatian name *Čubelić* are different for a Slavic speaker (although most English speakers would not hear the difference, since it is not a significant one in English).

On the morphemic level, English has prefixes and suffixes but does not generally have "infixes" such as those that can be inserted into the Hebrew stem *š-m-r* ("guard"), where the infix *-o-* forms *smor* ("he guards") while the infix *-a-a-* forms *samar* ("to guard"). And on the syntactic level, English adjectives normally precede the nouns they modify, while French adjectives often follow nouns (as in *the visible world* vs. *le monde visible*).

Of these three levels, the phonemic received the most attention. The morphemic level was being widely investigated in the middle 1950s. The level of syntax (or of tagmemes) was not subjected to as much analysis as the "lower

---

[1] The Bibliography provides a selective list of important publications by structuralist linguists.

[2] Readers not familiar with the term *phoneme* or with the system of writing phonemes may wish to consult Archibald Hill, *Introduction to Linguistic Structures* (New York: Harcourt Brace Jovanovich, 1958).

levels" because of the then generally held belief that linguistic research should proceed in an orderly fashion, that is, from the lowest level (the phonemic) to the succeedingly higher levels (morphemic, syntactic, and so on). Nonetheless some work was being done on the level of syntax, and it was the difficulty of this work that, in part, led to the development of transformational grammar.[3]

The structuralists assumed that each level could be defined in terms of a distinctive unit, for example, the *phoneme*. Moreover, they believed that, for each language, there were principles of combination that applied to each level English, for example, contains a phoneme $/ \eta /$, which represents the final consonantal sound in words such as *running*. Unlike most other consonantal phonemes, however, the $/ \eta /$ phoneme cannot occur as the initial sound of an English word. (In other languages, such as Vietnamese, $/ \eta /$ can occur as an initial sound in words.) The "principles of combination" (or **phonotactics**) that apply to English phonemes would indicate this fact. Similar principles of combination presumably existed for all other levels. Thus, on the morphemic level English contains plural suffixes but no plural prefixes (as some other languages do). And on the syntactic level, English is normally a subject-verb-object language. Presumably, the "principles of combination" could be expressed as rather simple rules. In practice, the structuralists paid less attention to the nature of these rules than they did to the system of classifying sounds and morphemes.

Specifically, we should note that phonemes, morphemes, and various structures of syntax are directly observable in sentences, whereas the rules governing the occurrence of these linguistic items cannot be observed directly. Some structuralists, therefore, assumed that the nature of the rules was primarily a subject for investigation by psychologists, and most structuralists assumed that the rules were best discussed within the framework of the *stimulus-response model* common in behavioral psychology.

In sum: the American structuralists focused chiefly only on observable language (that is, speech); their model of language was divided into a hierarchy of levels (for example, phonemic, morphemic, and syntactic); each level contained distinctive units; and presumably there were relative simple "principles of combination" which, however, were not as rigorously investigated as the taxonomic categories, that is, phoneme, morpheme, and—in some cases—tagmeme.

The transformational-generative grammarians challenged the assumptions that are inherent in the structuralist's model of language. We can state the challenges this way:

[3] Kenneth Pike and his followers provide an exception to this statement about work on the syntactic levels. Pike's version of structuralism shares certain features of a generative grammar and is, in fact, known as a "tagmemic grammar" (see the Bibliography). For beginning students, the best overview of structural linguistics is provided by James Sledd in *A Short Introduction to English Grammar* (Chicago: Scott, Foresman, 1959). Sledd, in this extremely readable book, also provides an excellent glossary of the key terms used by most structuralist linguists.

1. The fundamental object of linguistic study is not speech *per se.*
2. The syntactic level is more basic to the study of language than is the phonemic level.
3. The various "principles of combination" suggested by the structuralists are inherently inadequate to a description of any natural language.

We can also approach the challenges through the philosophical concept of "levels of abstraction." If we consider any physical object (for example, the solar system, or a spoken sentence), then at the first level of abstraction we have a simple description of the object (for example, the solar system comprises the sun, nine planets, and their various moons; an English sentence consists of sounds, which are arranged into morphemes, which—in turn—are arranged into phrases and clauses). We can say that, for all practical purposes, the American structuralists stopped at the first level of abstraction, whereas the transformationalists believed that linguists should consider higher levels. Thus, at the second level of abstraction, a scientist considers the "laws" that govern the behavior of the properties of the first level (for example, the laws of planetary motion, or the laws relating interrogative and declarative sentences). There is also a third level of abstraction on which the scientist considers the "laws" that govern the laws of the second level. (For example, are the laws of planetary motion a "special case" of a more comprehensive set of laws, and are the laws that apply to sentences determined, in any way, by other laws which may be an innate part of man's mental capacities?) In these terms, we can say that the transformationalists challenged the structuralists' assumption that linguistic research should be restricted to the first level of abstraction.

In the late 1950s and early 1960s, many structuralists accepted the validity of the transformationalists' challenge and, in fact, became transformationalists themselves. Other structuralists rejected the challenges, and it is toward this latter group of linguists that the arguments in the first chapter of *Aspects* are primarily directed. Specifically, and as alternatives to the structuralists' assumptions, the transformationalists proposed the following:

1. The fundamental object of linguistic study is the internalized knowledge of language possessed by a native "speaker-hearer."
2. The level of syntax is central; that is, it mediates between "meaning" and "sound." Moreover, the "spoken form" of a sentence can be defined by applying various phonological rules to the structures on the syntactic level.
3. Any adequate description of a language requires a unique kind of rule known as a "transformation," and such rules are different in kind from the "principles of combination" inherent in the descriptions of most structural grammars.

In Chapters 2 and 3, we examined the result of these transformationalist assumptions. Specifically, we defined a "grammatical model" which represented, in a highly simplified way, a part of the internalized knowledge possessed by a native speaker. Where a structuralist would discuss a spoken sentence by using a "first-level" vocabulary, we used a lexicon and some rules to develop a derivation of a sentence. In other words, the grammatical model was a "second-level" abstraction, since it focused not on the various parts of a sentence (for example, phonemes, morphemes, phrases, and clauses) but on the rules governing the operation of these parts.[4]

The first chapter of *Aspects* contrasts the transformationalists' assumptions with those of the structuralists. The main argument is presented within the context of a distinction we have already discussed, namely, that between *competence* and *performance* (see pp. 62-63). American structuralists have focused primarily on the results of performance. European linguists, in contrast, have generally recognized the importance of the distinction. The transformationalists, in keeping with the European tradition, do not ignore the existence of performance; rather, they assume that any discussion of performance must be based on an adequate theory of competence.

In other words, some structuralists claim that a linguist must restrict his investigations only to observable phenomena (that is, spoken sentences) and to the classification of these phenomena (that is, first-level abstractions). The transformationalists, in contrast, hope to characterize the mental rules that govern the operation of linguistic phenomena (that is, they hope to make second- and third-level abstractions). Ultimately, the disagreement is an empirical question: Which method—structuralist or transformationalist—provides a more adequate description of (and explanation for) language? At present, the weight of informed opinion seems to be on the side of the transformationalists.

The concept of competence, then, is a second-level abstraction. Also on the second level is an equally important abstraction, namely, the concept of a **universal grammar**. Again, this concept is not a new one; grammarians have considered the possibility for several hundred years.

Specifically, a transformationalist assumes that there are universal principles that apply to all human languages, and that such principles constitute a universal grammar. A grammar of a particular language, then, consists of two parts: a set of principles that are common to all languages, plus a set of particular rules and other items that are unique to the particular language.

At this point, we ascend to the third level of abstraction, which focuses on the question: How does the individual acquire a knowledge of the rules of lan-

---

[4] The transformationalists and structuralists did not even agree on the parts that comprise the first level. For example, the transformationalists dismissed the concept of the phoneme, since phonemes do not play an essential role in a generative-transformational grammar. In effect, the transformationalists claimed that the phoneme was a "second-level" abstraction (since, on the first level, a sound can be analyzed into various distinctive phonological features), and moreover, that—on the second level—the concept of phoneme was unjustified.

guage?[5] Most transformationalists assume that the principles of universal grammar are innate in the mind; that is, these principles are present—in some form—at birth. This hypothesis, if true, has extraordinary significance for teachers of English.

4.2 The Structure of a Transformational-Generative Grammar

We can now return to a consideration of the structure of a transformational-generative grammar; additionally, we can consider the nature of "grammatical evidence." In the preceding chapter, we examined a highly simplified version, which approximated the structure of the earliest generative grammars. The structure defined in *Aspects* is a more elaborate version of the type of structure we have already examined. (Some linguists refer to this more elaborate model as the *standard transformational grammar*; in the following pages, for the sake of variety, we shall sometimes adopt this terminology.)

Briefly, the *Aspects* model contains three major components: syntactic, phonological, and semantic. These terms have quite specific meanings which, in some instances, are at variance with the "ordinary language" use of the same terms. This variance confuses some persons who assume—because of other associations—that the "semantic component" provides the meaning of a sentence. But such an assumption is not correct. An example may clarify the distinction.

In the *Aspects* model, the syntactic component is divided into several parts which, for our purposes, we can illustrate as in Figure 4.1. First, the syntactic component is divided into two major subdivisions: (A) a **base** (which is further subdivided), and (B) a set of **transformational rules**. The base has two parts: (1) a set of phrase-structure rules, and (2) a lexicon.

Syntactic Component	
A. (*Base*)	B.
1. Phrase-structure rules	Transformational
2. Lexicon	rules

Figure 4.1 Syntactic component

[5] In the authors' experience, some readers have difficulty breathing the rarefied air on the third level of abstraction. For such readers, the following summary might prove helpful:

Reality: for example, a spoken sentence.
First Level: a vocabulary for classifying the elements in a given sentence.
Second Level: a generative grammar, containing rules, a lexicon, and other items, which defines the relationships existing among the items on the first level.
Third Level: a set of principles (sometimes called a "language acquisition device") that determines the structure of the second-level generative grammar.

In constructing a derivation, we first turn to the base subcomponent. We apply the phrase-structure rules to produce a branching tree, and this tree defines various grammatical relationships (for instance, "subject of a sentence"). Given a tree, we then insert items from the lexicon at each terminal node on the tree.[6] The product of these two operations is a deep structure that contains all the information required for an understanding of the sentence.[7]

Notice that, so far, we have used *only* the base subcomponent of the syntactic component. We have, however, derived a highly detailed deep structure, which contains all the information necessary for an understanding of a sentence. In other words, the meaning of a sentence inheres in the deep structure *before* the application of the so-called semantic component. Thus, in technical terms, the semantic component is strictly "interpretive."

Consider, now, a specific sentence:

Sentence 4.1 John took the train.

This sentence is ambiguous, as we can see by placing it within two different contexts:

Sentence 4.2 Although most of us drove, John took the train.
Sentence 4.3 Although we hoped he would choose some other toy, John took the train.

In each of the deep structures that underlie these three sentences, there is a verbal node that immediately dominates a lexical entry for the verb *take.* In the version of the theory we are now considering, this lexical entry is identical in all three sentences. The first sentence (Sentence 4.1) does not provide sufficient information for us to determine which of the several meanings of *take* is intended. Thus, the interpretive rules of the semantic component automatically provide us with all the possible meanings (and, for this reason, the sentence is ambiguous). In contrast, Sentences 4.2 and 4.3 do provide information that permits us to select single and specific meanings for *take.* The interpretive semantic rules, in each of these cases, provide nonambiguous readings; in technical terms, they "block" readings that are incompatible with other lexical items in the sentence.

In short, in the standard model each deep structure contains all the possible meanings associated with a particular branching tree and a particular set of lexical entries. The interpretive rules from the semantic component simply combine the various meanings of the lexical items using so-called **projection rules**, that is, rules that "project" meanings up the branches of the tree and combine

---

[6] In Chapter 5, we shall return to the question of lexical insertion and define the matter more precisely.

[7] This, too, is a simplification, but one that does not materially affect the present discussion. Currently, some linguists believe that the statement, as given, is correct; others prefer to modify the statement slightly.

two (or more) meanings when they meet at a particular node. And in the process of combining meanings, the projection rules suppress any elements of meaning (in a lexical item) that are incompatible with other elements of meaning in the sentence.

At the risk of belaboring the obvious, we can consider another example:

Sentence 4.4 Irving is our candidate.

This sentence is ambiguous since the word *our* may include or exclude the person being addressed. The ambiguity is resolved in the following sentences:

Sentence 4.5 Homer may be your candidate, but Irving is our candidate.
Sentence 4.6 I'm glad we all agree that Irving is our candidate.

In each of the trees that underlie these sentences, the lexical entry for the word *our* contains both the inclusive and the exclusive meanings. The interpretive semantic rules that apply to Sentence 4.5 block the inclusive meaning; in Sentence 4.6, the interpretive rules block the exclusive meaning.

Returning, now, to Figure 4.1, and to the process of constructing a derivation for a sentence. So far, we have been through the following steps: (1) We used the phrase-structure rules from the base component to derive a branching tree. (2) We selected lexical items from the lexicon and inserted these into the tree wherever there was a terminal node. As a result of these two steps, we produced a deep structure, and this deep structure contains the complete meaning of the sentence.

We can now continue with the following steps: (3) To the deep structure we apply the interpretive ("automatic") rules of the semantic component, and the result is a so-called **semantic reading** of the sentence. (4) Then we return to the syntactic component and apply the appropriate transformational rules.[8] These rules operate on the highly compact deep structure to produce a surface structure for the sentence. (5) Finally, we apply the rules of the phonological component, which are also "automatic" and interpretive; specifically, the phonological rules operate on the surface structure (produced in step 4) to give the phonetic—the "spoken"—form of the sentence.

Such an exposition frequently produces a resounding "so what!" from English teachers, and some teachers—those with a classical bent—quote Horace: *parturient montes, nascetur ridiculus mus*; "mountains will labor, and will give birth to only a silly mouse." In short, many teachers wonder if all this detail is really necessary. There are, however, good reasons for answering "yes" to any such question, and these reasons have to do with one of the major achievements of linguistic research during the last 20 years, namely, the evaluation of linguistic evidence.

[8] In the *Aspects* model, we have little—if any—choice in choosing particular transformations. Rather, the transformations are automatically chosen by the shape of the branching tree and also by the features contained within the lexical items. In other words, the deep structure completely determines which transformations are required to produce a surface structure.

Earlier statements about language—in both traditional and structural grammars—were generally based on intuition; within a generative grammar, statements about language require the support of evidence. In other words, linguistic statements are no longer "trained judgments" such as—for example—a critic might make about a work of literature (for instance, "Shakespeare's late plays have a resonance that bears the mark of suffering."). Rather, linguistic statements are now empirical propositions similar to statements in the physical sciences. Chomsky's three-part grammar provides a framework for formulating hypotheses about language, and language itself provides the evidence for accepting or rejecting these hypotheses.

Given a well-defined framework, four possibilities exist for formulating statements about language:

1. A linguist can make statements that are compatible with the framework and that are fully supported by all known evidence.
2. He can make statements that are compatible with the framework, that are supported by a considerable body of evidence, but that may—or may not—be contradicted by other evidence.
3. He can challenge the structure of the framework itself (the "model") by proposing another, equally detailed framework which satisfies at least as much of the evidence as does the original framework.[9]
4. He can make statements that are compatible with some theory, but that are impossible to falsify with *any* evidence. (Some such statements are necessary, such as definitions of technical terms.)

As an example of the first kind of statement, we have the hypothesis that grammatical transformations are necessary to linguistic descriptions. This hypothesis is rarely, if ever, challenged by generative grammarians, and all the known evidence seems to support the hypothesis. The various descriptions of the passive voice are an example of the second kind of statement. There are several different analyses that seem to be compatible with the general framework, and all of them are supported by some evidence; at this time, no single analysis of the passive is clearly superior to all others. In such cases, linguists interested in this problem must find additional evidence (that is, acceptable English sentences) that will demonstrate the superiority of one hypothesis over all others. As examples of the third kind of statement, we shall note (in Chapter 6) that some generative linguists have proposed alternative models to the standard transformation model. Such proposals raise empirical questions. That is, given the

[9] This third point relates to our earlier comparison between structural and transformational grammars. In particular, the framework of American structuralist grammars was never well defined. Most of them, however, seem to be simple phrase-structure grammars, that is, grammars that do *not* contain transformational rules. The lack of definition meant that the structuralists not only began but proceeded mostly by intuition. In contrast, a generative-transformational grammar (which, like any scientific model, has its source in intuition) attempts to make precise statements about many of the subjective judgments recorded in earlier traditional grammars.

case where a linguist proposes a different solution within the existing framework (for example, an alternative description of the passive voice), or else given the case where a linguist proposes a different framework (for example, a so-called **case grammar**), then the alternative proposals must be weighed in terms of the evidence—actual language. As noted above, definitions of technical terms are sometimes examples of the fourth kind of statement.[10]

We need to make two final remarks about the nature of linguistic research in general before turning to the important question of language acquisition (that is, questions on the third level of abstraction).

First, the field of generative linguistics is quite young in practice, even though its principles were established more than 300 years ago. For this reason—and also because the field of research is so vast—investigations proceed along many fronts simultaneously, and new ideas are advanced almost daily. This was particularly true during the first dozen years of research (that is, into the late 1960s). Nonetheless, and even in the face of the fact that we may eventually have to abandon many currently held beliefs, we now know considerably more about language than we did 20 years ago. It would be extremely shortsighted for English teachers to ignore those things we now believe to be true—or, if not "true," then at least reasonable and probable. Similarly, it would be unprofessional to continue teaching language in ways that are, at best, subjective and doctrinaire, and at worst, quite false and possibly even harmful.

Second, the *Aspects* model, partly because it is only a few years old, is an idealization that necessarily ignores some of the rough edges of reality.[11] More specifically, the present generative models of language aim to characterize the knowledge possessed by "an ideal speaker-hearer." Such an ideal person possesses a perfect knowledge of his language, and this knowledge is not affected by nonlinguistic considerations (such as fatigue, limitations on memory, and so on). As we have already noted, linguists use the term *competence* to refer to the knowledge possessed by any speaker-hearer. Unless otherwise noted, we shall use

[10]This kind of rigor seems to be—and probably is—a far remove from the kinds of lessons on English grammar usually taught in the schools and colleges. We can note here that the English class—particularly in the schools—is probably not the place to teach *linguistics* as a subject in itself. Rather, pupils in elementary and secondary schools can sometimes use (part of) the vocabulary of linguistics in discussing (1) their own linguistic competence, and (2) their writing and speech. Yet teachers need to have some understanding of recent developments in linguistic rearch, since such understanding can affect the attitudes they hold toward children and toward teaching children about language. As one teacher has said, "I used to think that our problem was getting language *into* the head of a child. Now I believe our chief problem is getting language *out*." Thus, a teacher who believes that the hypotheses of transformational grammar *might* be correct will probably want to help children recognize the extent of their intuitive knowledge of language.

[11]Similar idealizations can be found in nearly all scientific disciplines, particularly as they are presented in introductory courses. Thus, *pi* (which is an irrational number) is frequently "idealized" to 22/7 or to 3.14. Similarly, the paths followed by the planets in their orbits about the sun are frequently idealized to perfect ellipses. Such idealizations do not usually affect the kinds of generalizations that are important in an introductory course.

the term solely to refer to the knowledge possessed by an "ideal" speaker-hearer. But the use of "ideal" is not meant to deny the real. In other words, *competence* does not deny *performance*. Thus, most generative linguists assume that any useful model of actual performance must be based on an understanding of competence.

4.3   Language Acquisition

In the preceding section, we examined some issues that relate to the purposes of linguistic research, particularly those that distinguish transformational-generative grammar from American structuralist grammar. In this section, we shall reexamine some of the same issues but from a different perspective. Specifically, we shall consider the concept of linguistic universals more fully and shall see how these affect the goals of linguistic theory.

As already noted, linguists assume—that is, "hypothesize"—that certain linguistic universals exist. We can now distinguish two types of linguistic universals: **formal** and **substantive**. Formal universals, as the name suggests, are *conditions* that help to determine the form that any language may take. As a consequence, formal universals also determine, in part, the form that a grammar of a language may take. For example, the claim that "all speakers learn transformations" is a formal universal, since it requires that every grammatical description include transformations as a part of the description.

Substantive universals include statements about the kinds of elements a linguist uses in describing a language. For example, linguists claim that every sound in a language can be analyzed into certain "distinctive features" (for example, *voiced* or *unvoiced*). They claim, further, that there are comparatively few of these features (perhaps two dozen). Finally, they claim that speakers of all languages draw on the same basic set of features in forming the sounds of these languages.

In something of a simplification, we can say that substantive universals relate to the *items* of language, while formal universals relate to the *rules* that govern the use of these items.

The distinction between formal and substantive universals can help us see the difference between modern generative grammars and earlier theories—including traditional school-grammar. As already noted, the idea of universals is an old one, going back at least 300 years (and, thereby, antedating the original school-grammars of English). But most older hypotheses were concerned with substantive universals (for example, with the possibility that categories such as "noun" and "verb" exist in all languages). Some earlier grammars speculated about formal universals, but only in recent years (that is, only with the development of modern symbolic logic) has it been possible to give these speculations an explicit characterization.

Generative grammar is concerned with both types of universals. One major contribution of generative grammar has been in the area of formal universals which, by their very nature, are more abstract than substantive universals since they impose restrictive conditions not just on the elements of language but also on the structure of language.

Recent work in linguistic universals—both formal and substantive—permits us to discuss the question of how a child acquires language, and equally important, how a linguistic theory can represent the facts of language acquisition. The first chapter of *Aspects* lists five qualities of mind that a child "must have" if he is to learn a language. For our purposes, we can paraphrase the list as follows:

1. The mind must contain some method of distinguishing and representing the *sounds* of language, that is, a system of mental representation that is akin to—but vastly more complex than—a written alphabet.

This quality is fairly obvious. Even very young children quickly build up an inventory of sounds, as we can tell when we hear them make up a string of "nonsense words" (which they have never heard); for example, *ing, bing, ding, fing, ling, ming,* and so on. Perhaps this can be explained as simple memory, although the nature of memory is only poorly understood.

2. The mind must also contain a way of determining and representing so-called *structural information* about language, that is, a system of determining such things as class membership.

That children have such systems can be seen by the mistakes they make in the early stages of language acquisition. Consider a child who says, **This ball is gooder than that one.* In most cases, the child has never heard anyone say the word *gooder.* Yet the sentence reveals that the child knows that (1) adjectives can be compared, (2) the suffix *-er* is the normal way of comparing one-syllable adjectives, and most important, (3) the word *good* is an adjective. In other words, children obviously make mistakes in assuming that all adjectives are regular in comparisons; but children rarely—if ever—confuse adjectives with other classes of words. For example, a child will not say: **This red thing is baller than that one,* or **This is glasser than that.* Thus, while the child certainly does not know the word *adjective* (which is a first-level abstraction, that is, a category label), he does insert adjectives "where they belong" in English sentences.

3. The mind must contain some "initial delimitation" about the *nature of language structure,* that is, a system of separating sounds into those that do—and those that do not—exhibit characteristics of linguistic structure.

This third feature is a prerequisite to the fourth (which is concerned with the kinds of judgments a child makes about structures). Thus, the third feature states that the range of human languages is limited—in some sense "predetermined"—by the nature of the human mind. In other words, the mind itself imposes limits on those things we call languages.

4. The mind has some way of *determining the structural meaning* inherent in a given sentence; that is, each child has a system for identifying such notions as "subject of a sentence," "object of a verb," and so on.

Whereas the second feature is concerned with class membership (and thus relates to the lexicon of a generative grammar), the fourth feature is concerned with such things as syntactic relationships (and thus relates to the phrase-structure rules of a generative grammar). As early as age three, children will form sentences such as, "Daddy 'pank," and "'Pank Daddy," which clearly illustrate the subject-object distinction. By the time a child reaches maturity, he is able to perceive the same relationships in vastly more complex sentences such as, for example, two quoted by Chomsky[12]:

Sentence 4.7 John appeared to Bill to like himself.
Sentence 4.8 John appealed to Bill to like himself.

In the first of these sentences, *himself* (the direct object of *like*) refers to "John," while in the second sentence, *himself* refers to "Bill." The fact that a mature native speaker instantly recognizes the intended referent for *himself* in each sentence indicates that the speaker is able to determine the structural relationships that underlie these seemingly "almost identical" sentences.

The fourth feature is also a prerequisite for the fifth—and even more startling—feature.

5. The mind is able to make judgments about—to evaluate—various *syntactic relationships*; that is, while there may be an indefinite number of possible or imaginable descriptions, a child chooses one of a set of acceptable descriptions, specifically, those that conform to the total structure of language (according to the limitations indicated in the third feature, above).

Of all the features, this last is probably the most difficult to understand and accept. We can consider it in two contexts, one simple and the other more complex.

We have already noted that a child who says things like *gooder* (or *swimmed*) has formulated the hypothesis that adjectives and verbs are always regular in the formation of comparatives and the past tense. Such a hypothesis is false; that is, it does not conform to the evidence of actual language use. When the child recognizes this fact, he reformulates the hypothesis to admit irregularities. In short, every child is capable of formulating and then modifying hypotheses about language use until he constructs the single hypothesis that best conforms to the facts of language.

As a more complex example, we can consider the passive voice. Most children in the elementary school use passives rather freely. That is, they recognize the (near) synonomy of sentences such as the following:

[12]Noam Chomsky, *Problems of Knowledge and Freedom* (New York: Pantheon, 1971), p. 24.

Sentence 4.9 My brother made this cake.
Sentence 4.10 This cake was made by my brother.

By the age of ten or so, children are able to take simple active sentences and turn them into passive sentences. This fact suggests that, in technical terms, they may perceive a transformational relationship between active and passive sentences. Presumably, this relationship can be stated by a single transformational rule. But as we have noted, linguists do not agree on a description of passive sentences. Some linguists claim, for example, that such sentences are intimately (and necessarily) associated with manner adverbials; others claim that passives are similar (in underlying structure) to questions and negatives; and still others think that passives may be defined independently of active sentences. Nonetheless, it is possible to assume (and some linguists do) that English speakers all have one— and the same—set of rules that apply to passives. In brief, linguists have proposed alternative descriptions, but they are unable to agree on which of these descriptions most accurately fits the model; a language learner, however, seems to "choose" a single description (perhaps after formulating several alternatives, as in the case of comparative adjectives). The linguist believes that a language learner can choose from among hypotheses (and that is the point of the fifth feature), but the linguist does not know *how* the learner makes such choices (and that is one thing linguists hope to discover).[13]

These five features define the *minimum* linguistic abilities that the learner of a language must possess. Additionally, these features determine the goals of linguistic study, which can also be divided into five parts corresponding to the list of five features possessed by the learner.

1. The linguist must develop a "universal phonetic theory" that, in Chomsky's terms, defines the notion of "possible sentence."
2. The linguist must develop a definition of "structural information."
3. The linguist must define the limits of a possible language. (In essence, this would also be a definition of "generative grammar.")
4. Given goal 3, the linguist must define all possible structural meanings.
5. And given goal 4, the linguist must determine how a speaker chooses the best possible description from a variety of imaginable descriptions.

Again, this is a list of minimum goals for linguistics. For example, these goals deal only indirectly with performance—that is, with the conditions that prompt speech production as well as with the processes by which speakers actually produce sentences. Even so, this "minimal" task is enormous. In fact, defining the task has been among the major achievements of linguistics in the last 15 years.

---

[13]The fifth point is complicated by the fact that no two people have identical grammars, which suggests that there is some latitude in making choices. This topic remains to be investigated.

We should also note that both lists—the learner's abilities and the linguist's goals—are idealizations, since they ignore such factors as the rate of maturation (particularly of the brain), the possibility that—for example—the choice of a particular structural description (5) might also affect a child's notion of structural information (2), and so on. In this case (and in contrast to the reasons given in footnote 11), the idealization is chiefly a result of our lack of knowledge. As research progresses, we can assume that the lists of abilities and goals will become more particular.

We can summarize this section as follows. Linguists—in theory as well as in practice—propose alternative "generative grammars" which characterize the competence possessed by an ideal speaker-hearer. Linguists assume that each speaker-hearer is also capable of proposing (below the level of consciousness) alternative grammars that would enable him to use his language. Presumably, the grammars possessed by all speaker-hearers of a language are nearly identical (at least in form); that is, every speaker-hearer chooses—from the range of possible grammars—the one that best fits the evidence. Logically, then, we can conclude that each speaker-hearer has some means of evaluating possible grammars and choosing the most efficient.

In the simplest possible terms, then, linguistics has two goals: (1) to describe this "most efficient" grammar, and (2) to describe the means by which the speaker-hearer selects this grammar from the range of possible grammars.

In achieving this second goal, the linguist makes a common scientific assumption (sometimes referred to as the "simplicity metric"), namely, that significant generalizations which apply to a wide variety of cases are more valuable (in terms of the complete theory) than *ad hoc* statements which apply to only one case or, at best, a few cases. This assumption underlies the widespread use of **conventions** (for example, parentheses, brackets, and so on) in linguistic research. Such conventions permit a linguist to make explicit generalizations. In other words, the conventions are not "just a form of shorthand"; rather, they represent quite specific kinds of generalized statements.

As defined by generative linguists, the goals of linguistic theory differ significantly from those proposed by the American structuralists of the 1930s and 1940s, although they are similar to those proposed more than 300 years ago by the so-called *philosophical grammarians*. Thus, the structuralists were concerned chiefly with describing the *results* (but not the process) of linguistic performance, that is, with describing speech. In practice, they left the task of explaining language acquisition to the psychologists, or more particularly, to the behavioral psychologists. In contrast, many generative linguists define their field of research as a branch of *cognitive* psychology, and moreover, they insist that the goals of linguistics are vitally concerned with language acquisition.

In more specific—and somewhat technical—terms, linguists describe the situation as follows: Given a native speaker, we know he has learned a language by listening to more or less well-formed sentences. We can use the term *input* to refer to the sentences a speaker has heard (or read) in the process of acquiring a language. Additionally, we know that the speaker is capable of producing sentences in the language, and we can refer to these sentences as *output*. We also know that the output contains sentences the speaker has never heard or read as input. (It is in this sense that the normal use of language is "creative.") On the basis of this evidence, we can logically conclude that there is "something" between the input and the output that has processed the data from the input and, as a result of this processing, has produced a *grammar*. The speaker utilizes this grammar in determining the meaning of the input (for example, in determining which nominal is the logical subject of such a sentence as: *It is easy to understand*), and also utilizes the grammar in producing an output—that is, in producing English sentences.

In discussing this "something" that processes input data, linguists generally use the term *language acquisition device,* that is, a system (involving many different parts of the brain) that has the specific function of enabling humans to learn languages. A transformational-generative linguist is particularly concerned with defining the nature of this "device."[14] In other words, a generative linguist believes that the universal qualities of language are not accidental but are, rather, determined by the nature of the human mind.

In this sense, language is a special case of the larger question which is concerned with the acquisition of any kind of knowledge (as opposed to the acquisition of habits).[15] Many rationalist philosophers would assume, in Chomsky's terms, that "the general form of a system of knowledge is fixed in advance as a disposition of the mind" (*Aspects,* p. 51). In this book, however, we shall not be concerned with this larger question.

4.4   Categories and Relationships

The linguistic distinction between *categories* and *relationships* is an important one, but unfortunately, the nature of the distinction is frequently misunderstood, partly because the distinction is not carefully maintained in many so-

---

[14] A behavioral psychologist generally assumes that language acquisition is not different in kind from the acquisition of "habits" or "propensities," and, moreover, that habits can be explained in terms of generalized inductive principles. (Empirical philosophers hold a similar view.) A cognitive psychologist, like a generative linguist, believes that there are innate ideas and principles which are vastly more complex than "generalized inductive principles" and which help to determine the form that acquired knowledge (such as language) may take.

[15] Habits would include such things as "customary" ways of walking, of holding a coffee cup, and so on. Knowledge would include such things as the ability to solve arithmetic problems, to play chess, and so on. There is no *a priori* reason to assume, as some behavioral psychologists do, that the acquisition of habits and the acquisition of knowledge are the result of the same kind of mental behavior.

called traditional school-grammars, the kind of grammars most commonly used in American schools during the last 100 years.

We can move outside linguistics for an analogy. Terms such as *man, woman, boy,* and *girl* are categorical; thus, there is a large category of people called "men," another category called "women," and so on. In contrast, the terms *husband, wife, sister,* and *son* (among other possibilities) are relational terms; that is, (1) they presuppose the existence of at least two categorical terms; (2) they express a relationship between the two implied terms; and (3) in most cases the relationship is directional. Thus, *husband* (a relational term) refers to a *man* who exists in a specific relationship to a *woman*. And, to complicate things, (4) relational terms may also define categories; for example, there is a category of people called *husbands*.

Returning to language, such traditional terms as *noun, verb, adjective,* and so on, are categorical. In contrast, terms such as *subject of a sentence* and *object of a verb* express relationships; that is, they imply the existence of two categorical terms and, moreover, they define a relationship between these terms.

For years, traditional grammarians have used both categorical and relational terms in the kind of exercise known as **parsing**.[16] For the most part, parsing has been an intuitive process, and the skill could only be acquired through considerable trial-and-error practice. Consider, again, two sentences we have already discussed (renumbered here for convenience of discussion):

Sentence 4.11 John is easy to please.
Sentence 4.12 John is eager to please.

In parsing these sentences, we might say that *John* is a *noun* and, moreover, a *proper noun*. Additionally, in Sentence 4.11, *John* is the *object of the infinitive, to please*. Notice that a term such as *noun* is a categorical term, while a term such as *object of the infinitive* is a relational term. Notice also that categorical terms are more or less permanent (for example, *John* is always a noun), whereas relational terms apply to a specific context (for example, a specific sentence).

The question for linguists is, in essence: "How can we best incorporate this (and similar) information into a formal grammar?" Unfortunately, there is no simple answer nor, indeed, is there a single answer that all linguists accept at present. Again, this lack of agreement may seem alarming to teachers of English who—for more than 100 years—accepted the so-called traditional definitions of school-grammars without question. When, for example, such teachers were asked to explain how they knew that *John*, in Sentence 4.12, is the subject of the

---

[16] Because traditional parsing has fallen into disuse in the schools, it may be worthwhile to quote a definition:

> **parse** to describe (a word in a sentence) grammatically, by stating the part of speech, inflexion, and relation to the rest of the sentence; to resolve (a sentence, etc.) into its component parts of speech and describe them grammatically.
>
> —*Oxford English Dictionary*

infinitive, they were unable to give precise reasons.[17] Teachers with some knowledge of the history of science will be less alarmed, because they will recognize that there are virtually no scientific hypotheses that are universally accepted by all scientists. Moreover, all scientists will readily admit that any hypothesis is always a candidate for replacement by a more comprehensive hypothesis. While linguists hope to find the single best way to describe language and language acquisition (the kind of ambition that motivates any scientist), they recognize that, on practical grounds, they must be content with much less, namely, with descriptions that are more accurate and comprehensive than those of the past.

In brief, *Aspects* presents one hypothesis about a speaker's knowledge of language and, in addition, presents some arguments against alternative hypotheses. In Chapter 5, we shall develop the "standard" hypothesis in some detail, since this is of particular interest to teachers. We shall not, however, discuss the arguments against alternative hypotheses, leaving that task for interested readers who wish to consult *Aspects* itself.

Exercises

1. Three levels of abstraction beyond reality have been discussed for linguistics. Can you find examples of similar levels of abstraction in other fields? Are all three levels represented in these fields?

2. Choose six ambiguous sentences (such as *John took the train*, discussed on p. 76) and provide contexts that disambiguate them.

3. As explained on pp. 81-82, Chomsky has argued that a child must have at least five abilities if he is to learn a language. Is it possible to define five analogous abilities a person must have to learn to perform other activities, such as swimming, bicycle riding, playing a musical instrument, or playing bridge or chess? Is there a difference between the types of ability necessary for games (bridge, chess) and those necessary for physical activities (swimming, riding a bicycle)?

4. Linguistic study can be divided into five parts corresponding to the five types of ability possessed by the language learner. Can any of the activities discussed in Exercise 3 be studied in an analogous fivefold manner?

5. The distinction between *categorical* and *relational* terms in linguistics has been stressed (p. 86). How does this distinction apply to other fields? In baseball, is *batter* a categorical or a relational term? What about *shortstop*, *home run*, *Vida Blue*?

---

[17]They might say something like, " 'John' is the one who does the pleasing," but this is not an answer, since we can still ask: "How do you *know* he does the pleasing?" It is this latter question that linguists are trying to answer by formalizing the study of grammar.

CHAPTER 5

The *Aspects* Model: II

The speech of man is like embroidered tapestries, since like them this too has to be extended in order to display its patterns, but when it is rolled up it conceals and distorts them.

Attr. to THEMISTOCLES, in Plutarch's *Lives*

We can now turn to a more detailed examination of the syntactic component in the standard model of transformational-generative grammar. As we noted briefly in Chapter 4, the syntactic component consists of three subcomponents: a set of phrase-structure (or "categorical") rules, a lexicon, and various transformational rules.

5.1 Phrase-Structure Rules

Formally, phrase-structure rules are "categorical rules"; sometimes, they are also called "rewriting rules" or "branching rules." In terms of symbolic logic, they function to relate one symbol to "a string of one or more symbols." Thus, the familiar rule

PS 5.1 S → NP + VP

is a phrase-structure rule, since it indicates that the symbol S (representing **sentence**) consists of a string of two other symbols, namely, NP (**noun phrase**) and VP (**verb phrase**). Such a rule is a symbolic way of representing internalized knowledge. It expresses this knowledge in exactly the same way that the familiar geometric formula $C = 2\pi r$ expresses information about the relation between the circumference and the radius of a circle.

Some further redundancy may be in order here, since the nature of phrase-structure rules has been widely misunderstood. Thus, the geometric formula for the circumference of a circle does not *produce* circles; rather, it expresses knowledge that defines the relationship between the categorical notions of *circumference* and *radius*. This is knowledge that a mathematician must have if he is to work with circles. Similarly, a phrase-structure rule, in itself, does not tell us how to *produce* sentences; rather, such a rule expresses the kind of knowledge we must have before we can produce sentences.

A few additional terms will facilitate discussion. In particular, we need to define *major category, lexical category, terminal symbol,* and *grammatical formative*; additionally, we need to define the meanings of two symbols: ⌢ and Δ. The necessary definitions can be given in terms of the following simplified rules:

PS 5.1a S → NP⌢VP   **PS 5.6** N → Δ

PS 5.2 VP → Aux⌢V (*NP*)   **PS 5.7** V → Δ

PS 5.3 NP → N   **PS 5.8** Modal → Δ

PS 5.4 Aux → Tense⌢(Modal)

PS 5.5 Tense → $\begin{Bmatrix} Present \\ Past \end{Bmatrix}$

The symbol that resembles a parenthesis lying on its side is called a **concatenation symbol**: ⌢ . This symbol indicates that the two symbols it connects can occur only in the order given.[1] The Greek letter delta, Δ, which is generally called a "dummy symbol," always represents a **terminal symbol** (see below).

Lexical category: any symbol that, in a phrase-structure rule, is necessarily rewritten as a "dummy symbol." In the simplified rules, above, *N, V,* and *Modal* all symbolize lexical categories.

Grammatical formative: any symbol that, in a phrase-structure rule, does *not* lead ultimately to a "dummy symbol." For convenience, some grammatical formatives are usually printed in italics. In the simplified rules, *Tense, Present,* and *Past* are grammatical formatives.

Terminal symbol: the "dummy symbol," Δ, which results from any rule that rewrites a lexical category symbol.

Major category: any symbol, except for a grammatical formative, that appears to the left of an arrow in a phrase-structure rule. (Thus, all lexical categories are also major categories, but all major categories are not lexical categories.) In the simplified grammar, *S, NP, VP, Aux, V, N,* and *Modal* all refer to major categories.[2]

---

[1] Logically, the use of a plus sign (rather than a concatenation symbol) in many early transformational grammars was incorrect since, for example, 3 + 2 = 2 + 3; that is, addition is commutative. In contrast, NP⌢VP ≠ VP⌢NP, since concatenation requires that the ordering of symbols be maintained.

[2] The system of using Δ is one of two that Chomsky presents in *Aspects*. In the other system, the symbol for a lexical category (for example, *N*) is rewritten as a so-called complex symbol. (The choice of one system over another relates to the concept of "subcategorization," which is discussed later in this chapter.) There is also an alternative to the use of grammatical formatives in the phrase-structure rules, but this alternative was not developed until after the publication of *Aspects*. The alternative is also discussed below.

There are several fragmentary grammars scattered throughout *Aspects,* and these fragments sometimes contain different versions of the same rule (for example, the rule for rewriting *VP*). The fact that there are different versions reminds us that the precise rules for the base component have not yet been established. For example, different transformational grammarians have offered the following version of the first rule:

PS 5.1a S → NP⌢VP
PS 5.1b S → NP⌢Predicate phrase
PS 5.1c S → NP⌢Aux⌢VP
PS 5.1d S → P⌢NP⌢(NP)   (where P represents "proposition")

Other versions may also be possible. But since we are concerned primarily with the significance of the theory, the variety is irrelevant. No matter what precise rule the linguists finally agree on, it will certainly be similar to all the versions proposed. Thus, it will have an *S* to the left of the arrow, at least one *NP* to the right of the arrow, and some other symbol which will lead, ultimately, to a verb. (Some linguists would say "to a verb or adjective"; we shall consider this distinction below.)

For our purposes, then, we shall select a few rules from the different fragments in *Aspects*; moreover, we shall simplify some of these rules. In particular, we shall omit some items from various rules (for example, those that underlie adverbs), and we shall also use the system of "dummy symbols" (rather than "complex symbols"—see footnote 2—which are used in most of the fragmentary grammars in *Aspects*). In sum, we are concerned with the general shape of the grammar rather than with particular rules. Our second grammatical model incorporates the following phrase-structure rules:

PS 5.1a S → NP⌢VP

PS 5.2a VP → Aux $\left\{ \begin{array}{l} \text{Copula⌢Predicate} \\ \text{V⌢(NP)⌢(NP)} \end{array} \right\}$

PS 5.3a NP → (Det)⌢N⌢(S)

PS 5.4   Aux → Tense⌢(Modal)

PS 5.5   Tense → $\left\{ \begin{array}{l} \textit{Present} \\ \textit{Past} \end{array} \right\}$

PS 5.6   N → Δ

PS 5.7   V → Δ

PS 5.8   Modal → Δ

PS 5.9   Predicate → $\left\{ \begin{array}{l} \text{Adjective} \\ \textit{(like)}⌢\text{NP} \end{array} \right\}$

PS 5.10 Det → Δ

PS 5.11 Copula → *be*

PS 5.12 Adjective → Δ

Notice that in PS 5.3a there is an *S* on the right of an arrow. This *S* makes the

Major Categories	Lexical Categories	Grammatical Formatives	Terminal Symbol
S NP VP	N V Det	*like Past*	Δ
Predicate	Adjective	*Present be*	
Aux Det N	Modal	Copula	
Copula V		Tense	
Adjective			
Modal			

set of rules recursive. Figure 5.1 is a derivation of Sentence 5.1 that has been constructed from these rules.[3]

Sentence 5.1 The boy who ate the pie is sad.

In Figure 5.1, notice that the end result of the derivation is a series of "dummy symbols" and grammatical formatives. For illustrative purposes, words have been inserted into the dummy symbols in Figure 5.1; additionally, three syntactic transformations have been performed: (1) to produce *who* from the second occurrence of *the* and *boy*, (2) to combine *Past* and *eat* into *ate*, and (3) to combine *Present* and *be* into *is*. By choosing different words to insert into the positions occupied by the dummy symbols, we could produce any of the following sentences:

Sentence 5.2 The dog that found the bone is happy.
Sentence 5.3 The teachers who received a raise are delighted.
Sentence 5.4 The professor who corrected the test was angry.

In other words, the branching tree given in Figure 5.1 underlies these and thousands of other sentences. That is, the branching tree represents the syntactic *structure* (before lexical insertion) of many different sentences.

Before turning to the process of lexical insertion, we need to consider some additional facts about the phrase-structure rules. Specifically, we need to note

---

[3] The same information contained in the branching tree can also be indicated in a "labeled bracketing" as follows:

```
[ [the] [boy] [ [ [the] [boy] ] [ [ [Past] ] [eat] [ [the] [pie] ] ] ] [ [ [Present] ] [be] [ [sad] ] ] ]
 S N D    N     S N D    N       V A T   V    N D    N      V A T    C      P A
 P e            P e             P u e         P e          P u e     o      r d
 t              t              x n            t           x n        p      e j
                                s                          s      .  u      d
                                e                          e         l
                                                                     a
```

Such a bracketing has advantages, particularly when a linguist wishes to apply phonological rules. First, he applies all relevant rules to the items within the "innermost bracket"; then he erases the boundaries of this bracket and applies the phonological rules to the new "innermost bracket"; he continues in this way until all the boundaries are erased. In the authors' experience, however, many teachers find the bracket system confusing, and for this reason, we shall continue to use branching trees (which present exactly the same information).

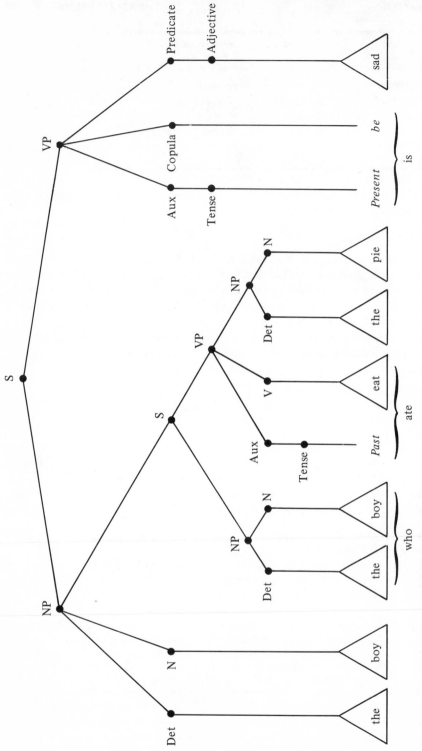

Figure 5.1 Derivation from a pedagogical model based on *Aspects*

that each rule operates independently of all the other rules. To speak figuratively, we can say that each rule is "ignorant" of any other rules that have been applied—or that will apply—within a derivation. For a rule to apply, it is only necessary that there be an appropriate node on the tree, that is, a node which corresponds to the symbol on the left of the arrow in the rule. In more technical terms, the rules are "context free." For example, consider the first *NP* node in Figure 5.1 (the one produced when the uppermost *S* is "rewritten"). As the tree shows, we actually chose to rewrite this *NP* as a sequence of *Det, N,* and *S.* We could, however, have chosen any of the following sequences: (1) *Det* and *N,* (2) *N,* (3) *N* and *S.* Of course, if we had chosen one of these different sequences, we would have produced a different tree from the one given in Figure 5.1, and consequently, we could not have derived the same sentences.

Again, we have touched on a topic that some teachers find confusing. Such teachers might ask: "In deriving a sentence (for example, *The boy who ate the pie is sad*), how can the rules be context free?" The answer is: they can't be. That is, given a nonambiguous sentence, there is only one fundamental syntactic structure which underlies the sentence. But the term *context free* is not meant to apply to such a situation. Rather, the term refers to the general properties of phrase-structure rules. If, for the moment, we ignore actual sentences and concentrate only on those "objects" we have called branching trees, then perhaps the situation will be clearer.

Suppose, then, that we begin with *S* and go through the rules and derive a tree; at each node we apply the rule that relates to the node, but if the rule gives us an option, we make a random choice. We would ultimately produce a string of "dummy symbols" and grammatical formatives which, for discussion purposes, we can label derivation 1. This derivation will underlie thousands of different sentences. Then suppose we start again with *S,* this time making several different choices as we go through the rules and finally producing derivation 2 (different from derivation 1). This second derivation would also underlie thousands of sentences, each one different from those related to derivation 1. Quite literally, we could repeat this process indefinitely, producing derivations 3, 4, 5, and so on, up to infinity. Each derivation would underlie thousands of sentences which are different *in structure* from those related to any other derivation.

Thus, when we say *context free,* we mean that any choice we make can eventually lead to some grammatical sentence, and the structure of such a sentence is different from any sentence produced by making alternative choices. While it may seem that we are making one more mountain out of yet another molehill, the point is nonetheless an important one. In particular, the point relates to the difference between phrase-structure rules and transformations. Phrase-structure rules are context free; transformations, in contrast, are "context sensitive."

The distinction is important for several reasons. First, it marks one of the major differences between transformational-generative grammars and American structuralist grammars. Second, it indicates that speakers of a language actually know two different kinds of rules, a distinction which is important in discussing dialects. Third, it suggests that phrase-structure rules may be identical for all languages, or to put the matter another way, that learning a language means learning the transformations of that language. And fourth, it suggests, at least as a possibility, that phrase-structure rules are—in some sense—innate at birth (whereas transformations are learned in the process of acquiring a particular language). As bizarre as this last statement may sound, there is—at present—no reason for rejecting it as impossible.

Finally, we can note again that phrase-structure rules can be used to define certain fundamental grammatical notions, such as *subject of a sentence* and *object of a verb*. In this sense phrase-structure rules make precise many of the intuitions that earlier grammarians applied in the process of parsing a sentence.

5.2   The Lexicon

At the end of Chapter 3, we noted briefly that the phonological theory of "distinctive features" contributed to the first major revision of transformational theory in two ways. First, it provided a basis for incorporating transformations into the phonological component of the grammar (and thus provided independent justification for postulating the existence of transformations). Second, it suggested a system for incorporating both syntactic and semantic features (which are analogous to phonological features).

We then noted, again briefly, that every item in the lexicon of a transformational-generative grammar is *marked* for each of these three kinds of features: phonological, syntactic, and semantic. Phonological features are quite independent of both syntactic and semantic features, but—as many transformationalists have noted—the line between syntactic and semantic features is difficult (and perhaps impossible) to draw. Thus, in English the feature *male* has both syntactic and semantic importance. Syntactically, it affects the form of third-person-singular pronouns (that is, *he, him, his*); semantically, it refers to one of the two sexes. The question is an important one, and there seem to be four possible solutions:

1. There is a definite line between syntactic and semantic features (which remains to be determined).
2. Some features are syntactic, some are semantic, and some are both.
3. All features are syntactic (or, alternatively, all are semantic).
4. The theory of syntactic and semantic features is basically flawed and must be replaced by some other theory.

At the present stage of our knowledge, we can do no more than identify the problem, note its importance, and make an *ad hoc* choice for purposes of further discussion. Thus, on strictly *ad hoc* grounds, we shall choose the second possibility. We can now represent a *lexical item* by two sets of features: (1) phonological, and (2) syntactic/semantic. The word *man* might be entered in the lexicon as in Figure 5.2. The phonological features of the word are indicated by the "distinctive feature matrix" on the left of Figure 5.2. Each sound of the word is represented by a column which indicates the presence—or absence—of various universal phonological features (for example, "voiced" or "not voiced"). The first column represents the sound normally written as *m*; the second column represents the "low front vowel" which, in a phonetic alphabet, is normally written in dictionaries as *æ*; and the third column represents the sound normally written as *n*.[4]

If the word contained two or more syllables, we would also indicate which syllables received stress. And we need to note that the stress of the underlying form (that is, the stress given in the lexicon) might be different from the stress assigned to the word in a sentence.

By way of example, consider *photo.* In the lexicon, we might use the representation *fo' to,* with the stress on the first syllable. (Alternatively, it might be that—in this case—both syllables receive equal stress in the underlying representation.) Now suppose that we combine the morpheme *photo* with various other morphemes to produce the following words:

photograph photography photographic

In the act of combining these morphemes to produce these words, both the stress and the vowel sounds in *photo* are sometimes changed. Thus, in *photograph* the first "o" retains its underlying form of /o/ and the primary stress in the word remains on the first syllable, but the second "o" is reduced to the "schwa" sound, /ə/. In the word *photography,* the first "o" is reduced to /ə/, the second "o" is pronounced /a/, and the primary stress shifts to the second syllable. And in *photographic,* the first "o" remains /o/, the second "o" is again

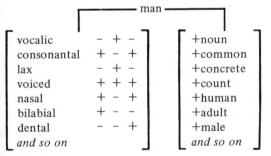

	man
vocalic	− + −
consonantal	+ − +
lax	− + −
voiced	+ + +
nasal	+ − +
bilabial	+ − −
dental	− − +
and so on	

+noun
+common
+concrete
+count
+human
+adult
+male
and so on

Figure 5.2 The lexical item *man*

[4] In the lexicon, distinctive features are the most accurate way of representing underlying sounds. But for practical purposes, it is frequently more useful to indicate sounds in a phonetic alphabet, with the understanding that each symbol in such an alphabet actually represents a column of distinctive features.

reduced to /ə/, and the primary stress is shifted to the following morpheme: *graph.*

All of these changes are governed by phonological rules that are consistent throughout the language. By way of example, consider the nonsense morpheme *dubi,* which, we shall assume, has the underlying pronunciation /dubi/. Suppose we combine this morpheme with others to produce

dubigraph   dubigraphy   dubigraphic

These nonsense "words" have the same stress patterns as those we have just discussed, which we can represent as follows:

/du' bə græf/   /də big' grə fiy/   /du bə græf' ik/

In sum, a lexical entry provides an *underlying phonological representation* for the words and morphemes of a language. This representation includes a column of distinctive features for each sound as well as stress markers for entries containing more than one syllable. Additionally, a grammar contains a set of phonological rules which come into operation as the entries are combined into words, and also as the words are combined into phrases, clauses, and sentences. The phonological rules are sometimes dependent on syntactic information. Thus, in a simple sentence such as the following, the primary stress normally occurs on the last noun:

2   3   1

Sentence 5.5 The people saw the thief.

In this example, the numbers indicate primary, secondary, and tertiary stress. Suppose, however, that we replace the nominal *the thief* with a pronoun, and add a contextual sentence. We might get

Sentence 5.6 (A thief ran down the street.)

2   1   3

The people saw him.

Notice that the primary stress (in normal intonation) shifts to the verb. In other words, the phonological rules need to "know" whether a word is a noun, a verb, a pronoun, and so on; moreover, the rules also need to "know" where—in what position—a word occurs in a sentence, and this kind of information is syntactic rather than phonological.[5]

Returning now to Figure 5.2, the syntactic/semantic features are indicated by the set of items on the right of the figure. In general, these are identical with those already discussed on pp. 67-68. Moreover, the set is incomplete—for two reasons: (1) Since we are concerned with the general outline of the theory, a full

---

[5] As noted earlier, we shall not consider either the phonological or the semantic component of the "standard" transformational-generative grammar in any detail. Interested readers will find additional references in the Bibliography.

representation is not necessary; (2) transformational linguists have yet to devise a complete listing of all possible syntactic and semantic features.

We can assume, however, that there are syntactic and semantic features which are linguistic universals. For example, the syntactic category of *noun* seems to be universal, as does the semantic feature of *male*. Additionally, we can also assume that these features are closely related to the terms lexicographers have (intuitively) used for centuries. Thus, a "dictionary definition" of *man* would indicate that (in one sense) the word is a noun, that it refers to a male, and furthermore to an adult male, that the noun has a plural form (which, in English, is irregular), and so on. Other features would be negatively indicated by reason of their absence from the definition. Thus, *man* is not a proper noun, is not an abstract noun, does not refer to an inanimate object, and so on.

So far, we have looked closely only at the system for representing nouns. We now need to turn to the means of representing verbs and adjectives. In particular, we need to note that the lexical entries for verbs and adjectives differ from those for nouns.[6] To see why, we can return, again, to phrase-structure rules.

The phrase-structure rules we have examined introduce a node marked *V* (for *Verb*). As we have noted, such a rule is also called a "branching rule" since it produces nodes and branches on a tree. Moreover, branching rules operate "blindly," that is, without regard for any other rules that have applied in a derivation. Now suppose we have produced the (simplified) tree shown in Figure 5.3. At this point, we are ready to select items from the lexicon. In theory, we have several alternatives. As our first lexical item, we can choose (1) the subject noun, (2) the verb, or (3) the object noun. And this is the important point: *Once we have selected the first lexical item, our choice of other lexical items is constrained.*

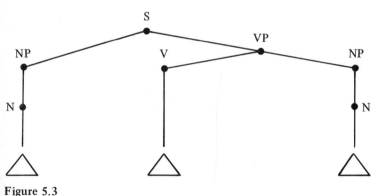

Figure 5.3

---

[6] In *Aspects,* Chomsky discusses various ways of categorizing verbs; he pays less attention to adjectives. As in the earlier discussion of nouns, we shall choose the "dummy symbol" form of the theory (rather than the "complex symbol" form). For reasons that will be developed more fully later, we shall assume that adjectives are classified in much the same way as verbs.

For example, suppose we choose the lexical item *hat* for the subject position. Our choice of verb is now constrained to those that can occur with inanimate subjects. Thus, we cannot choose *sleep* as a verb, since it requires an animate subject. Similarly, suppose we first choose a verb, in particular, the verb *elapse*. Now our choice of a subject noun is constrained. We cannot choose an animate noun; rather, we must choose one that has the feature **time** (as in: *An hour elapsed*). Moreover, if we choose *elapse,* then we cannot choose a direct object at all, since the verb is intransitive. Finally, suppose our first choice of a lexical item is the noun that functions as a direct object and, in particular, the abstract noun *happiness.* Again, our choice of a verb is constrained to those that can occur with abstract direct objects. (Thus, we can say *Irving sought happiness* but not **Fred cooked happiness.*[7]) Speakers of English know these facts. That is, they know that certain words do not normally occur with other words. We must, therefore, include this information in the grammar. The question is: How?

In the first place, one category must be dominant over other categories—either noun over verb, or verb over noun. This permits us to define the "subdominant category" in terms of the "dominant category." While arguments can be presented for either choice, the strongest seem to be those that favor noun as the dominant category, and we shall adopt this alternative.

Moreover, we shall follow *Aspects* in distinguishing two kinds of restrictions on verbs: (1) those that relate to category symbols (for example, *NP, Adj,* and so on), and (2) those that relate to features that are used in defining nouns (for example, *animate, abstract,* and so on). Borrowing terms from *Aspects,* we shall refer to the first kind of restriction as a **strict-subcategorization restriction**, and to the second as a **selectional restriction**.

The following rule, therefore, is a strict-subcategorizational rule:

PS 5.7a $\quad V \rightarrow \Delta / - \begin{cases} NP \\ \text{Adjective} \\ that \text{ Sentence} \end{cases}$

The rule may be read as follows: rewrite *V* as a "dummy symbol" in the context of either *NP,* or *Adjective,* or *that Sentence.* The "slash" (/) represents "in the context"; the dash that follows the slash indicates that the verb precedes the contextual items; the braces, as before, indicate a choice.

Now consider the means for representing the following verbs in the lexicon: *see, feel, expect.* Among other features, the lexical entries for these verbs will contain the following information:

$$\begin{bmatrix} \text{see} \\ +V \\ +-NP \\ and\ so\ on \end{bmatrix} \qquad \begin{bmatrix} \text{feel} \\ +V \\ +-Adj \\ and\ so\ on \end{bmatrix} \qquad \begin{bmatrix} \text{expect} \\ +V \\ +-that\ \text{Sentence} \\ and\ so\ on \end{bmatrix}$$

---

[7] We can probably provide a metaphorical reading for this latter sentence, but the point here is that the sentence does not have a *literal* meaning.

In each case, the feature $+V$ indicates, obviously, that the lexical item is a verb. The second feature for *see* indicates that this verb occurs in the context of a following noun phrase; that is, the verb takes a direct object. The second feature for *feel* indicates that this verb can occur in the context of a following adjective (for example, *Sam feels happy*); thus, this verb is different from the homophonous verb *feel*, which takes direct objects (for example, *Belle felt the pain*). Finally, the second feature under *expect* indicates that this verb can occur in the context of a complement (for example, *Marvin expected that we would go*).

When we insert verbs into a branching tree, we must be certain to follow the strict-subcategorization restrictions, since these are part of the meaning of the verbs themselves. Thus, we cannot insert the verb *see* into a tree that contains an adjective node immediately dominated by *VP*. Consequently, *feel* would fit into the tree shown in Figure 5.4, but *see* would not.

As the name implies, strict-subcategorization restrictions apply to subcategories of verbs including those traditionally designated as *transitive, intransitive, linking,* and so on. Selectional restrictions apply to verbs within these subcategories. Thus, a verb may have the feature $(+-NP)$; that is, it may be a transitive verb, but it may also be further restricted to occur only with animate direct objects.

Consider the verb *please*. The lexical entry might contain the following features (among others):

$$\begin{bmatrix} \text{please} \\ +V \\ +-NP \\ +-(+\text{animate}) \end{bmatrix}$$

As above, the first feature indicates that *please* is a verb; the second feature is a strict-subcategorization restriction which indicates that *please* takes a direct object; the third feature is a selectional restriction which indicates that we can choose *please* only if the direct object (a noun) contains the feature *animate* as part of its lexical entry.

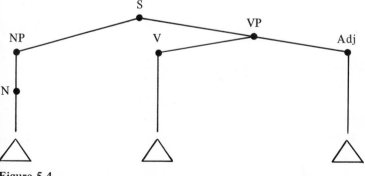

Figure 5.4

Again, some readers may think that we are picking nits where no nits are. But—also again—there is a reason for distinguishing between grammatical facts in such a precise way. Consider the following semigrammatical sentences:

Sentence 5.7 *Muriel pleases hungry.
Sentence 5.8 *Myke pleases the hat.

While neither sentence is fully grammatical, they deviate from full grammaticality in different ways. Sentence 5.7 incorporates an adjective (*hungry*) where the sentence requires a noun; thus, this sentence violates a strict-subcategorization rule. Sentence 5.8 has a noun in the required position (and thus does *not* violate a strict-subcategorization restriction), but the noun is inanimate whereas the verb can occur only with direct objects that are animate; thus, this sentence violates a selectional restriction.

This distinction permits us to introduce the notion of "degrees of grammaticality" (or, perhaps more properly, "degrees of ungrammaticality"). Most traditional school grammars treat all ungrammatical sentences alike; that is, in such grammars, a sentence either is—or is not—grammatical. By distinguishing between strict-subcategorization restrictions, on the one hand, and selectional restrictions, on the other, we can state that some "imperfect sentences" are less grammatical ("more ungrammatical") than others.

Thus, some strings of words are completely ungrammatical; we can get no meaning from them at all. Sentences that violate strict-subcategorization restrictions are more grammatical than completely meaningless strings of words. And sentences that violate selection restrictions are even closer to full grammaticality:

Sentence 5.9   *if happy the and however shoe.
Sentence 5.10 *This sentence seems Irving.
Sentence 5.11 *Stella saw the happiness.

The first of these violates the basic phrase-structure rules (that is, major categorical restrictions), the second violates strict-*sub*categorical restrictions, and the third violates selectional restrictions.

Finally, we can note that some selectional features refer to the subject noun (rather than, for example, to the object noun, as in the case of *please*). Thus, we can insert the verb *admire* into a tree only if the subject noun contains the feature *animate* (or, perhaps, *human*). Consequently, the first of the following sentences is grammatical; the second is not:

Sentence 5.12 The boy admired the picture.
Sentence 5.13 *The rock admired the boy.

Such a selectional restriction can be indicated in the set of features that (partially) defines *admire,* as follows:

$$\begin{bmatrix} \text{admire} \\ +\text{V} \\ +\text{—NP} \\ +\text{Det } (+human)\text{—} \end{bmatrix}$$

The first of these features indicates that *admire* is a verb; the second is a strict-subcategorization restriction which indicates that *admire* takes a direct object; the third feature is a selectional restriction which indicates that the subject of *admire* must contain the feature (+*human*) as part of its lexical entry.

In sum, the lexicon of a transformational-generative grammar contains entries for all the "lexical items" in the language. In the preceding discussion, we have made a pedagogical simplification in assuming that these "items" are, in effect, the same as "words." In Chapter 6, we shall consider the possibility that, for example, such words as *graphic, biography, graphite* (and so on) are not separate items in a lexicon; in place of such "full-word items," we would have items that are prefixes, suffixes, and stems, and also rules for combining these items into full words.

In any case, each entry contains, first, a set of distinctive phonological features, and second, various syntactic/semantic features. If the lexical items are "full words," the syntactic/semantic features indicate the category (for example, *N, V,* and *Adj*) to which the word belongs; they also indicate, for nouns, such features as *common, animate, abstract,* and so on. The listings for verbs and adjectives contain similar features and, in addition, others which we have designated as strict-subcategorization features and selection features.

The lexical entries for articles (for example, *the, a*) and similar "minor category" words are not discussed in any detail in *Aspects.* Presumably, such words are assigned features similar to those for nouns and verbs. Thus, the entry for *the* might contain the feature *definite*; *that* might contain the features *demonstrative, singular,* and *far.* We shall not discuss such entries here, however, since—in a few paragraphs—we shall examine a slightly different system of representing such minor categories in the grammar.

5.3 Transformational Rules

As its third subcomponent, the base component of a transformational-generative grammar contains various transformational rules. We have already demonstrated two types of transformations: (1) general transformations, and (2) lexical-insertion transformations.

Simplifying somewhat, we can say that general transformations apply to a tree as it is generated by the phrase-structure rules. Thus, the question transformation applies to *any* tree that contains the presentence element: *Question.* In contrast, lexical-insertion transformations permit us to insert lexical items into a tree, provided these items satisfy the strict-subcategorization and selectional restrictions. (In earlier examples, for example, those on pp. 91 and 92, we tacitly assumed the existence of lexical-insertion transformations.)

We now need to consider another type of transformation, the so-called **local transformation** (which is also called a "segment transformation"). This transformation is most easily understood if we place it against a backdrop of an earlier form of the theory. Thus, the first edition of this book contained the following phrase-structure rules, among others:

$$\text{NP} \rightarrow \left\{ \begin{array}{c} \text{NP}_s \\ \text{NP}_p \end{array} \right\} \qquad \text{NP}_s \rightarrow \text{T} + \text{N} + \phi \qquad \text{NP}_p \rightarrow \text{T} + \text{N} + \text{Z}$$

The new symbols have the following meanings:

NP_s: noun phrase singular
NP_p: noun phrase plural
T: article
ϕ: the singular morpheme ("zero morph")
Z: the plural morpheme

Notice, in particular, that the singular and plural morphemes were introduced into a tree by the phrase-structure rules. For example, these three rules could produce either of the tree "segments" shown in Figure 5.5.

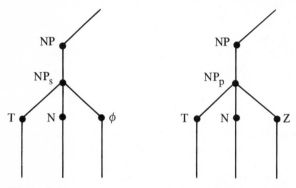

Figure 5.5

At this point, using an early model, we would turn to the lexicon and select suitable words and morphemes to insert into the tree. (The system of using syntactic/semantic features had not yet been developed.) Two of the many possibilities are shown in Figure 5.6.

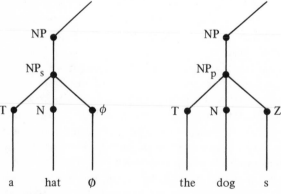

Figure 5.6

The incorporation of syntactic/semantic features into the grammar permits us to simplify these rules. Specifically, and following the *Aspects* model, we can reduce the three rules for writing noun phrases to a single new rule. To do this, we indicate—in the lexicon—that a noun either can or cannot be counted. Thus, we may have *one boy, two boys,* and so on, but we cannot have **one wheat,* **two wheats,* and so on. In terms of features, we say that *boy* is +*count,* whereas *wheat* is -*count.*

If a noun has the feature +*count,* then—when we insert that noun into a branching tree—we must indicate whether, in the particular sentence, the noun is +*singular* or -*singular* (that is, "plural"). If the noun is +*singular,* then no new transformations apply. But suppose the noun is -*singular*; that is, suppose we have a tree segment with an attached lexical entry, as in Figure 5.7.

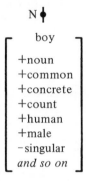

Figure 5.7

In this case, the presence of the -*singular* feature activates a "local transformation." This transformation produces a new segment to the right of the noun segment. The new segment contains the features +*affix* and -*singular,* and is immediately dominated by the *N* node. In Figure 5.8, the double arrow indicates the operation of the transformation.

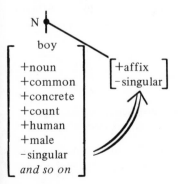

Figure 5.8

In the post-*Aspects* model, local transformation becomes increasingly important.[8]

In constructing a derivation based on the *Aspects* model, we go through the following steps. (1) We use the phrase-structure rules to produce a branching tree. (2) We select nouns from the lexicon and, using transformations, we insert these in place of the "dummy symbols" on the tree. (3) We then choose other lexical items that are compatible with the strict-subcategorization and selectional restrictions imposed in steps 1 and 2. (4) We apply all the necessary general transformations. (5) We apply all the necessary local transformations. (6) Finally, we apply the phonological transformations to produce a surface structure.

To repeat the familiar caveat again: These steps refer to a model of competence (that is, they represent knowledge a speaker *has* in his head); they are not a model of performance (that is, they do not indicate what a speaker *does* in producing sentences).

5.4   Observations and Corollaries

In developing the general outline of the *Aspects* model, and in particular, the base component of this model (the phrase-structure rules, the lexicon, the transformations), we have passed over some sections of the book that also concern some teachers of English. We can return to a few of these in this section. (There is no particular sequence to the following comments.)

1. The phrase-structure rules of the *Aspects* model have one basic role: they define the grammatical relations expressed in the deep structure (for example, *subject of . . . , direct object of . . . ,* and so on). Moreover, these are functional concepts; that is, they define the functions of particular grammatical categories (for example, *NP*) within a given sentence. Finally, it seems probable that such functional notions (for example, *subject of . . .*) are defined only for major categories. This last observation is consistent with the practice of traditional grammars.

2. In the *Aspects* model, restrictive relative clauses are a product of the determiner system (that is, they derive from a determiner node), while nonrestrictive relative clauses are complements of a full noun phrase.

In the examples below, the first sentence contains a restrictive relative clause (one *not* set off by commas), while the second contains a nonrestrictive relative clause.

Sentence 5.14   The boy who cut your grass is my brother.
Sentence 5.15   The book, which I thoroughly enjoyed, is a best-seller.

Both of these sentences contain embedded clauses, but in the *Aspects* model, these clauses derive from different sources. The tree segments in Figure 5.9 indicate, in a simplified manner, these different sources.

---

[8] One text that presents a number of segment transformations is Roderick Jacobs and Peter Rosenbaum, *English Transformational Grammar* (Lexington Mass.: Xerox College Publishing, 1968).

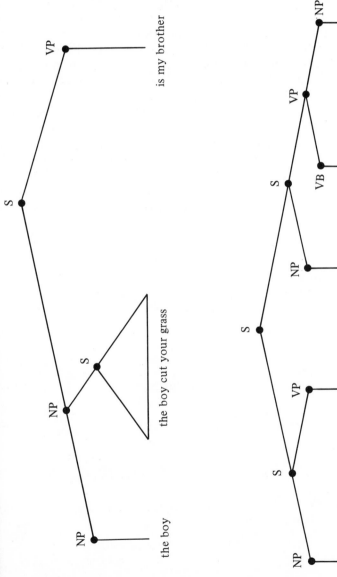
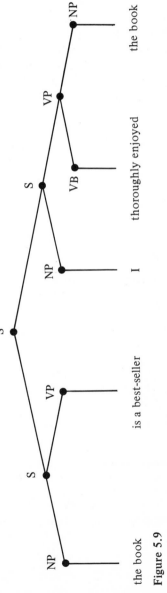

Figure 5.9

Note that, in the case of the restrictive clause, the embedded sentence derive
from the *same* noun phrase as the word—*boy*—that it "modifies." It is thus an
intimate part of the meaning of *boy* in this sentence. In the case of the nonre
strictive clause, the embedded sentence does not derive from the same noun
phrase, but rather from another sentence that also contains the noun phrase
Thus, it is not intimately connected with the meaning of *book* in the sentence
rather, to use a nontechnical term, the nonrestrictive clause is a kind of "after
thought."

3. There appear to be (at least) two types of adverbial constructions in
English: (a) those that can occur quite freely with almost any type of verb
phrase (in particular, adverbials of time and place), and (b) those that appear to
be closely associated with particular verbs. Moreover, it seems that we can treat
all adverbials as prepositional phrases (for example, *at the beach, in the morning,
with alacrity*); single-word adverbs can be transformationally derived from such
constructions (for example, *there, yesterday, quickly*).

Those adverbials that occur freely with verb phrases—(a) in the preceding
paragraph—do not affect the choice of particular verbs in sentences; that is, they
do not impose strict-subcategorization restrictions. In contrast, those adverbs
that are closely associated with particular verbs—(b), above—do affect the choice
of verbs in sentences and are, therefore, incorporated within the strict-subcategorization restrictions. For example, certain "stative" verbs (that is, those which
define states rather than actions—*know* as contrasted with *solve*), cannot occur
freely with adverbials of manner; nonstative verbs can occur with such adverbials. Thus, the first two sentences below are grammatical; the third violates
strict-subcategorization restrictions:

Sentence 5.16 John solved the problem very rapidly.
Sentence 5.17 Sue knows the answer.
Sentence 5.18 *Sue knows the answer very rapidly.

Although these observations about adverbials seem correct, the category is still
not well understood. A sentence from *Aspects* provides a necessary caveat:

Adverbials are a rich and as yet relatively unexplored system, and therefore
anything we say about them must be regarded as quite tentative (*Aspects*,
p. 219).

4. As noted in the first edition of this book, transformations may delete only
items that are "recoverable," that is, those that are understood by a listener or
reader as being part of the meaning of the sentence. This notion of "recoverabil-
ity" is a formal way of expressing the traditional notion of words being "understood" in a sentence.

For example, we can represent the derivation of a comparative sentence with
the following informal structures:

Sentence 5.19 Paula has eaten snails (*Comp*) David has eaten snails
                   Paula has eaten snails (more . . . than) David has eaten snails

Paula has eaten more snails than David has eaten (snails)
Paula has eaten more snails than David has.

In the final version of this sentence, we have deleted two "words" that appeared in the deep structure, namely, *eaten* and *snails.* This can be deleted because they are fully recoverable—fully understood—by the listener or reader.

Similarly, all imperative sentences have—in the deep structure—a logical subject: "you." Because, by convention, this is understood, it may be deleted from the surface structure in most imperatives.

5. *Aspects* also distinguishes between "stylistic" and "nonstylistic" transformations. We shall return to this distinction in a later chapter; here, we can simply note that transformations such as the question transformation are nonstylistic. Thus, when the question constituent occurs in a deep-structure tree, we *must* apply the appropriate transformation. In contrast, consider the following sentences:

Sentence 5.20 This is the car I want to buy.
Sentence 5.21 This is the car that I want to buy.

The deletion of *that* from the first of these sentences is achieved by applying a stylistic transformation, that is, one which is optional rather than obligatory. Stylistic transformations are probably activated by optional "markers" in the deep structure.

6. The rules relating to reflexivization are interesting in themselves, and they also raise interesting problems. Consider:

Sentence 5.22 I bought a present for myself.
Sentence 5.23 I put a present next to me.

Apparently, Sentence 5.22 consists of a single sentence—that is, one which does not contain an embedded sentence. In such cases, reflexivization is obligatory for coreferential pronouns. In contrast, Sentence 5.23 seems to be derived from two sentences—a matrix containing *I,* and an insert containing *me.*[9] In this case (at least in some dialects of English), reflexivization does not occur, because the two pronouns (*I* and *me*) do not originate in the same sentence. There may, however, be some exceptions to this observation. If so, the observation may be incorrect, or else speakers of the language may be changing the rule.

7. After reconsidering the various types of transformations discussed in the body of *Aspects,* Chomsky concludes that all transformations consist of one or more "elementary operations," namely: substitution, deletion, and adjunction. While the technical details of this conclusion are not particularly important for teachers of English, the conclusion itself reinforces the notion of a "language acquisition device"; thus, when faced with a new transformation, a language learner needs only to decide which of the three "elementary operations" may be

---

[9] Quite informally, we can represent these two sentences as: I put a present SOMEPLACE (SOMEPLACE is next to me).

involved. Presumably, it is easier for young children to learn those transformations that involve only one elementary operation (such as *you* deletion in imperatives). Transformations that involve all three elementary operations would, in contrast, be more difficult to learn (as in the case of the passive transformation).

8. Throughout *Aspects,* and particularly in the final chapter, Chomsky mentions several unresolved problems that require additional analysis. Some of these will be discussed in Chapter 6, when we examine various proposals for revising the *Aspects* model. One question, for example, relates to the role of surface structure in determining meaning. In general, the *Aspects* model assumes that all meaning resides in the deep structure, after the insertion of lexical items. Yet in the final chapter of *Aspects,* Chomsky suggests that—in some cases—surface structure may play a role in determining meaning, particularly in the case of such "quantifiers" as *even* and *only.*

The problem of paraphrase is also a major one in current research. Consider:

Sentence 5.24 I know that John is your brother.
Sentence 5.25 I am aware that John is your brother.

Aspects offers no suggestions for relating the meanings of these sentences. Some linguists, writing after *Aspects,* claim that *know* and *be aware* are identical in underlying meaning and that the surface differences (that is, the different spellings and pronunciations) are given by transformations.

Part of the importance of *Aspects* resides in the fact that problems such as these are brought to the reader's attention. That is, we have gone beyond the days when linguists—and teachers—can sweep intractable problems under an obfuscating rug. In an earlier chapter, we noted that linguistics moved into an adolescent stage during the early 1960s. The intellectual integrity that is part of the fiber of *Aspects* clearly marks a transition into maturity.

5.5   *Aspects* in Retrospect

The theory of transformational-generative grammar grew very rapidly during the ten years that preceded the publication of *Aspects,* and the book itself represents the culmination and most comprehensive statement of that growth.

In the late 1950s, much energy was devoted to two topics: (1) the debate between the transformational and the structural linguists, and (2) the means of formalizing the theory within the framework established in the field of symbolic logic.

There is still some interest in the first topic, but the debate has narrowed in some respects. Most structuralists now recognize the value of using transformations to describe language, but they also believe—sometimes in apparent contrast to their own earlier statements—that semantics must play a more important role in research than it does in the *Aspects* model.[10] Additionally, some structuralists deny the importance of linguistic competence as an object of scientific investigation, preferring instead to focus on performance. Nonetheless, the vast

[10] See, in particular, Charles Hockett, *The State of the Art* (The Hague: Mouton, 1968).

majority of linguists readily admit that Chomsky has made significant contributions to our understanding of language.

The second topic—developing the means for formally expressing the theory in logical terms—has also been accomplished, at least in general outline. This means that any alternatives to the standard theory must also be expressed in formal terms before they can be considered as viable. In brief, the standard theory of transformational grammar (as defined in *Aspects*) provides the starting place for future research into the nature of language.

These are major advances in our attempt to understand the world around us, and more particularly, to understand ourselves. But advances only bring us to resting—and not stopping—places. As we shall see in the next chapter, linguists are already beginning to move beyond *Aspects*. The fact of movement is clear, but the direction is obscure.

Exercises

1. Give five sentences having the structure represented by the branching tree in Figure 5.1.
2. Based on Figure 5.1, rewrite the noun phrases and verb phrases (that is, make different choices in the phrase-structure rules) to produce five different trees.
3. Using the phrase-structure rules on p. 90, produce branching trees for six deep structures.
4. Choose six verbs and give the strict-subcategorization and selectional restrictions which apply to them.
5. The selectional restrictions discussed in the text relate to the syntactic/semantic features of nouns. To shift ground slightly, are there any verbs that require plural subjects? Plural objects?
6. Look up the definitions of restrictive and nonrestrictive relative clauses in a school grammar. How do the differences given there correspond to the different derivations provided for them by the *Aspects* model?
7. What "understood words" have been deleted from the following sentences?

   a. Go home!
   b. Sam is taller than John.
   c. Mark is studying for the exam and Sam is too.
   d. Jim can juggle five china cups while reciting *Paradise Lost* longer than Bill can.

8. Find the various circumstances under which *myself* can be used in your dialect. Can other reflexives (for example, *yourself, himself, herself*) be used in all of these constructions?

CHAPTER 6

After *Aspects*

Of such deep learning little had he need,
Ne yet of Latin, ne of Greek, that breed
Doubts 'mongst Divines, and differences of texts,
From whence arise diversity of sects,
And hateful heresies.
SPENSER, *Mother Hubbard's Tale*

A dozen years ago, the number of transformationalists was quite small, and their arguments were mainly with the structuralists who formed the dominant group in linguistic studies. Today, the majority of American linguists accept the basic goals of transformational theory; that is, (1) they believe that the primary goal of linguistics is to demonstrate how sound (the surface structure of a sentence) relates to meaning; (2) they generally agree that grammars must satisfy the same kinds of formal requirements as other scientific descriptions (that is, they must, ideally, be internally consistent, complete, and as simple as the facts permit); and (3) they all seem to agree that the kind of rule known as a *transformation* is essential to an adequate descriptive grammar. Nonetheless, there are doubts, differences, and diversities among the transformationalists. The fundamental issues in most of these disagreements are quite technical, and for the most part beyond the scope of an introductory text such as this. We can, however, put the major issues into the historical context that we have been developing, and additionally, suggest some of the ways that these issues relate to the practical concerns of teachers.

But before looking at the disagreements, we must emphasize the many similarities that exist among all the so-called generative schools. And again, we can also consider the analogy with astronomy, originally presented in Chapter 1. Thus, contemporary astronomers work, almost exclusively, within the same basic paradigm—the same "framework for research." Yet as we noted, they propose conflicting theories about the origin of the universe. The theories are more or less equally compatible with the available data, and the question of which theory is "best" is an empirical one—that is, one which, presumably, can be decided on the basis of evidence that is not yet available, or alternatively, evidence that has been ignored or misinterpreted. In Thomas Kuhn's term, this is "normal science"[1]—that is, research conducted *within* a generally accepted paradigm. No astronomer has proposed a totally new paradigm, nor has any educator proposed that we ignore the discoveries of modern astronomy in teaching science to children.

Similarly, most research now going on in linguistics is also "normal science." That is, most linguists are working within the same basic paradigm, the same formal method of describing and explaining data.[2] The nature of their differences seems to be of two kinds: Some of them may simply be terminological (that is, some of the proposals may be "notational variants" of other proposals), other differences may be empirical (that is, genuine differences which can be resolved on the basis of evidence). But no linguist would deny that, in the past two dozen years, we have learned a great deal about language and about the methods of studying language; and to the best of the authors' knowledge, no educator has denied that much of this information (for example, that concerning the extent of a child's linguistic competence) is relevant for teachers of English.

6.1 Challenging the *Aspects* Model

The initial challenge to the standard theory came before the theory itself was published.[3] While younger linguists had certainly discussed their objections

---

[1] Thomas Kuhn's book, *The Structure of Scientific Revolutions,* 2nd ed. (Chicago: University of Chicago Press, 1970), examines the changes that have taken place in such fields as chemistry and astronomy. (He mentions linguistics in passing.) This highly readable book is particularly valuable for teachers with little training in the sciences.

[2] Some linguists might dispute this statement, but only—in the opinion of the authors—if its meaning is construed too narrowly. While, as we shall see, some linguists believe that the *Aspects* model should be abandoned in favor of one that more closely resembles the propositional nature of symbolic logic, these same linguists still accept the *Aspects* assumption that linguistic rules must meet certain requirements of symbolic logic—an assumption the structuralists, for example, did not consider. We shall return to this question later.

[3] This fact relates to a major problem. Much of the literature relating to transformational research circulates informally through a kind of underground; that which is published is sometimes out of date since—even after a paper has circulated underground for a while—there is still a lengthy period between acceptance and publication in a scholarly journal (although some newer journals have cut this time down somewhat). Nonetheless, and with a few exceptions that are noted in the text, the discussion in this book is based exclusively on published materials to which most readers can have access. For this reason, the reader should not consider the discussion as "a final word" on transformational linguistics. But

among themselves, the first written "underground" statement was probably made by George Lakoff in his dissertation, "On the Nature of Syntactic Irregularity," which was completed in the fall of 1965.[4] For our purposes, we can note that Lakoff raised several important challenges to the standard theory, and because of these challenges the field of transformational linguistics has since divided into two major "schools." We shall return to these schools after introducing two of Lakoff's challenges.

First, Lakoff suggested that the number of grammatical categories should be reduced. He would retain only those major categories that truly seemed to be linguistic universals. For example, since some languages do not distinguish between *verb* and *adjective,* Lakoff proposed that they were both members of a single category. This suggestion has been developed by other linguists including, for example, Paul Postal, who suggests that *pronouns* are really *articles* in English.[5] (*Cf., Henry V,* IV, iii, 60: "We few, we happy few, we band of brothers.")

Second, Lakoff also suggests that Chomsky's definition of *deep structure,* as given in *Aspects,* is artificial. In particular, Lakoff raised doubts about the standard claim that all lexical insertion must precede the application of any transformations, and he proposed underlying structures that were more semantic and less syntactic than those of standard theory.

Lakoff also raised other important issues that we shall consider later, but our discussion will be facilitated if we first consider the "schools" that developed after his challenges.

The central issue in the current debate among transformationalists concerns the relationship between syntax and semantics in a descriptive grammar. In the standard model of transformational theory (the *Aspects* model), the semantic component is strictly interpretive (see pp. 76-77), and proponents of this model comprise the school of "interpretive semantics." The primary spokesman for this school is Chomsky, aided by Ray Jackendoff and Jerrold J. Katz. Opposing this position is a group known as the school of "generative semantics," which rejects the theory of deep structure as being artificial and unnecessary to an adequate description of English. The major spokesmen for this second school are Lakoff, Postal, John Ross, and particularly James McCawley.[6]

---

because the book is intended primarily for teachers rather than linguists, because the structure of this section follows the historical development of transformational theory, and—finally—because any attempt to make the discussion fully current would be futile (since research is still going on), the restriction to publicly available material seems reasonable.

[4] Lakoff's dissertation has since been published in a slightly revised form as *Irregularity in Syntax* (New York: Holt, Rinehart and Winston, 1970). References to this work will, hereafter, be cited in the text as *IiS.*

[5] "On So-Called 'Pronouns' in English" (1966). See the Bibliography for a full citation.

[6] Chomsky and McCawley are not "leaders" of the schools. (As we shall see, there is disagreement within each school.) Rather, in the published materials Chomsky and McCawley have carried the brunt of the direct debate. Most beginning students find McCawley's articles comparatively easy—and enjoyable—to read.

But the names of these schools are not fixed. In the late 1960s, the school of interpretive semantics was also known as the "lexicalist" school, while the school of generative semantics was known as the "transformationalist" school. While the reasons for these earlier names will become clear in the following discussion—and while, even now, linguists are proposing still other names for the two schools—we shall continue to refer to the two positions as those of "interpretive semantics" and "generative semantics."

Consider, now, the hypothesis (not the "fact") that adjectives and verbs are members of a single category, which we shall call **verbals**. We can note, first, that in *Aspects* verbs and ajectives are not treated as members of the same category (although there may be a suggestion that such classification is possible). And we can note, second, that some languages do not (always) distinguish between these two kinds of words.

In many cases, speakers of English can choose between a verb and an adjective in saying, approximately, "the same thing":

Sentence 6.1 I hunger for fame.
Sentence 6.2 I am hungry for fame.

As a slightly different pair, consider:

Sentence 6.3 The boy saddened when he heard the news.
Sentence 6.4 The boy became sad when he heard the news.

These examples certainly suggest a close relationship between verbs and adjectives. Moreover, there is additional evidence. Thus, as traditional grammarians have known for years, verbs and adjectives can be **stative** or **nonstative**. That is, they can refer to "states" or to "actions." The set of stative verbs would include *know, perceive, resemble.*

For our purposes, we can note that stative verbs differ from nonstative verbs in two important ways: (1) Normally, stative verbs do not occur as the main verb in an imperative sentence, and (2) normally, stative verbs do not occur with *be* in a progressive (*-ing*) form. Thus, the following sentences are odd—not fully grammatical—in some way:

Sentence 6.5 *Know the recipe.
Sentence 6.6 *Resemble a good man.
Sentence 6.7 *I am knowing the recipe.
Sentence 6.8 *I am resembling a good man.

Grammarians knew these facts long before the advent of transformational grammar. Similarly, they also knew that certain adjectives can occur (with *be*) in imperatives, whereas others cannot. Those that cannot are stative, for example,

Sentence 6.9   *Be short. (Contrast: *Be good.*)
Sentence 6.10 *Be empty.

These same stative adjectives do not normally occur in progressive constructions:

Sentence 6.11 *I'm being short. (Contrast: *I'm being good.*)
Sentence 6.12 *The glass is being empty.

These facts suggest that verbs and adjectives, in the lexicon, must both be marked as stative or nonstative. That is, two kinds of words, normally considered different, share the same features.

Adjectives and verbs are alike in other ways as well. For example, some adjectives and verbs require animate subjects:

> **Sentence 6.13** John is hungry. (Contrast: *The hat is hungry.*)
> **Sentence 6.14** John hungers for affection.

Moreover, some adjectives seem to take direct objects (which follow prepositions), and these objects are restricted in the same way as those that follow verbs. For example, the verb *please* (in the sense it has in *I will try to please you*) is nonstative; that is, it expresses an action. Moreover, it is transitive and the direct object must be animate (generally, human). Thus, we can have

> **Sentence 6.15** John pleases me.

(where *pleases* has its active meaning). Similarly, we can have

> **Sentence 6.16** John is pleasant to me.

(where *me* can be considered as the direct object—in traditional terms, "the receiver of the action"—of "being pleasant"). Notice that, if we change the object to an inanimate noun, both sentences deviate from grammaticality in the same way[7]:

> **Sentence 6.17** *John pleases the hat.
> **Sentence 6.18** *John is pleasant to the hat.

Suppose we now wish to incorporate this information into a formal grammar of English. In the context discussed in earlier chapters, we would begin by reformulating the phrase-structure ("categorical") rule that rewrites *VP*. A simplified version of this new rule might be

PS 6.1 VP → Aux $\widehat{VB}$ (NP)

(where *VB* represents **verbal** and symbolizes a category that includes both adjectives and verbs). In the lexicon, every verb would be marked +*VB*, +*V*; while every adjective could be marked +*VB*, -*V*. In constructing a derivation, verbs would be treated as in the previous grammatical models. But adjectives would require a different treatment. In particular, given PS 6.1, we would no longer introduce **copula** as a major category in the phrase-structure rules. Rather, we would use the presence of (-*V*) in the feature matrix of an adjective to activate a transformation that would introduce **copula** into a branching tree.

Suppose, then, that we have a tree such as the one in Figure 6.1. The lexical-insertion rule attaches lexical items to this tree. Simplifying where possible, we can represent the tree after lexical insertion as in Figure 6.2. Now we apply the third

---

[7] For additional and considerably more technical arguments, see *IiS*, pp. 115-133.

type of transformation we discussed in the preceding chapter, namely, the **segment transformation** (or **local transformation**). Such a transformation is activated by the presence of one or more features in the matrix that defines a lexical item. Thus, the presence of the feature $(-V)$ in Figure 6.2 activates a copula segment transformation which introduces a new segment into the tree, as in Figure 6.3.

Through a series of other transformations which are irrelevant here, the *Present* of the *Aux* combines with the (*Copula*) to produce—in this sentence—the surface word: *are*. And the final sentence is *Gnats are small*.

This segment transformation differs slightly from the one discussed in the preceding chapter (that is, the one which is activated by the presence of a –*singular*) feature in the lexical entry for a noun). In the former case, the new segment that was created came under the immediate domination of the *N* node which also immediately dominated the noun. In the present case, the segment comes under the immediate domination of a different node—that is, different from the node which immediately dominates the feature that activates the transformation.

As a useful (if inelegant) pedagogical label, we can refer to various features that activate segment transformations as **loose features**. In general, loose features are sometimes (but not always) associated with particular lexical items in actual sentences.[8] In other words, the term "loose features" refers to elements that may—or may not—be associated with a major lexical category in a particular sentence.

Thus, the word *boy* always has such features as *male, human, young,* and so on. In a given sentence, we may also wish to indicate that we are referring to a definite boy (*the boy*) or an indefinite boy (*a boy*), to one who is near (*this boy*) or one who is not (*that boy*), and so on. In each of these cases, the word *boy* retains its primary meaning and, in addition, acquires supplementary meanings.

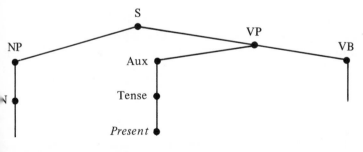

Figure 6.1   Using PS 6.1

[8] Thus, any noun that has the feature *count* must, in a given sentence, be either +*singular* or –*singular*. A feature such as *count* is invariant since it comprises part of the permanent lexical definition of a word. In contrast, "loose features" are optional since they relate only to the use of a word in a given sentence.

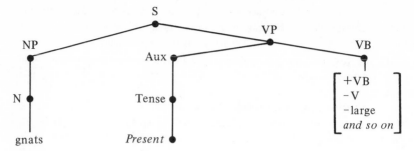

Figure 6.2 Inserting a $+VB$, $-V$ matrix

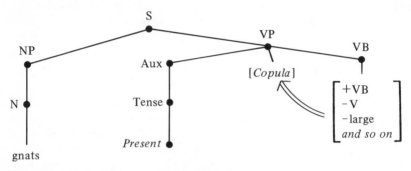

Figure 6.3 Introducing a copula segment

Similarly, in a particular sentence, we might want to refer to only one boy or, alternatively, to more than one. These occurrences can be definite, indefinite, or demonstrative, as the following pairs indicate:

| a boy | the boy | this boy | that boy |
| some boys | the boys | these boys | those boys |

Again, in each of these cases, the word *boy* retains its primary meaning and, in addition, acquires supplementary meanings. Earlier, we represented the basic meaning of *boy* as in Figure 6.4.

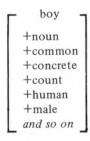

Figure 6.4 *Boy*

Now suppose that, in the lexicon, we also have the following "loose features":
singular, ±definite, ±demonstrative, ±near. The second, third, and fourth fea-
ures are hierarchical, as we can see from the branching tree in Figure 6.5. If we
hoose "minus definite," then we do *not* choose any other determiner features.
f we choose "plus definite," then we must choose either "plus demonstrative"
r else "minus demonstrative." If we choose "minus demonstrative," then we do
ot choose any other features. But if we choose "plus demonstrative," then we
1ust choose either "plus near" or else "minus near." We could also draw a
imilar tree for plural nouns with *a*; *some, the*; *the, that*; *those, this*; *these.*

Now suppose that, in a particular derivation, we want to insert the lexical item
oy into a tree. At the same time that we insert *boy*, we also add various loose
eatures to the matrix which represents *boy*. Figure 6.6 illustrates some of the

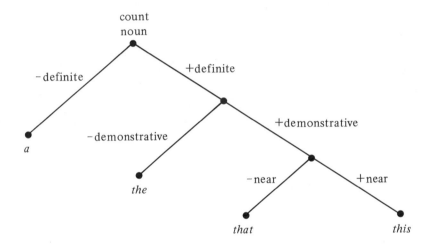

Figure 6.5   Determiner features for singular nouns

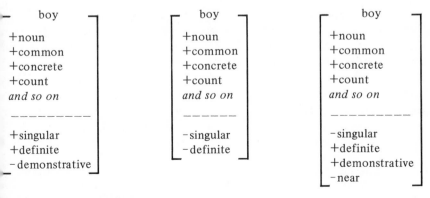

Figure 6.6   *Boy* plus various loose features

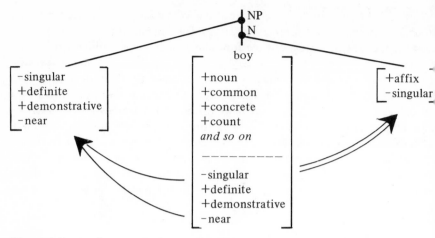

Figure 6.7   Applying segment transformations

possibilities available to us. (The dashed lines are added for convenience o
discussion only. The features above the dashed lines are invariable features tha
are always part of the meaning of *boy*; those below the lines are the ones tha
may be added in particular sentences.)

Given any of these possibilities, we then apply various segment transforma
tions. If we choose the third set, we would produce the (partial) tree in Figur
6.7, where the double-stemmed arrows represent the application of transforma
tions.

Following the procedure outlined in these examples, we can simplify th
phrase-structure rules still further, for example, by representing *perfect* an
progressive aspect as potential "loose features" which can be added to the lexica
entries for certain verbals in particular sentences. This system, in fact, is a
improvement over the earlier system since—as we noted in discussing stative an
nonstative verbals—there are some verbals that do not, normally, occur in th
progressive. Most linguists in the school of generative semantics also believe tha
the remaining auxiliaries can be deleted from the list of major categories.[9] Thi
proposal, which is supported by considerable evidence, would remove *Aux* fron
the phrase-structure rules. Moreoever, the proposal is in keeping with the intui
tions of earlier grammarians, including the structuralists, who (for example
treated auxiliaries as well as articles and prepositions as "structure words." (Se
Appendix 1.) As additional support for the proposal to reduce the number o
categories which are represented in phrase-structure rules, we can note that ther
are many languages which do not include articles, prepositions, or auxiliaries a
distinct words in surface sentences. Rather, the information that, in English, i

[9] See, in particular, John R. Ross, "Auxiliaries as Main Verbs," and James McCawley
"Tense and Time Reference in English," both listed in the Bibliography. Ross's pape
circulated "underground" for two years before its publication in 1969.

conveyed by separate "structure words" is, in these languages, conveyed by a system of affixes attached to major category items.

Lakoff's proposal to reduce the number of categories mentioned in phrase-structure rules has had a great impact in linguistics studies. And as Postal has noted, the few categories that remain can "lay some claim to universality" (*IiS*, p. v). But we need to note one fact, namely, that the simplification of the phrase-structure rules entails a complication of other components in the grammar, particularly of the transformational component. Thus, the matter of simplification relates to the overall organization of any descriptive grammar and is, therefore, a central issue in the debate between the school of interpretive semantics and that of generative semantics.

We can now turn to the second of Lakoff's challenges: his questioning of the deep structure that is defined in *Aspects*. In the *Aspects* model, every lexical item underlies a real English word. If we insert a lexical item into a tree, then that item will eventually be realized as an English word in the surface structure. Lakoff proposed a different system: one that inserts into a tree features that may *or may not* be realized as English words in a surface structure. The original proposal has been extended by several generative semanticists, including Lakoff himself. The development of the original proposal is of considerable historical interest, but it will suffice for our introductory purposes to examine only some recent versions.[10]

In the simplest possible terms, the *Aspects* model consists of three basic components: (1) the syntactic component (which contains the "base" of the grammar, that is, the phrase-structure rules and the lexicon); (2) the phonological component; and (3) the semantic component. As we noted earlier, these latter two components are strictly interpretive. The syntactic component thus mediates between the spoken form of a sentence and the meaning of the sentence. (Remember, here, that a primary goal of linguistics is to demonstrate how sound relates to meaning.) The phrase-structure rules of the base generate trees; transformational rules insert lexical items onto the tree; semantic "projection" rules provide a "reading" (that is, the "meaning") of the sentence; and phonological rules provide the spoken form of the sentence.

The generative semanticists, as we have noted, reject this organization of a descriptive grammar. In its place (and particularly, in place of the phrase-structure rules of the standard theory), they propose extremely "deep" rules which correspond closely to the so-called "formation rules" of symbolic logic.[11] Thus, there is one—and only one—basic rule in the grammar of generative semantics (in

[10] Interested readers may consult the essays in Charles J. Fillmore and D. Terence Langendoen, Eds., *Studies in Linguistic Semantics* (New York: Holt, Rinehart and Winston, 1971), which also contains an extensive bibliography of other relevant papers.

[11] James D. McCawley, "Where Do Noun Phrases Come From?", p. 171. See the Bibliography for a full citation.

contrast with the dozen or more rules in *Aspects* and the four or five rules in the model presented in Jacobs and Rosenbaum's *English Transformational Grammar*).[12]

6.2   Defending — and Revising — the *Aspects* Model

Most defenders of the *Aspects* model admit that some of the details must be revised, but they claim that once these revisions are made, there is no substantial difference between the model of interpretive semantics and that of generative semantics. In their terms, generative semantics is only a "notational variant" of interpretive semantics (that is, merely a different way of saying the same thing). But before looking at the claims made by the interpretive semanticists, we should (once again) reconsider the definition of *generate*. In an article that argues in support of generative semantics, McCawley offers the following informal but memorable distinction between the popular and technical meanings of the word. (We referred to this passage in Chapter 1.) Specifically, he cites the case of a linguist who incorrectly:

> uses "generate" in the sense of "causes to come off the assembly line in a sentence factory" rather than in the mathematical sense of "specify what the members of —— are."[13]

For our present purposes, this means that we should *not* judge the merits of the models by considering them as "sentence-producing machines." Rather, we should compare them solely on the basis of how well they define the relationships that exist between sound and meaning.

Such a comparison requires that the two competing proposals be presented within the same "general framework"; otherwise formal comparison is impossible.[14] But a difficulty immediately arises since, in Chomsky's opinion, "there is no reasonably concrete or well-defined 'theory of semantic interpretation'" ("Deep Structure . . .," p. 183). In other words, while some transformationalists assume that such a theory can be developed, they also believe it is "still to be discovered" ("Deep Structure . . .," p. 183).

We can recall now that, in the *Aspects* model, there is a categorical component (containing phrase-structure rules) and a lexicon. (We are, for the moment, ignoring the other components of the *Aspects* model.) The rules of the categorical component, which are "context free," generate a structure that can be repre-

[12] Appendix 1 presents a brief discussion of two changes suggested by the generative semanticists. The details are rather technical and, therefore, beyond the scope of most introductory courses.

[13] "Interpretive Semantics Meets Frankenstein," p. 295.

[14] As we have noted in several places, this insistence on formalism has been, perhaps, the major fact of recent linguistic research. Chomsky emphasizes this point in "Deep Structure, Surface Structure, and Semantic Interpretation." See the Bibliography for a full citation.

sented in a branching tree, in particular, one that contains terminal symbols indicated by Δ. Lexical-insertion transformations then insert lexical items onto this tree, and such insertion occurs before any nonlexical transformations apply (for example, before we apply such things as the question transformation). These "postlexical structures" (that is, a tree with lexical items attached) are known as deep structures. Moreover, once the process of inserting lexical items into the basic tree has been completed, we turn immediately to the transformational component. That is, the lexical items are inserted as a group, and subsequent to this insertion we cannot insert additional lexical items at some later stage in a derivation. To put the matter in still another way, according to the *Aspects* model, once we have begun to apply general transformations (for example, question, extraposition, and so on), then we can no longer insert lexical items.[15]

In contrast to the standard theory, that of the generative semanticists starts with a structure called a "propositional tree" into which we can insert various so-called predicates, which more closely resemble semantic features than words. Through a series of transformations, these predicates are combined so that various semantic groupings come under the domination of a single node, and subsequent transformations would produce a surface structure.[16]

At this point we can, with Chomsky, ask two questions: (1) Are the systems genuinely different? (2) Are representations of the generative-semantics model better or worse than those of the standard model?

Chomsky's answer to the first question is "no." Each system expresses the interrelationships among four entities: (1) a semantic interpretation (S, as in footnote 15); (2) an underlying representation (P_i), where associated semantic information is grouped together under a dominating node; (3) a surface structure (P_n); and (4) a final phonetic representation (P).[17] In other words, both systems

---

[15]Stated formally, the *Aspects* theory "specifies for each sentence, a syntactic structure $\Sigma = (P_1, \ldots, P_i, \ldots, P_n)$ (where P_i is the deep and P_n the surface structure), a semantic representation S, and a phonetic representation P. It asserts, furthermore that S is determined by P_i and P by P_n" ("Deep Structure . . .," p. 185). In this formulation, P_1 is the structure defined by the branching tree before lexical insertion; P_i is the tree after lexical insertion and before "nonlexical" transformations; and P_n is the surface-structure tree produced from P_i by nonlexical transformations. Projection rules apply to P_i to give the semantic representation of the sentence, and phonological rules apply to P_n to give the phonetic representation.

[16]In formal terms similar to those in footnote 15, P_1 is a propositional tree that contains all the semantic information necessary to an interpretation. Through transformations, P_1 becomes P_2 (for example, referring to the example cited in Appendix 1, p. 262, joining *alive* and *not* under a single V node), then P_2 becomes P_3 (for example, joining *become* to *not* and *alive* under a single V node), and so on, finally becoming a structure comparable to P_i of the standard theory, that is, a structure where associated semantic information is grouped together under a single dominating node. Additional transformations apply to produce P_n, which underlies the phonetic representation.

[17]Formally, each system "generates quadruples (S, P_i, P_n, P). There is no precise sense to the question: which of these is selected 'first' and what is the 'direction' of the relations among the formal objects?" ("Deep Structure . . .," p. 196).

express the interrelationships among the same entities, and thus they are only formal "variations" of each other.

The answer to Chomsky's second question is: "Nobody knows." If Chomksy's answer to the first question is correct, then we have two variations that describe the same "formal objects," and the choice between these variations is an empirical one. And thus we have an impasse.

1. McCawley believes that the system of generative semantics is different in kind from that of interpretive semantics, and thus, that the burden of proof rests with the interpretive semanticists.
2. Chomsky believes that the two systems are merely notational variants of each other, and thus, that the burden of proof rests with those (that is, the generative semanticists) who propose an alternative variation.

The impasse, however, has not prevented additional research, and hopefully, this research will eventually provide a solution to the problem.[18]

We can turn, now, to one of the key questions of contemporary research: Do transformations change meaning? And we can best begin a consideration of this question with a brief review of the history of the hypothesis. In the early model of transformational grammar, namely, that presented in *Syntactic Structures* (1957), transformations did affect the meaning of sentences. In the *Aspects* model (1965), all meaning was given in the deep structure of a sentence, and consequently, transformations did *not* affect meaning. Similarly, in the model proposed by the generative semanticists (first suggested by Lakoff in 1965), all the meaning is given by what we have called the "propositional structure" of the sentence, and consequently, transformations do not affect meaning in this model.

But recently, Chomsky and others who reject the model of generative semantics have argued that all meaning does not inhere in the deep structure; some meaning, they claim, also inheres in the surface structure of sentences. For this reason, Chomsky has proposed a revision of the standard model.[19]

Specifically, Chomsky claims that "there are cases in which semantic interpretation seems to relate more directly to surface structure than to deep structure"; that is, "grammatical structure plays a part in specifying" such notions as **presup-**

---

[18]The impasse has been debated (in the authors' opinion, inconclusively) in various articles. See, in particular, Jerrold J. Katz, "Interpretative (*sic*) Semantics vs. Generative Semantics," and James D. McCawley, "Interpretive Semantics Meets Frankenstein," full citations for which are given in the Bibliography. (The "Frankenstein" in McCawley's title reflects his belief that Katz has created a kind of "straw monster" which he substitutes for the "real" model of generative semantics.

[19]Chomsky's claim, if true, would be an argument against generative semantics as an adequate "notational variant," since the standard model can incorporate the proposed revision more readily than can the model of generative semantics, at least in Chomsky's view. See "Deep Structure, Surface Structure, and Semantic Interpretation."

position and **focus.**[20] We can first examine *focus* and related notions of *topic* and *comment.* Consider the following sentences:

Sentence 6.19 Mary gave a book to the boy.
Sentence 6.20 Mary gave the boy a book.

In terms of standard theory, these two sentences have identical deep structures, and the difference in surface structures is determined by whether or not the so-called indirect-object inversion transformation has been applied. Nonetheless, the two sentences have slightly different meanings, or, to borrow a term from rhetoric, the two sentences differ in *focus.* Chomsky has defined *focus* as "the phrase containing the intonation center ("Deep Structure . . .," p. 199). Thus, *the boy* is the focus in Sentence 6.19, whereas *a book* is the focus in Sentence 6.20.

Now consider, in two examples adapted from Chomsky ("Deep Structure . . .," p. 210), the rhetorical distinction between *topic* and *comment*:

Sentence 6.21 Pancakes are easy to cook on this griddle.
Sentence 6.22 This griddle is easy to cook pancakes on.

Presumably, the grammatical relations expressed in these two sentences are also identical and are provided by the deep structure, but the sentences do not have identical meanings. Thus, Sentence 6.21 provides a "comment" on the "topic" of *pancakes,* whereas Sentence 6.22 provides a "comment" on the "topic" of *this griddle.*

On the subject of *presupposition,* consider:

Sentence 6.23 John likes my cooking.
Sentence 6.24 Even John likes my cooking.
Sentence 6.25 John likes even my cooking.

If we take Sentence 6.23 as a norm, then the other two sentences contain presuppositions not inherent in the norm; namely, that John is generally fussy about other people's cooking (Sentence 6.24); and that John is *not* generally fussy and, moreover, that "my" cooking is not very good (Sentence 6.25). Such presuppositions are obviously involved in the meanings of these sentences.

In commenting on examples similar to these. Chomsky states:

it seems that such matters as focus and presupposition, topic and comment, reference, scope of logical elements, and perhaps other phenomena, are determined in part at least by properties [of sentences] other than deep structures, in particular, by properties of surface structure ("Deep Structure . . .," p. 213).

Another revision proposed by Chomsky relates to the lexicon of the standard

---

[20] Among transformational grammarians, the earliest statements on such matters as *topic* and *comment, presuppositions,* and *focus* seem to have been made by Paul and Carol Kiparsky, John Robert Ross, and Thomas Moore, all in the mid-1960s. Chomsky's comments, quoted above, are from "Deep Structure, Surface Structure, and Semantic Interpretation," p. 199.

model. As we noted earlier, the school of interpretive semantics is also known as the "lexicalist school," and the reasons for this alternative name relate to the proposed revision.

As we noted briefly in Chapter 5, Chomsky proposes to "enrich" the lexicon by introducing transformations that combine prefixes, suffixes, and stems into English words. For example, the lexicon would contain an entry for the stem *-graph-*; that is, it would contain the phonological and syntactic/semantic information which relates to this stem as well as a set of constraints which determine the words that can be formed using this stem: *autobiography, biographical, digraph, epigraph, graphic, graphite, mimeograph, monograph, paragraph, physiograph, telegraph, telegraphy,* and so on. In other words, *some* of the things that the generative semanticists would accomplish through propositional structure would—in the "lexicalist hypothesis"—be part of the lexicon itself. On the other hand, this revision of the standard lexicon does not relate to words such as *buy, sell, own, barter, trade; kill, murder, assassinate, behead;* and so on—that is to words that have related semantic features but do *not* have related phonological features.

The "revised standard theory," then, has the following organization: (1) a base that contains phrase-structure (categorical) rules as well as a lexicon that incorporates word-forming transformations; the base generates deep structures; (2) a transformational component that relates deep structures to surface structures (3) a phonological component that relates a surface structure to a phonetic representation; and (4) a semantic component that relates *both* the deep structure and, when necessary, the surface structure to a semantic representation; but the grammatical relations expressed in a sentence are invariably inherent in the deep structure.[21] At the risk of antagonizing some readers through too great redundancy, we need to realize—again—that the numbered sequence of this paragraph does not relate to a performance model (whereby sentences "come off the assembly line in a sentence factory"). Neither the standard theory nor the revision of the standard theory specifies an "order" for producing sentences. Rather the standard theory and the revision both posit a base, transformational rules phonological rules, and semantic (interpretive) rules *as well as* the relationships that exist among these entities.

6.3   Other Problems, Other Factors

The generative semanticists are not the only linguists who have challenged the standard theory. Charles J. Fillmore, in 1968, published "The Case for Case," [22]

[21] In the formal terms of footnote 15, the revised standard model still generates quadruples S, P_i, P_n, P. Before the revision, S (the semantic interpretation) was directly related to P (the deep structure) but not directly related to P_n (the surface structure); after the revision S is directly related to *both* P_i and P_n.

[22] In Emmon Bach and Robert T. Harms, Eds., *Universals in Linguistic Theory* (New York Holt, Rinehart and Winston, 1968), pp. 1-88.

which develops some suggestions made by traditional grammarians and which argues for a case grammar that, presumably, eliminates the need for the standard deep structure. Case grammar resembles generative semantics in many respects (for example, in its claim that basic sentence structures involve a logical "proposition"), but there are some differences. In particular, where McCawley uses "indices" to define propositions and provides for subordinate structures to define the indices, Fillmore (in contrast) provides for an underlying structure that incorporates a verbal and one or more noun phrases, where each of the noun phrases stands in a particular "case" relationship to the verbal. Moreover, Fillmore does not raise the question of the lexicon.

Fillmore initially suggested (at least) six cases:

Agentive (A), the case of the typically animate perceived instigator of the action identified with the verb.

Instrumental (I), the case of the inanimate force or object causally involved in the action of the state identified with the verb.

Dative (D), the case of the animate being affected by the state of action identified with the verb.

Factitive (F), the case of the object or being resulting from the action or state identified by the verb, or understood as a part of the meaning of the verb.

Locative (L), the case which identifies the location or spatial orientation of the state or action identified by the verb.

Objective (O), the semantically most neutral case, the case of anything representable by a noun whose role in the action or state identified by the verb is identified by the semantic interpretation of the verb itself. . . . The term is not to be confused with the notion of direct object, nor with the name of the surface case synonymous with accusative.[23]

In Fillmore's system, these are all "deep case relations" which may have different representations in the surface structure (particularly in a language such as English, which has few inflections). We can cite a few examples to give some flavor of the system. The capital letters over the noun phrases in the following sentences are those defined by Fillmore (above); they identify the deep-structure cases for these phrases:

         A   O   I

Sentence 6.26 Penelope deflated my spirit with her denial.

         I   O

Sentence 6.27 Her denial deflated my spirit.

         O

Sentence 6.28 My spirit deflated.

---

[23]"The Case for Case," pp. 24-25. Later in the article, Fillmore suggests *Benefactive*. Other candidates for inclusion obviously include *Time*.

As the latter two sentences indicate, the surface-structure subject need not, in the deep structure, be in the agentive case.[24]

Fillmore's proposal underscores a point we have already discussed, namely, that the factors involved in the current dispute among linguists are complex. Nonetheless, in its most basic form, the dispute seems to focus on the question: Is syntax autonomous? Thus, interpretive semantics, generative semantics, and case grammar all assume that any fully adequate description of English must incorporate rules which define whether or not a sentence is syntactically well formed (and, if it is not, how it deviates from "well-formedness"). If such syntactic rules are autonomous, then the argument would favor the school of interpretive semantics; if they are not—if syntactic "well-formedness" is completely determined by semantic constraints—then the argument favors the generative semanticists and, in a different way, the case grammarians.

Exercises

1. Find six pairs of verbs and adjectives that express approximately the same meaning.
2. Find more examples of stative verbs and adjectives.
3. The matrices given on p. 117 represent the phrases *the boy, some boys,* and *those boys.* Give the matrices for the other possibilities—*a boy, this boy, that boy, the boys,* and *these boys.*
4. The focus of a sentence is usually the last noun, verb, or adjective in it. Thus the focus of (a) is *John,* while the focus of (b) is *Jane*:

   a. Jane saw John.
   b. John was seen by Jane.

   In normal pronunciation, it is this last major category that is stressed most heavily. Give five sets of sentences that seem to mean approximately the same thing but that differ in focus.
5. Give five sets of sentences that mean approximately the same thing but that differ in topic and comment.
6. What are the presuppositions of the following sentences?

[24]In 1968, Robert Stockwell and others at the University of California, Los Angeles, published a two-volume government document (ESD-TR-68-419) which combines Fillmore's case grammar with Chomsky's lexicalist hypothesis. While this is hardly an underground publication, distribution of the study has nonetheless been quite limited, although it is probably available in the libraries of most major universities. Besides being a highly detailed presentation of a case grammar (as of 1968), the study is also a good source of example sentences relating to determiners, pronominalization, negation, conjunction, reflexivization, complementation, cleft and pseudo-cleft structures, and so on. See the Bibliography for a full citation.

a. John's murderer was never found.
b. Even Ralph can play backgammon.
c. Ralph can even play backgammon.
d. I wish I were in Paris.
e. John only thinks he's sick.

PRACTICE

CHAPTER 1

Introduction

In this second part of the book, we shall present a formal transformational grammar. Before we do so, however, it might be useful to review briefly what we expect a transformational grammar to do. As we have said, transformational grammar attempts to describe a speaker's competence. The most startling aspect of a speaker's competence is the ability to produce and understand a limitless number of sentences of the language. Slightly less startling is the ability to distinguish sentences of the language from all other things in the universe. It is easy, of course, to tell a sentence from a horse, but more difficult to distinguish a sentence from other noises. And it is not just a matter of words—a sentence using scientific terminology strange to us is recognized as a sentence of English, as is *'Twas brillig, and the slithy toves did gyre and gimble in the wabe.* We may not know what the words mean, but the sentence is clearly English, and given the meanings of the words we would understand it perfectly. Even without knowing what the words mean, we have a good idea of how they relate to each other. We know that *brillig* describes the general conditions, of time or atmosphere ('Twas evening, 'twas raining) and so on, that *toves* are things of some sort and are furthermore described as *slithy;* that these *toves* are performing the actions of *gyring* and *gimbling,* and that they are performing these actions in a particular place—the *wabe.* Furthermore, we know that these actions took place in the past. Such a sentence is to be sharply distinguished from a group of familiar words that do not "fit together" to produce a message at all, such as

Note: In Part Two, the exercises are in four groups, as follows: (1) The first exercises follow the discussion of the base component (phrase-structure rules and lexicon); they appear at the end of Chapter 6, on p. 161. (2) The exercises that cover the transformations that apply to simple sentences appear at the end of Chapter 12, on p. 196. (3) The exercises that cover the transformations that produce complex sentences appear at the end of Chapter 14, on p. 224. (4) The exercises that cover compound sentences and pronominalization appear at the end of Chapter 16, on p. 243.

boys the quickly was a. Here we recognize all the words, but have no idea how they fit together. When we talk about language, then, we are talking primarily about the structure of language—the way the words are put together or are related to each other. This is why we can claim that a six- or seven-year-old has learned his language, even though his vocabulary is not as large as it will become (though even at six, a child's vocabulary is nothing to sneer at).

A second ability a person who knows a language has is the ability to tell when a sentence is ambiguous—when it means more than one thing. Again, we may not be immediately aware of all ambiguities, in fact in daily conversation we tend to block them out, but we can be made more aware of them. There are three types of ambiguity. The simplest is called **lexical ambiguity**, and arises when one word can mean several things: *meet me by the bank* might mean *meet me by the First National bank* or *meet me by the river bank,* since *bank* can refer either to a place to keep money or to the earth immediately adjacent to a river. The second type is called **constructional ambiguity**, and usually occurs when a word can modify more than one other word. Thus, *the old men and women left* can mean either *the old people left (but the young ones stayed)* or *the old men and all the women left (but the young men stayed).* In the first instance, *old* is interpreted as modifying *men and women;* in the second, it modifies only *men.* The third type of ambiguity we might call (for want of a better term) **derivational ambiguity**, a term whose precise meaning will become clearer shortly. Thus, *the shooting of the soldiers was terrible* can mean either that the soldiers were terrible marksmen, or that it is terrible that the soldiers were shot. Here the ambiguity arises not from a word having two or more meanings, or from *of the soldiers* modifying or not modifying *shooting* (which it does in either case), but from something else, something we shall analyze in some detail below.

When we say that these sentences are ambiguous, we mean that in isolation they can be assigned more than one meaning. Our competence allows us to do this. In actual usage, however, it will usually be clear which meaning is meant—in the middle of a wilderness, it will be pretty clear that *river bank* and not *money bank* is meant; and continuations will disambiguate the third set—*the shooting of the soldiers was terrible; they couldn't hit a thing.* But remember that we are studying *competence,* not *performance,* and also that one may not always be aware, perhaps because of social pressures, of the possible ambiguities he can see once they are pointed out to him: *John is too hot to eat* would be more obviously ambiguous (in a rather macabre way) if we were cannibals.

A third ability included in competence is the ability to detect **paraphrases**—to tell when two sentences mean the same thing. It is fairly easy to agree that Sentences 1.1a and 1.1b mean the same:

Sentence 1.1a It bothers John that Sally dates Sam.
Sentence 1.1b That Sally dates Sam bothers John.

But it is a bit more difficult for most speakers of English to agree that Sentences 1.2a and 1.2b or 1.3a and 1.3b mean the same:

Sentence 1.2a It seems that Sam left.
Sentence 1.2b Sam seems to have left.
Sentence 1.3a Sam loves Sally.
Sentence 1.3b Sally is loved by Sam.

In these cases there seems to be a difference in meaning: Sentence 1.2a makes a statement about a general condition, but Sentence 1.2b is talking about Sam; Sentence 1.3a says something about Sam, while Sentence 1.3b says something about Sally. The "a" and "b" Sentences in 1.2 and 1.3 have different *topics*. But they convey the same information, so we shall consider them paraphrases, overlooking the different emphases.

We can distinguish two different kinds of paraphrase: lexical and syntactic (or derivational). **Lexical paraphrase** occurs when two sentences mean the same thing because a word or phrase in one is replaced by a different word or phrase in the other. Thus, Sentences 1.4 and 1.5 mean the same because *storyteller* and *raconteur* mean the same:

Sentence 1.4 The storyteller was amusing.
Sentence 1.5 The raconteur was amusing.

Syntactic or **derivational paraphrase** occurs when two sentences have the same meaning even though they have different syntax. A sentence and its passive counterpart are good examples of this:

Sentence 1.6a John bought the boat.
Sentence 1.6b The boat was bought by John.

These sentences mean the same even though they have different surface subjects, Sentence 1.6a has a direct object and Sentence 1.6b a prepositional phrase, and Sentence 1.6a has a simple verb while Sentence 1.6b has a complex verb.

The fourth ability included in competence is a knowledge of the internal structure of sentences. This knowledge is especially difficult to get at, since it is usually not conscious. But consider the following examples (the first pair was discussed in Part One, p. 10):

Sentence 1.7a John is easy to please.
Sentence 1.7b John is eager to please.
Sentence 1.8a John promised Sam to behave himself.
Sentence 1.8b John asked Sam to behave himself.

In Sentence 1.7a we know that *John* is in some sense the object of *please*—that John is the one who is going to be pleased. But in Sentence 1.7b we know that John is going to do something to please somebody not specified—that *John* is in some sense the subject of *please*. Similarly, in Sentence 1.8a *John* is the subject of *behave*, and *himself* refers to *John,* while in sentence 1.8b Sam is the one who is going to behave, and *himself* refers to *Sam.* It is difficult to see how these differences can be related to different meanings for *easy* and *eager,* or for *promise* and *ask.* Rather, it seems that we have knowledge of the structure of the sentences from some other source.

Closely related to this knowledge of the internal structure of sentences are two other kinds of knowledge. Consider the following sentences:

Sentence 1.9a   Bill slept late, and Sam did too.
Sentence 1.9b   Bill ran a mile, and Sam did too.
Sentence 1.10a   Bill is tall, and Sam is too.
Sentence 1.10b   Bill is a doctor, and Sam is too.
Sentence 1.11a   *Bill slept late, and Sam is too.
Sentence 1.11b   *Bill is a doctor, and Sam did too.

We know that the clause *Sam did too* in Sentence 1.9a means that Sam slept late, but in Sentence 1.9b, exactly the same clause means that Sam ran a mile. Likewise with Sentences 1.10a and 1.10b. Sentences 1.11a and 1.11b show that the two clauses *Sam did too* and *Sam is too* cannot be substituted for each other. Two things are interesting about these examples. First, Sentences 1.9a and 1.9b and Sentences 1.10a and 1.10b show that the meaning of a clause or a phrase may not be represented directly by the words in that clause, since in each case we have repeated clauses that mean entirely different things. Second, we know, probably without ever consciously learning it, that *did too* and *is too* are very different in terms of where they can be used.

The second kind of knowledge we have about the internal structure of sentences is also fairly complex: We know, again not consciously in the sense that we can necessarily explain it, when two clauses or phrases are units of the same type. Units of the same type can be joined together (or **conjoined**) to form grammatical sentences. Thus, *the boy* and *Sarah* are both units of the same type, since they can be conjoined: *The boy and Sarah went home.* Now consider the following:

Sentence 1.12a   The inference that John drew was wrong.
Sentence 1.12b   The inference that Sam objected to was wrong.
Sentence 1.12c   The inference that John lied was wrong.

Sentences 1.12a and 1.12b have the same internal structure, as we can tell by conjoining them: *The inference that John drew and Sam objected to was wrong.* But Sentence 1.12c, which looks exactly the same as Sentence 1.12a, has a different structure, as is shown by the fact that Sentences 1.12c and 1.12a cannot be conjoined: **The inference that John drew and John lied was wrong.* It is important to recognize that we know that the internal structures are different even though we may not know quite how to explain the difference.

Finally, a speaker of a language knows when he is presented with a grammatical sentence of his language, and also when a sentence is ungrammatical; in the latter case he can often tell what causes the ungrammaticalness, even though he may not know why.

Sentence 1.13a   Is Sam here?
Sentence 1.13b   Should Sam go home?
Sentence 1.13c   *Went Sam home?
Sentence 1.13d   Did Sam go home?
Sentence 1.13e   *Did Sam be home?

Speakers of English know that Sentences 1.13a, 1.13b, and 1.13d are grammatical, and that Sentences 1.13c and 1.13e are ungrammatical because an incorrect verbal form begins the sentence. With some thought, many speakers would be able to construct a rule for predicting the correct forms and incorrect forms. More complex are the following examples:

Sentence 1.14a   John kept the car in the garage.
Sentence 1.14b   What did John keep the car in?
Sentence 1.15a   John kept the car that was in the garage.
Sentence 1.15b   *What did John keep the car that was in?

Speakers of English know that the phrase *the garage* can be questioned in Sentence 1.14a to produce Sentence 1.14b, but that the same phrase in Sentence 1.15a cannot be questioned—if it is, the ungrammatical Sentence 1.15b results. It would be somewhat more difficult to produce a rule predicting correct and incorrect forms for these examples, and yet everybody can point to the source of the ungrammaticalness. What this indicates is that although speakers of a language have knowledge of what is and is not grammatical in their language, they frequently do not know how to express that knowledge. And that knowledge is likely to be a kind that is never taught—it would be strange for somebody to know that Sentence 1.15b is ungrammatical because he had been taught (say, in school) that it was; more likely is that he knows it is ungrammatical without knowing exactly why.

We are using the term **grammatical** in a specialized meaning. What we do not mean is "good grammar": We do not especially want to call *We don't got none* ungrammatical, since it is a perfectly acceptable dialect form. When we call a sentence grammatical, we mean that it is accepted as a perfectly normal sentence by the speakers of the dialect of the language we are describing. This means that sentences employing metaphor or figurative language are considered ungrammatical, even though they may be understandable and perhaps even brilliantly insightful. For instance, Sentence 1.16a is grammatical, but Sentence 1.16b is not:

Sentence 1.16a   They perform their duty with diligence.
Sentence 1.16b   *They perform their leisure with diligence.

Part of the force of Sentence 1.16b stems from the substitution of *leisure* for *duty*; the author suggests that some people have the attitude about leisure that is normally reserved for duty (for further discussion of Sentence 1.16b and similiar sentences, see *Aspects*, p. 149). This definition of "grammatical" implies that much poetic language is ungrammatical; but that helps explain why it is so powerful: It is a calculated stretching of the normal language.

The competence of the native speaker, then, can be said to include at least these five abilities: (1) to produce and understand an infinite number of sentences, (2) to understand the internal structures of these sentences, (3) to detect ambiguity, (4) to detect paraphrases, and (5) to tell when and why a sentence is ungrammatical. To study the nature of language, the linguist constructs his grammar, which is a *model* of the native speaker's competence. By a

model we mean a device that will produce exactly the same results as the original, so the linguist's grammar will have to provide information on the five aspects of the native speaker's competence. Notice that there is no guarantee that the linguist's grammar and the native speaker's grammar are the same—in fact, the grammar we shall be studying most likely is not the same as whatever mechanism we have inside our heads. However, the model will give the same results as our internalized grammars: It will produce and understand an infinite number of sentences, it will provide descriptions of the internal structures of those sentences, it will detect ambiguities and paraphrases, and it will tell when and why a string of words is not grammatical. (Our language is, of course, anthropomorphic: The grammar will not actually "tell" us these things, but it will provide a means by which we can make these judgments without recourse to the grammars in our heads.)

In addition to performing these duties, the model must meet the general standards for any scientific theory. It must be *complete*—it must explain everything that it is supposed to explain: A grammar that could not produce questions, for example, would not be a particularly good grammar. It must be *explicit*: It must not rely on our intuitions about how to use it, but rather must contain complete instructions so that it can be operated mechanically. The easiest test for this is to computerize it: Since a computer has no "intuitions"— no "mind"—it will do only what it is told. If a grammar can be fed into a computer and produce the correct results, we can be sure it is completely explicit. (Notice that this does not imply any interest in computerizing language—it is just an easy test for explicitness). And it must be *simple*: Given two grammars of equal completeness and explicitness, the simpler one will be the better one (although this sounds straightforward, it is not, since we are not sure how simplicity is to be measured). Finally, it is the final model that counts, not how it is arrived at. Whether the theory comes to one in a dream, or as the result of using opium, or after years of careful thought and study makes no difference to the value of the final product, although one suspects the last method will, in general, be more efficacious than the others.

CHAPTER 2

The Model

Another way to look at language is to see it as an infinite set of paired sounds and meanings. In the case of ambiguity, we have one sound that is paired with more than one meaning. In paraphrase the opposite is true: Several different sounds are paired with one meaning. What we need, then, is a model that *generates* (or provides the rules for relating) an infinite number of pairs of sounds and meanings, and explains how sometimes one meaning gets mapped onto several different sounds, or vice versa, and how some sounds have no meanings provided by the mapping system (these would be ungrammatical sentences or strings of sounds not in the language). Transformational grammar accomplishes this by positing two distinct levels for each sentence: the level of **deep structure** (or DS), which represents the meaning of a sentence, and the level of **surface structure** (or SS), which represents the sound, or phonology, of a sentence. Ordinarily, one deep structure is related to one surface structure; in ambiguity, however, two or more deep structures are related to one surface structure; and in the case of paraphrase, one deep structure is related to more than one surface structure. This provides an explicit representation of ambiguity as several meanings in one sequence of sounds, and of paraphrase as several sequences of sound expressing one meaning.

Once we have two levels, one a representation of the meaning and the other a representation of the sound, there are four obvious questions to ask:

1. How do we get deep structures?
2. How do deep structures represent meaning?
3. How are deep structures related to surface structures?
4. How do surface structures represent the sound of a sentence?

Since we want our model to be completely explicit, we state it in terms of *rules* that are followed. There are four different types of rules:

Exercises are on p. 161.

1. Phrase-structure (PS) rules, which, when followed, produce the deep structure.
2. Semantic interpretation (SI) rules, which "interpret" the deep structure to reveal its meaning.
3. Transformational (T) rules, which change deep structures into surface structures.
4. Phonological interpretation (PI) rules, which "interpret" the surface structure to tell us how it sounds.

Schematically, we may put each of these types of rules together, and arrive at the model shown in Figure 2.1. All of the PS rules taken together are called the **phrase structure** or **base component** of the grammar. Likewise, all the T rules are called the **transformational component**, all the SI rules are called the **semantic component**, and all the PI rules are called the **phonological component**. The base component and transformational component taken together are called the **syntactic component**. From Figure 2.1 one can see that the grammar provides a way of relating sound and meaning, although a bit indirectly. What is not immediately obvious from the diagram is that the rules are of different types. The PS rules are *generative*, that is, they provide the means for deriving deep structures. The other three components are interpretive: The semantic component interprets deep structures, the phonological component interprets surface structures, and the transformational component, although it does not actually interpret deep structures, takes them as a starting point. So for all the components except the base, one must put something in to get something out. For the base, all one has to do is start it working. We shall be studying primarily the syntactic component (that is, the base and transformations).

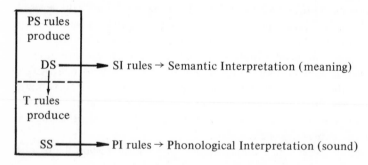

Figure 2.1

CHAPTER 3

Phrase-Structure Rules

The phrase-structure rules are all of the form $A \rightarrow B + C$, where A is a single symbol, B and C are either single symbols or strings of symbols (a **string** is a series of symbols joined together by the concatenation symbol +, which indicates that the symbols are connected to each other, not added) and the arrow is the instruction to replace whatever occurs on its left by whatever occurs on its right. Thus, $A \rightarrow B + C$ says that A is to be replaced by (*rewritten as*) $B + C$. Let us consider a simple set of rules:

Rule 1 $A \rightarrow B + C$
Rule 2 $B \rightarrow D \; (E)$
Rule 3 $C \rightarrow \begin{Bmatrix} F \\ G \end{Bmatrix}$
Rule 4 $E \rightarrow H + K$

To use these rules, we begin with the **initial symbol** A. Rule 1 says that A is to be replaced by $B + C$. Rule 2 states that B is to be rewritten either by D or by $D + E$: Parentheses around a symbol indicate that its choice is optional. Rule 3 says that C is to be rewritten as either F or G: Braces indicate that one line must be chosen. Rule 4 says that E is rewritten as $H + K$. Below are the possible *derivations* based on these rules (a **derivation** is the result of applying the rules from first to last until there are no symbols in the string that appear on the left of a rule):

I.		II.		III.		IV.	
1.	A	1.	A	1.	A	1.	A
2.	$B + C$	2.	$B + C$	2.	$B + C$	2.	$B + C$
3.	$D + C$	3.	$D + C$	3.	$D + E + C$	3.	$D + E + C$
4.	$D + F$	4.	$D + G$	4.	$D + E + F$	4.	$D + E + G$
				5.	$D + H + K + F$	5.	$D + H + K + G$

Exercises are on p. 161.

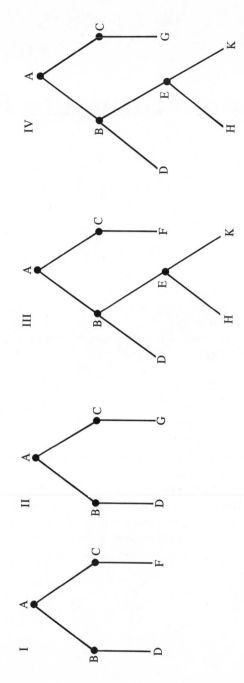

Figure 3.1

To get from one line of a derivation to the next, we apply only *one* PS rule: Only one symbol at a time is rewritten. In I and II, B is rewritten as D, in accord with one option of Rule 2; in III and IV, it is rewritten as $D + E$, the other option. C is rewritten as F in I and III, and as G in II and IV. Notice that Rule 1 and Rule 4 offer no options, while Rule 2 and Rule 3 do. The last line of the derivation is called the **terminal string**, since it comes at the end of the derivation.

From these derivations we can follow the whole process step by step: in derivation IV, for example, we can see that to get from step 3 to step 4, C was replaced by G. An equivalent way to represent a derivation is by means of a **phrase-structure tree**. Figure 3.1 shows the PS trees corresponding to the four derivations. The trees provide exactly the same information as the written derivations except that they do not indicate the order in which the PS rules have applied: From tree IV one cannot tell whether E was rewritten as $H + K$ before or after C was rewritten as G. But this difference is not very crucial, since the PS rules themselves will give us the correct order. We shall in general use trees to represent derivations because they are quick and very clearly represent the relations among the symbols.

To refer to the trees more easily, we label the parts. Each symbol is called a **node**; a line joining two nodes is called a **branch**. The relations between the nodes is stated in terms of **dominance** and **immediate dominance**. One node dominates another if a path between the two can be traced always moving down the tree (away from the initial symbol). In tree IV, B dominates D, E, H, and K, but not G, because a line cannot be traced from B to G without going *up* the tree. D, E, H, and K are *dominated by B. E dominates H* and K; K is *dominated by E, B,* and *A.* One node *immediately dominates* another if it dominates the second and no nodes intervene between the two. Thus, B *immediately dominates D* and E but not H or K, because the node E intervenes between B and H or K. Likewise, K is *immediately dominated by E,* but not by B, since node E intervenes between K and B. One further useful relation: All the nodes dominated by a node *is a* whatever the latter node is. Thus, $D + E$ is a B, $D + H + K$ is a B, G is a C. $D + E + H + K$ is not a B, because we must remain on one level—we can consider either E or what it dominates, but not both. Applying this terminology, the entire terminal string *is a* initial symbol.

Below are the phrase-structure rules we shall use for our grammar, followed by an explanation of each rule:

PS   3.1 $S \rightarrow (SM) \; NP + Pred \; P \; (Place) \; (Time)$

PS   3.2 $Pred \; P \rightarrow Aux + VP$

PS   3.3 $Aux \rightarrow Tn \; (M) \; (have + en) \; (be + ing)$

PS   3.4 $VP \rightarrow \begin{Bmatrix} be + Pred \\ V \; (NP) \; (NP) \; (Manner) \end{Bmatrix}$

PS   3.5 $Pred \rightarrow \begin{Bmatrix} Adj \\ NP \\ Place \end{Bmatrix}$

PS   3.6 $NP \rightarrow \begin{Bmatrix} NP + S \\ N \; (S) \end{Bmatrix}$

PS   3.7 $Tn \rightarrow \begin{Bmatrix} Past \\ Pres \end{Bmatrix}$

PS   3.8 $N \rightarrow [\pm Common]$

PS   3.9 $[+Common] \rightarrow [\pm Pro, \pm Pl]$

PS 3.10 $[-Pro] \rightarrow [\pm Def]$

PS 3.11 $[+Def] \rightarrow [\pm Dem]$

PS 3.12 $[+Dem] \rightarrow [\pm Near]$

Explanation. PS 3.1 states that the initial symbol S must be rewritten as a **noun phrase** (*NP*) and a **predicate phrase** (*Pred P*). These may be optionally preceded by a **sentence modifier** (*SM*), either a lexical sentence modifier such as *yes, no, probably,* and so on, or a dummy symbol which indicates that the terminal string will become a question, negative, or emphatic. Also, there may be optional adverbs of either time, such as *now* or *yesterday,* or place, such as *here, there,* and so on.

PS 3.2 states that the predicate phrase consists of an **auxiliary** (*Aux*) and a **verb phrase** (*VP*).

PS 3.3 states that each auxiliary must contain at least **tense** (*Tn*), as we can see from PS 3.7, either **past** or **present**. It may optionally include a modal (*M*) auxiliary (*may, shall, will, can, must*). It may also optionally include a marker for perfect constructions (*have + en*) and/or the marker for the progressive constructions (*be + ing*). The various combinations allow a sentence with just tense,

> John goes
> John went.

with tense and a modal,

> John will go.
> John would go.

with tense and the perfect,

> John has gone.
> John had gone.

with tense and the progressive,

> John is going.
> John was going.

or with any combination of these,

> John may have been going.
> John will be going.
> John will have gone.
> John has been going.

Notice that what is usually called the "future tense" is treated as a modal construction: Although a construction with *shall* or *will* often refers to future time, it is structurally exactly the same as a construction with *may, can,* or *must*.

PS 3.4 states that the verb phrase may consist of *be* plus a **predicate**, which we can see from PS 3.5 must be either an **adjective** (*Adj*), *or* a **noun phrase** (*NP*), *or* an **adverb of place** (*Place*):

> John is sick.
> John is a doctor.
> John is here.

Alternatively, the verb phrase may consist of a verb by itself (an intransitive verb), a verb followed by a noun phrase called its direct object (a transitive verb), or a verb followed by one noun phrase called its indirect object followed by another noun phrase called its direct object (a double transitive verb):

> John arrived.
> John saw the girl.
> John gave the girl a book.

If an intransitive, transitive, or double transitive construction is chosen, it may optionally be followed by an adverb of manner, such as *quietly, immediately, off-handedly,* and so on.

PS 3.5 has been treated under PS 3.4.

PS 3.6 states that a noun phrase may consist *either* of a noun phrase followed by a sentence (this configuration will produce restrictive relative clauses), *or* a noun optionally followed by a sentence. Examples of restrictive relative clauses are

> The boy *who broke the window* ran away.
> The boy *I saw* ran away.

If only the noun is chosen under the second option, we may get a **proper noun**, a **common noun,** or a **pronoun**:

> *John* left.
> *The boy* left.
> *He* left.

(For the source of *the*, see the discussion of PS 3.8–PS 3.12 below). If the sentence following the noun is chosen, we have a **noun phrase complement**. The noun can be either the pronoun *it* or one of a small class of nouns such as *argument, idea, conclusion,* or *fact*:

> John presented *the argument that Leif discovered Newfoundland.*
> *The fact that John left quickly* should not incriminate him.
> *It* is likely *that Leif discovered Newfoundland.*
> *It* is strange *that John left quickly.*

Noun phrase complements and relative clauses are treated in more detail in Chapters 13 and 14.

The optional *S* included in this rule is what allows us to derive an infinite number of sentences from a finite number of rules, since whenever *S* is chosen the PS rules must be applied over again. First the original S is finished, then the new S is treated as the beginning of a new run through the rules. Clearly, a sentence can be made indefinitely long in this way, since each time a new S is introduced it will contain at least one *NP* (by PS 3.1) and thus the opportunity of choosing S again by PS 3.5. This ability to run through the rules again is called the **recursive** property of the grammar.

PS 3.7 states that the grammatical tense of the sentence must be either **past** or **present**. Sentences with *will, may, shall, can, must,* present progressives, present perfects, or verbs in the present tense, have *Present*:

John works every day.
John will work every day.
John has worked every day.
John is working every day.

Sentences with *would, might, should, could* (note that there is no past form for *must*), past perfects, past progressives or verbs in the past, have *Past*:

John worked every day.
John would work every day.
John had worked every day.
John was working every day.

Notice again that the "future tense" is treated as a modal construction (see PS 3.3 above); and that present and past, as used here, are grammatical categories rather than references to time. Thus, a sentence with grammatically present tense may refer to future, past, or present time:

John will work tomorrow.
John has worked every day.
John works all day.

PS 3.8–PS 3.12 are **segment-structure rules**. They differ from phrase-structure rules in two important ways: First, phrase-structure rules, as the name implies, determine the structure of entire phrases, while segment-structure rules determine instead the internal structure of one segment or part of speech (here the noun). Second, while phrase-structure rules *replace* the symbol on the left of the arrow with the string of symbols on the right, segment-structure rules *add* the symbols on the right of the arrow to what is already present. To compare these two differences: Phrase-structure rules are branching rules—they add new branches to the tree. Segment-structure rules are not branching: Instead of adding new branches, they specify more completely the internal structure of one branch.

To consider the rules separately:

PS 3.8 states that any segment already marked N will have added to it the information that it is either a **proper** noun, such as *John, Rome, Susan* (symbolized [−*Common*]) or a **common** noun, such as *cat, dirt, virtue* (marked [+*Common*]). The major differences between proper and common nouns—

proper nouns generally do not follow determiners or occur in the plural—are captured by the following rules.

PS 3.9 states that any segment marked [+*Common*] may be either a pronoun ([+*Pro*]) or a regular noun ([−*Pro*]) *and* either singular ([−*Pl*]) or plural ([+*Pl*]). *I, you* (singular), *she, he, it* are [+*Pro, −Pl*]; *we, you* (plural), *they* are [+*Pro, +Pl*]; *dog, idea, desk* are [−*Pro, −Pl*]; and *dogs, ideas, desks* are [−*Pro, +Pl*]. All, of course, are [+*Common*].

PS 3.10 states that any segment that is not a pronoun (that is, that is marked [−*Pro*]) may be either definite (marked [+*Def*]) or indefinite ([−*Def*]). In English, the definiteness of the noun is indicated by the kind of determiner that precedes it: *a* and *some* are indefinite, while *the, this, that, these,* and *those* are definite. Notice that this rule and the preceding one capture the characteristics of proper nouns: Only segments that are [+*Common*] can be plural, thus excluding proper nouns; and the only segments that can be preceded by determiners are those marked [−*Pro*]. But since proper nouns are not marked either [+*Pro*] or [−*Pro*] (they are marked only [−*Common*]), they will never have determiners before them. (In those proper nouns having determiners, such as *The George Washington Bridge,* the determiner seems to be part of the noun.)

PS 3.11 states that if a noun is definite, it may be demonstrative ([+*Dem*]) or not ([−*Dem*]), another quality indicated in English by the determiner. A noun marked [+*Dem*] will be preceded by one of the demonstratives—*this, that, these, those*; one that is marked [−*Dem*] will be preceded by *the.*

PS 3.12 states that among the demonstratives there is a distinction based on the proximity (temporal, spatial, or referential) of the noun to the speaker. If [+*Near*] is chosen, the demonstrative will be either *this* ([−*Pl*]) or *these* ([+*Pl*]); *that* ([−*Pl*]) and *those* ([+*Pl*]) are [−*Near*].

Again it should be emphasized that the segment-structure rules are additive: Each feature is added to the features already present.

These phrase-structure rules will give us something to work with, though they are obviously not detailed enough to describe English fully. For one example, there is no provision for prepositional phrases. But rather than spending too much time on any one component, we shall try to get a general idea of how the entire grammar works.

CHAPTER 4

The Lexicon and Lexical Insertion

After all the phrase-structure and segment-structure rules have been applied, we shall have a terminal string of the type shown in Figure 4.1. There are two types of symbols in the terminal string: **lexical category symbols,** such as N_1, N_2, and V, which must have lexical items substituted for them, and **grammatical category symbols,** such as *Past,* which do not require lexical items. In this section we shall deal with the problem of substituting lexical items for the lexical category symbols.

To insert lexical items into a PS tree correctly, we must ensure three things:

1. That the correct part of speech is inserted in the correct position; that any lexical item inserted under either of the N nodes, for instance, is a noun.
2. That the correct subcategory of the part of speech is inserted. In Figure 4.1, the V is followed by a NP, so whatever verb is inserted must be a transitive verb (*eat, read*) rather than an intransitive verb (*arrive, awake*).

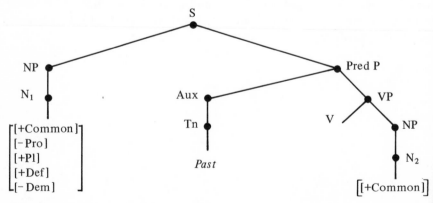

Figure 4.1

Exercises are on p. 161.

. That the verb and the nouns with which it occurs fit together in another way. Consider:

Sentence 4.1   The thunder frightened John.
Sentence 4.2   *The thunder frightened the rocks.

Frighten requires that its direct object be a certain type: A person or animal can be frightened, *rocks* or an idea cannot.

We ensure correct lexical insertion by having a **lexicon**—a complete listing of all the lexical items in the language—and a **lexical-insertion rule**—a formal procedure for putting lexical items into trees. We shall first look at the structure of the lexicon and then at the lexical-insertion rule.

The lexicon of a language consists of a large list of **lexical entries**, one for each lexical item. Each entry contains two types of information: (1) an abstract representation of the pronunciation of the item (a **phonological representation**), and (2) information on the syntactic behavior of the item. The phonological representation contains in a very abstract way (presently envisioned as a matrix of pluses and minuses) all the information the phonological component needs to specify the pronunciation of the item in a sentence. To simplify matters, we shall just write out the word in traditional spelling, although an example of how the phonological component works is given in Chapter 6 (p. 159).

The syntactic component of the lexical entry will be treated in somewhat more detail. As we have seen, there are at least three kinds of information that must be given for each lexical item:

1. Category information. Each lexical item must be classified according to its lexical category, or part of speech. Thus, *boy, girl, John, tree, rock* will be classified as nouns (represented +*N*); *love, arrive, give, frighten* as verbs (+*V*); *tall, ambitious, interesting* as adjectives (+*Adj*); *the, a, these* as determiners (+*Det*); and so on.

2. Subcategory information. Each lexical item will be further classified on the basis of which other categories it can occur with. Verbs, for instance, are subcategorized in terms of the lexical categories by which they can be followed. A verb that cannot be followed freely by a *NP* is called **intransitive**—for example, *arrive, sleep, die, escape, go.* (Notice the qualification "freely": Some intransitive verbs may take a direct object, called a **cognate object**, that is closely related to the verb—for example, *He died a horrible death.*) These can all be optionally followed by a manner adverbial, such as *quickly, peacefully, painfully*, so we represent them as +_(*Manner*), which states that the verb can occur before a manner adverbial, but not before a *NP*. A verb that can be followed by a *NP* is called **transitive**, and the *NP* is its **direct object**. Such verbs are *eat, read, see, hate, own, possess.* If these verbs can be followed by a manner adverbial as well, as *eat, read, see, hate* can, they are +_*NP* (*Manner*), indicating that they can be followed by a *NP* and a manner adverbial. If they cannot be followed by a manner adverbial (for example, *own, possess*) they are +_*NP*, which indicates that they can be followed by a *NP* but not a manner adverbial. Notice that many of these verbs can occur without a *NP* following them: They are still transitive,

since they *can* have a following *NP* (and, in fact, *do* in deep structure, as we shall see). A verb that can be followed by two *NP*s is called **double transitive**; the first *NP* is its indirect object, while the second is its direct object. Such verbs are *give, buy, sell, owe*. Again, if they allow a manner adverbial, as *give, buy, sell,* they will be listed + _*NP* + *NP* (*Manner*). If they do not allow the manner adverbial, as *owe*, they will be listed as + _*NP* + *NP*.

Similarly, nouns are subcategorized by whether they allow a following *S* (a noun phrase complement). Proper nouns never allow a following sentence, and would thus be marked − _*S*. But the pronoun *it* and certain common nouns do allow a following *S*; they would not be marked at all, indicating that they can occur no matter what follows.

3. Selectional information. Selectional information includes information that is used in two ways. First we shall discuss information that is directly related to the segment-structure rules proposed in Chapter 3 (p. 142). The segment-structure rules further specified the noun in two ways, one depending on features inherent in the noun itself and one depending on how the noun is used in a particular sentence. Thus, a noun is inherently either **proper**, such as *Sally, Rome,* or *Jupiter,* or **common**, such as *bird, idea, flour*; similarly, it is inherently a **pronoun**, such as *I, you, they,* or a plain noun, such as *butter, girl, truth.* But whether a common noun is definite or indefinite depends only on how it is used in a sentence, not on anything inherent in the noun itself; we can refer either to *the dog* or *a dog*, to *some flour* or *this flour*. Of the features added by the segment-structure rules, [±*Common*] and [±*Pro*] refer only to features inherent in the noun; [±*Def*], [±*Dem*], [±*Near*] refer only to how the noun is used in a particular sentence; and [±*Pl*] has a shady kind of existence between them. For some nouns, plurality is an inherent feature: Nouns that are always singular, such as *dirt, flour, homework,* are called **mass nouns**; those that are always plural, such as *tweezers, scissors, trousers,* are called **pluralia tantum**. Most common nouns, though, can be either singular or plural; we can talk about *one dog* or *many dogs*, about *one idea* or *several ideas*.

We represent this information about the inherent characteristics of nouns in the lexicon by means of **inherent syntactic features**, so called because they are inherent in the lexical item and have syntactic consequences. One of the syntactic consequences of being a proper noun [−*Common*] is that such a noun cannot, in normal circumstances, be preceded by a determiner. We ensure that a proper noun is not preceded by a determiner by marking the lexical entry [−*Common*]; this entry can then be put into a terminal string only if the segment-structure rules have specified a +*N* segment in the string as [−*Common*] also. But if something is marked [−*Common*] by the segment-structure rules, it cannot be marked either plus or minus definite, and thus no determiner will precede it. Thus, a combination of segment-structure rules and inherent syntactic features ensures that we get the desired results. The lexical entry for each noun will thus have to specify whether the noun is common ([+*Common*]) or proper ([−*Common*]) and whether it is a noun ([−*Pro*]) or a pronoun ([+*Pro*]). If a noun is a mass noun, it will be marked ([−*Pl*]) to indicate that it cannot be pluralized; if it is a *pluralia tantum,* it will be marked ([+*Pl*]). The great majority of nouns will not be inherently marked for plurality at all, indicating that they can be either plural or singular. Likewise, nouns will not be marked either plus or minus for *definite, demonstrative,* or *near,* indicating that they can be either definite or indefinite, and so on, depending on the particular sentence in which they are used.

The second type of information contained in the inherent features concerns the relation between nouns and the verbs and adjectives with which they occur.

Sentence 4.3　John contemplated the idea.
Sentence 4.4　John lifted the box.
Sentence 4.5　John frightened the dog.
Sentence 4.6　John embarrassed the girl.
Sentence 4.7　*John lifted the idea.
Sentence 4.8　*John frightened the box.
Sentence 4.9　*John embarrassed the dog.

All the verbs are transitive, and all are followed by direct objects. But there is some relation between a verb and its direct object we have not accounted for: Sentences 4.7–4.9 are deviant because this relation is violated. Notice that the direct object in Sentences 4.4–4.6 can be substituted in a lower numbered sentence than its own, but cannot be used in a higher numbered one.

The same type of relation holds between the subject *NP* and its verb:

Sentence 4.10　The idea surprised John.
Sentence 4.11　The desk stood in the corner.
Sentence 4.12　The dog walked away.
Sentence 4.13　The boy read the book.
Sentence 4.14　*The idea stood in the corner.
Sentence 4.15　*The desk walked away.
Sentence 4.16　*The dog read the book.

Here any subject of Sentences 4.10–4.13 can be substituted in a sentence with a lower number than its own, but not in one with a higher number.

Similarly, there is a relation between the subject *NP* and the predicate adjective:

Sentence 4.17　The idea was interesting.
Sentence 4.18　The desk was heavy.
Sentence 4.19　The dog was intelligent.
Sentence 4.20　The boy was indiscreet.
Sentence 4.21　*The idea was heavy.
Sentence 4.22　*The desk was intelligent.
Sentence 4.23　*The dog was indiscreet.

Again, a subject *NP* from Sentences 4.18–4.21 can be substituted in a lower numbered sentence but not in a higher one.

To account for these relations, we postulate that nouns have more inherent syntactic features, and that verbs and adjectives are selected in terms of the inherent features of the nouns with which they occur. This gives primacy to nouns—they must be chosen first, and then verbs and adjectives that go with them are chosen. It would, of course, be possible to do it the other way around, ascribing inherent syntactic features to verbs and adjectives, inserting them first, and then choosing nouns on the basis of the verbs and adjectives already present; but that would be more complicated, because any noun can occur in several places in a sentence—subject, direct object, indirect object—while verbs and adjectives occur in only one.

The important features are listed below.

A. *Abstract* vs. *Concrete.* A noun may be either abstract, such as *idea, proposal, thought,* and so on, or concrete, such as *dirt, desk, dog, boy.* As we have seen, abstract nouns cannot be the direct objects of verbs such as *lift, frighten,* and *embarrass,* or the subjects of verbs such as *stand, walk, read,* and so on. Abstract nouns are [−*concrete*]; concrete nouns are [+*concrete*].

B. *Animate* vs. *Nonanimate.* Among the concrete nouns, some can be the subject of verbs such as *walk, move,* and so on, and the object of verbs such as *frighten, annoy,* and so on, while others cannot. Those that can, such as *dog, boy, Jane,* are [+*animate*]; those that cannot, such as *tree, desk, dirt,* are [−*animate*].

C. *Human* vs. *Nonhuman.* Among the animate nouns, some can be subjects of verbs such as *read, write, converse,* and the objects of verbs such as *outrage, embarrass.* The ones that can are [+*human*]; the ones that cannot are [−*human*]. This distinction is not as clear as one would wish, since animals, especially pets, are often anthropomorphized. What must be remembered is that these are syntactic distinctions that are being drawn, not biological ones.

D. *Masculine* vs. *Feminine.* We must also list among the other syntactic features the distinction between masculine and feminine, which has syntactic consequences not only for the proper choice of pronoun (*he* vs. *she*), but also for the verbs and adjectives that can be used with them:

Sentence 4.24   The bull sired the calf.
Sentence 4.25   *The cow sired the calf.
Sentence 4.26   They milked the cow.
Sentence 4.27   *They milked the bull.
Sentence 4.28   The woman is pregnant.
Sentence 4.29   *The man is pregnant.

A masculine noun is [+*masc*], a feminine noun is [−*masc*].[1]

Although these are the most important features, there are undoubtedly many others. For instance, physical state is important:

Sentence 4.30   The ice cracked.
Sentence 4.31   *The water cracked.
Sentence 4.32   John boiled the water.
Sentence 4.33   *John boiled the gas.

[1] The reader is reminded of the distinction between sex and gender, and that syntactic categories do not necessarily correspond to biological categories in either fact or name.

In fact, we would have to account for many other features in a complete description; this is possible in principle but has not been done, probably for two reasons: (1) The effect of inherent features on a grammar can be illustrated with only a small number of oppositions, and (2) the line between syntax and semantics (meaning) is a very difficult one to draw—some people have suggested that all of these selectional features are a matter for the semantic component, and do not properly belong in the syntactic component at all.

Some of these features are **hierarchically ordered** with respect to others: If a noun is [+*human*], it must also be [+*animate*] and [+*concrete*]. Obviously, the reverse is not true: A noun can be [+*concrete*] without being either [+*animate*] or [+*human*]. Some features are **cross-classifying** with respect to others: [+*masc*] can be either [+*human*] (*boy*) or [−*human*] (*bull*); [−*masc*] can be [+*human*] (*girl*) or [−*human*] (*cow*). Notice that a particular feature can be cross-classifying with respect to some features and hierarchically ordered with respect to others: [±*masc*] is cross-classifying with respect to [±*human*], but hierarchically ordered with respect to [+*animate*] and [+*concrete*]. If features are hierarchically ordered, we need mention only the most specific in the lexical entry, and the other features will be predicted by a general **redundancy rule** for the entire lexicon, which will say, for example, that all items marked [+*human*] are also to be marked [+*animate*] and [+*concrete*]. This information can be represented on a tree. For common count nouns (that is, those that are [+*Common*], we would have the tree in Figure 4.2. This tree represents *boy* as being [+*masc*], [+*human*], [+*animate*], [+*concrete*], and so on, and shows clearly which features are hierarchically ordered and which are cross-classifying: Any feature occurring twice is cross-classifying with respect to the feature immediately above it.

The lexical entry for each noun, then, will contain a list of its inherent syntactic features. To get the proper verbs and adjectives into strings with these nouns, their lexical entries will indicate their **selectional features**—a list of the inherent features required of the nouns with which they occur. If a verb requires a human direct object, as *embarrass* or *outrage,* it will be represented [_[+*human*]], indicating that the noun following it must be [+*human*]; if it requires a concrete object, as *lift,* it will be [_[+*concrete*]]. If there are no restrictions on its object, as *contemplate,* it will state nothing. The formalism for subject noun restrictions is similar: A verb requiring a human

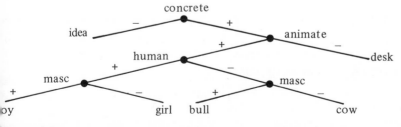

Figure 4.2

subject will be marked [[+*human*] _] to indicate that the preceding *NP* must be [+*human*] ; one requiring a masculine subject (*father, sire*) will be [[+*masc*] _] , and so on. Similarly, adjectives will be selectionalized: one requiring a feminine subject (*pregnant*) will be [[–*masc*] _] ; one requiring a concrete subject (*heavy, solid*) will be [[+*concrete*] _] , and so on. How these features will be used to ensure the correct relations between nouns and their verbs and adjectives will be treated in the section on the lexical-insertion rule.

4. Syntactic idiosyncrasies. In addition to the information listed above, the syntactic idiosyncrasies of the lexical item must be listed in the lexical entry. For example:

Sentence 4.34a   John ate the steak.
Sentence 4.34b   John ate.
Sentence 4.35a   John fixed the car.
Sentence 4.35b   *John fixed.

From Sentences 4.34a and 4.34b, it is obvious that some transitive verbs can occur without a following *NP*; from Sentences 4.35a and 4.35b, it appears that this is not true of all transitives. We have to indicate that *fix* and verbs like it do not allow deletion of the direct object *NP* (or, alternatively, that *eat* and verbs like it do) as one of the syntactic idiosyncrasies of the verb. The notation would be something like [–*Obj Del*].

For another example, consider:

Sentence 4.36a   John saw the car.
Sentence 4.36b   The car was seen by John.
Sentence 4.37a   John had a car.
Sentence 4.37b   *A car was had by John.
Sentence 4.38a   John weighs two hundred pounds.
Sentence 4.38b   *Two hundred pounds is weighed by John.

Most transitive verbs, such as *see*, can undergo the passive transformation, which relates Sentences 4.36a and 4.36b. However, there is a small class of transitive verbs, known as **middle verbs**, which cannot be passivized, including *have, resemble, cost, weigh* (in the sense of Sentence 4.38a, not as in *John weighs the letter*) and *marry* (in the sense of *John married Jane* rather than *the preacher married John and Jane*). The lexical entry for the middle verbs will include the information that they cannot go through the passive transformation, in some notation such as [–*Passive*].

To summarize: Each lexical entry consists of two parts: (1) a phonological representation, and (2) syntactic information, including (a) category membership, (b) subcategorization information, (c) inherent syntactic features for nouns, selectional features for verbs and adjectives, and (d) syntactic idiosyncrasies. Such entries might look like these:

boy, +*N*, –_*S*, [+*Common*], [–*Pro*], [+*human*], [+*masc*]
Sally, +*N*, –_*S*, [–*Common*], [+*human*], [–*masc*]
scissors, +*N*, –_*S*, [+*Common*], [–*Pro*], [+*Pl*], [+*concrete*]

dirt, +N, −_S, [+*Common*], [−*Pro*], [−*Pl*], [+*concrete*]
fact, +N, [+*Common*], [−*Pro*], [−*concrete*]
they, +N, −_S, [+*Common*], [+*Pro*], [+*Pl*]
frighten, +V, +_NP (*Manner*), [_[+*animate*]], [−*Obj Del*]
kick, +V, +_NP (*Manner*), [[+*animate*] _], [_[+*concrete*]]
have, +V, +_NP, [−*Passive*] [−*Obj Del*]
arrive, +V, +_(*Manner*), [[+*concrete*] _]
pregnant, +Adj, [[−*masc*] _]

We now need a method for inserting the lexical entries into terminal strings. In general, nouns are inserted first, and a lexical item can be inserted under a lexical category if no information in the lexical entry conflicts with the PS tree into which the entry is being inserted. Thus, in Figure 4.3, only a lexical entry marked +N, [+*Common*] [−*Pro*] can be substituted for N_1, and only an entry marked +N, [−*Common*] for N_2. Once the nouns have been inserted, we insert the verb. This must be +V, +_NP to fit the tree. Further, its selectional features must not contradict the inherent features of either N_1 or N_2. Suppose we substitute *dog* for N_1. Then the verb cannot be marked [[+*human*] _], because the tree into which we are inserting it already has a subject noun marked [−*human*], and there would thus be a contradiction between the lexical item and the tree.

Let us make this process a bit more formal. Suppose that at the end of the PS rules we have a series of rules that rewrites each lexical category as the dummy symbol Δ. The lexical-insertion rule is an operation that substitutes a lexical entry for an occurrence of Δ if the syntactic part of the lexical entry contradicts nothing in the tree. This operation is actually a transformation, because it has the power to look around, so to speak, to see what Δ *is* (in terms of domination) and what environment Δ is in (in terms of other categories and inherent features already in the tree). Suppose, then, that we have Figure 4.4. The lexical-insertion rule can substitute a +N, [+*Common*], [−*Pro*] for $Δ_1$, and any +N [−*Common*] for $Δ_3$ (actually, this is a bit simplified: since N_1 is marked [+*Pl*], a mass

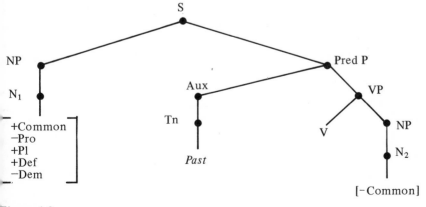

Figure 4.3

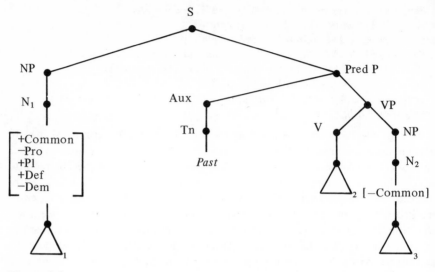

Figure 4.4

noun—one lexically [–*Pl*]—cannot be substituted). Suppose that *dog* and *Joan* are chosen. After substitution, the tree is as shown in Figure 4.5. The lexical insertion rule can now substitute for Δ_2 any entry that does not conflict with any of the information contained in the tree. Thus, the item must be +V, +_NP must allow an animate but nonhuman subject (it cannot be *write* or *read*), an

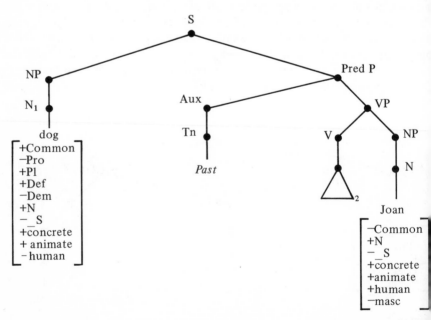

Figure 4.5

must allow a human and feminine object (thus, *formulate* is out, because it requires [*−concrete*] objects, and *castrate* because it requires [*+masc*] objects). *Frighten, see, outrage, eat,* and so on are all acceptable. The lexical rule operates as often as necessary to insert lexical items: When there are no longer any dummy symbols (Δ), it has nothing further to operate on, and so stops.

Once lexical items have been substituted for all the dummy symbols, we have a *deep structure* (DS). The deep structure is a representation of the meaning of the sentence, and the starting point for transformations. Theoretically, every deep structure contains fully specified lexical items; in practice, we shall list only the syntactic information in the lexical item that is necessary to the derivation.

CHAPTER 5

The Semantic Component

Although there are questions about every aspect of transformational grammar
nothing has raised more unanswered questions than the structure of the semantic
component. Our discussion will be extremely sketchy, merely suggesting how a
semantic component might work.

We have said that the semantic component is interpretive—that it interprets the
deep structures that are fed into it. If we consider a deep structure such as
Figure 5.1, the semantic component must specify its meaning. There are at least
two aspects to this: (1) The semantic component must have a list of the
meanings of all the lexical items and grammatical categories, and (2) The
semantic component must be able to tell how the lexical items are related to
each other in the DS under consideration.

Considering first Figure 5.1, it is clear that part of the "meaning" of the NP
dog is contained in the syntactic information already present in the deep
structure, that is, that it is plural and definite, and also animate, concrete, and
nonhuman (although, as we have already said, these syntactic terms may not
exactly match semantic categories). In addition to this information, the semantic
component must link the item *dog* with the meaning "domestic canine" or some
such thing. Similarly, the semantic component must represent the meaning of
frighten as something like "cause to become afraid." And *Past* must be interpreted as meaning that the action took place at some time previous to the
present. Thus, one part of the semantic component must be a large dictionary
that gives the meanings of all the lexical items and grammatical formatives in the
language.

The second function of the semantic component is to put the meanings of the
lexical items and grammatical formatives together in the correct way. That is
given the information that *dog* refers to a domestic canine, that *Joan* refers to a
particular human female, that *frighten* means "cause to become afraid," and that

Exercises are on p. 161.

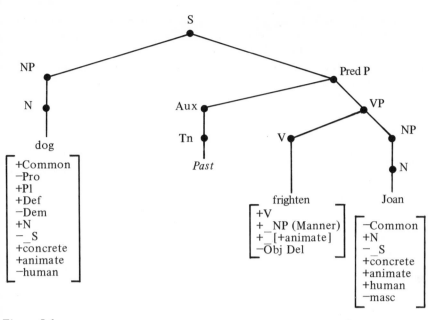

Figure 5.1

the tense *Past* indicates that the action took place at some previous time, the semantic component must combine these to give 5.1 rather than 5.2 as the meaning (a **semantic reading**) of Figure 5.1.

5.1 At some time in the past, specific domestic canines caused a particular human female to become afraid.

5.2 At some time in the past, a particular human female caused specific domestic canines to become afraid.

In traditional terms, the semantic component must be able to identify the subject of the sentence and assign it a meaning such as "instigator or performer of action," and it must identify the object and assign it the meaning of "receiver of action, or entity affected by action." Identifying the subject from the structure of the DS tree is quite simple: It is the *NP* immediately dominated by *S*. Likewise, the direct object is a *NP* immediately dominated by *VP*. To distinguish between a direct and an indirect object, we might define direct object as the right *NP* daughter of *VP* (one node immediately dominated by another is a "daughter" node), and the indirect object as the left *NP* daughter of *VP*. Whatever our exact definition, the important point is that the deep structure represents not only the lexical items but also the functions they fulfill—subject, direct object, indirect object, and so on—in the sentence.

To summarize roughly how the semantic component works: The deep structure represents the lexical items in the sentence and the functions they fulfill. The semantic component contains a dictionary giving the meaning of all the lexical items and grammatical formatives in the language, and a characterization of the semantic relation between verb and direct object, verb and indirect object, subject and verb, subject and predicate adjective, subject and predicate nominative, and so on. First the semantic component looks up each of the lexical items and grammatical formatives in its dictionary and assigns the meaning. Then it combines the meanings, drawing on the structural information contained in the deep structure and its own characterization of the meaning of the various structural relations. When it is finished, it has interpreted the meaning of the entire deep structure.

CHAPTER 6

The Phonological Component

As we have said, each lexical entry consists of two parts, one an abstract phonological representation of the item, the other a characterization of its syntactic behavior. The function of the phonological component is to interpret the surface structure: Beginning with the abstract phonological representations of the individual items and the syntactic structures the items are in, it will fully specify the pronunciation of the sentence. Even a partial explanation of how the phonological component works would require more time than we have, but perhaps a simple example can be presented.

Although English is a stress language, it seems that the stress is fully predictable. That is, stress will not be represented in the underlying phonological representation but will rather be added by the phonological component. Consider the two phrases *the black bird* and *the blackbird*. The first has major stress on *bird,* secondary stress on *black,* and no stress on *the,* and refers to any bird that happens to be black. The second, which refers to a particular type of bird, has primary stress on *black*, tertiary stress on *bird*, and no stress on *the*. The surface structures of the two phrases will presumably be as in Figures 6.1 and 6.2. The structure under N in Figure 6.2 just represents the internal structure of the compound *blackbird*. Another way to represent the same information is to use labeled brackets:

1 $[_{NP}[\text{the}]_{Det}\ [\text{black}]_{Adj}\ [\text{bird}]_N]_{NP}$

2 $[_{NP}[\text{the}]_{Det}\ [_N[\text{black}]_{Adj}\ [\text{bird}]_N]_N]_{NP}$

We begin by assigning heavy stress (represented by 1) to each lexical category (such as noun, verb, adjective, and so on). After we have applied stress, we erase the innermost brackets:

Exercises are on p. 161.

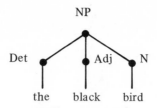

Figure 6.1

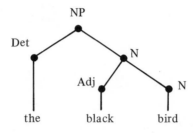

Figure 6.2

$$\overset{\text{1}\quad\text{1}}{\textbf{1a}\ [_{NP}\text{the black bird}]_{NP}}$$

$$\overset{\quad\quad\quad\text{1}\quad\text{1}}{\textbf{2a}\ [_{NP}[\text{the}]_{Det}\ [_{N}\text{black bird}]_{N}]_{NP}}$$

Now we work on the innermost brackets again. Two rules could apply here: (1) the **nuclear stress rule**, which assigns heavy stress to the rightmost heavily stressed element in *NP*s, *VP*s, and so on, and (2) the **compound stress rule**, which assigns heavy stress to the leftmost heavily stressed element in nouns. (Assigning heavy stress again is equivalent to reducing the other stresses by 1—the higher the number, the lower the stress.) The nuclear stress rule can apply to 1a, since we are considering the entire *NP*, to give 1b:

$$\overset{\text{2}\quad\text{1}}{\textbf{1b}\ [_{NP}\text{the black bird}]_{NP}}$$

However, this rule cannot apply to 2a, since the innermost brackets there indicate that it is a noun and not a noun phrase that is to be stressed. So the second rule, the compound stress rule, which applies to nouns, must apply, giving 2b:

$$\overset{\text{1}\quad\text{2}}{\textbf{2b}\ [_{NP}\text{the black bird}]_{NP}}$$

Now the nuclear stress rule can apply to 2b. It puts heavy stress on the rightmost heavily stressed element, adding another degree of stress to *black*, since that is the only heavily stressed element left. After this, we shall get 2c:

$$\overset{1\quad\ \ 3}{\text{2c} \ [_{NP}\text{the black bird}]_{NP}}$$

But these are just the results we wanted: In 1b, we have secondary stress on *black* and primary stress on *bird*; in 2c we have primary stress on *black* and tertiary stress on *bird*.

The phonological component, then, takes as input the abstract phonological representation of the lexical items and the syntactic information represented in the surface structure and applies its rules to produce the pronunciation of the sentence.

Exercises (Chapters 1–6)

1. Derive the following terminal strings and give the phrase-structure trees for them. Notice that the nouns are not specified at all: You will not have to apply PS rules 3.8–3.12.

   a. *N + Past + V + N*
   b. *N + Past + be + ing + V + N + Place*
   c. *N + Past + M + be + Place*
   d. *SM + N + Pres + have + en + be + ing + V + N + N*
   e. *N + Pres + be + ing + V + NP + Manner*
   f. *N + Pres + be + NP*
   g. *N + Pres + M + have + en + V + N + Manner + Place*
   h. *N + Pres + be + Adj + Place + Time*

2. In the discussion on inherent features in nouns, it was stated that many other features would have to be included in a complete description (p. 150). What are some of these additional features?

3. Provide the lexical entries for the following items (if an item belongs to more than one major category, provide more than one entry): *run, walk, girl, brave, man, table, masculine, dance, contemplate, deciduous.*

4. We have said (p. 144) that *tense* is used as a grammatical category rather than as a reference to time, and showed that grammatically present tense could refer to present, future, or past time. Even more surprising are examples such as *The rocket might come down,* where grammatically past tense can refer only to future time. Find more examples of this disparity between grammatical tense and time reference.

5.* A line from "The Jabberwocky" was used (p. 131) to illustrate that one does not necessarily need to know what a word means to know how it is functioning. How could this approach be generalized in the classroom to teach the distinctions among nouns, verbs, adjectives, and adverbs?

*Exercises preceded by asterisks are more advanced and/or more theoretical than the others.

6.* We have accounted for the fact that nouns often occur with determiners (*a, the, this, that, these, those*) or in the plural by means of segment-structure rules (PS rules 3.8–3.12). An alternative method is to introduce the determiner and/or plural ending as segments in their own right by a PS rule, such as

$$NP \rightarrow \begin{Bmatrix} NP + S \\ (det) \; N \; (Pl) \; (s) \end{Bmatrix}$$

which would replace our PS rule 3.6. If we were to adopt this method, how would we have to change the selectional restrictions to prevent determiners with proper nouns or pronouns (**the Peter, *the she*), plurals of mass nouns (**dirts*), and singulars of *pluralia tantum* nouns (**scissor*)?

7.* We shall have little to say about adverbs in this grammar because they are so complex. The complexity arises from the fact that an adverbial of time may be a word (*now*), a phrase (*in ten minutes*), or a clause (*after John had left*); conversely, a word, phrase, or clause may be either an adverbial of time or serve some other function. In short, our category *time* seems to be the name of a function rather than of a construction. Ideally, we would like to treat *time* like the other functions, such as *subject* and *direct object*, defining it in terms of configurations of PS trees. But this does not seem to be possible, since *time* and *place* may be realized by the same construction—say, a prepositional phrase—so, on the basis of construction alone, we would not be able to distinguish between them. Is there any way out of this dilemma?

8.* As stated, the phrase-structure rules allow one Place adverbial to be chosen in PS 3.1 and another in PS 3.4 and PS 3.5, thus producing a string like *NP + Aux + be + Place + Place*. Are there any sentences like this? If not, how could the PS rules be changed to ensure that *be* is followed by at most one Place adverbial?

CHAPTER 7

Segment-Structure Transformations

The transformations, as we have seen, change, or transform, the deep structure into the surface structure. Each transformation consists of two major parts, a **structural description** (or **structural index**, abbreviated SI) and a **structural change** (abbreviated SC). The structural index indicates which strings the transformation applies to; the structural change tells how the transformation changes the string. In addition, each transformation is either **optional** (if its structural description is met, it may or may not apply), or **obligatory** (if its structural description is met, it must apply).

At the outset, we must distinguish two different types of transformations: **local**, or **segment-structure** transformations, and **general**, or **syntactic** transformations. Local transformations (discussed on p. 103) are used to produce the determiners and plural markers in our model. Above (p. 156) we claimed that the structure shown in Figure 7.1 was the deep structure for *The dogs frightened Joan*. Two of the most obvious differences between this deep structure and the sentence is that the deep structure contains neither the article *the* nor the marker for the plural of *dog*. The local transformations will add these elements.

First the determiner transformation: A local transformation will apply obligatorily to every noun in the string that contains either [+*Def*] or [−*Def*]. (Notice that this excludes the noun *Joan*, which is not specified at all for [*Def*].) The transformation will produce a new segment, attached to the *NP* node, which is labeled *Det*, and which contains all the information specified for the noun by the segment-structure rules. Thus, from Figure 7.2, this transformation will produce Figure 7.3. In these figures, notice that [+*concrete*], [+*animate*], and [−*human*] are not copied; this is because they are inherent features of the noun rather than features added by segment-structure rules.

Now we have all the specifications for the determiner, but not the phonological representation. So we must have a **second lexical lookup**: After all the

Exercises are on p. 196.

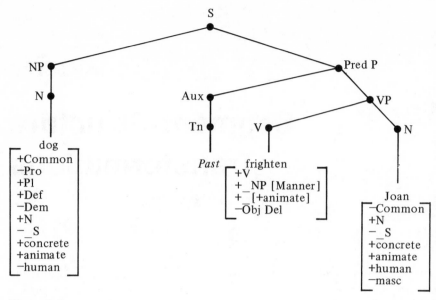

Figure 7.1

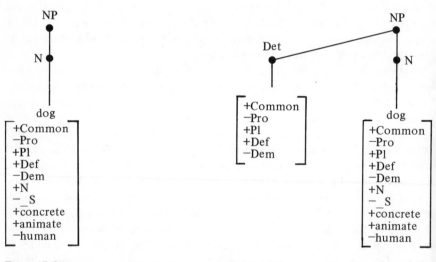

Figure 7.2   **Figure 7.3**

transformations have applied, the lexicon is consulted a second time, and phono-logical representations are supplied for any segments that have been either cre-ated or changed by transformations (for an example of the latter, see Chapter 15). In this case, the representation supplied will be *the* (remember that we are using conventional spelling as a substitute for phonological representation), since the determiner is [+*Def, -Dem*]. The other possibilities have been given above

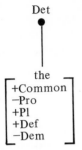

Det

$$\begin{bmatrix} \text{the} \\ +\text{Common} \\ -\text{Pro} \\ +\text{Pl} \\ +\text{Def} \\ -\text{Dem} \end{bmatrix}$$

Figure 7.4

(pp. 116-118, p. 145). After the second lexical lookup, then, the determiner segment will be as in Figure 7.4.

This solves one of our problems but leaves the other: We still have no overt representation of the plurality of *dog*. Another obligatory local transformation produces this segment: To any noun marked [+*Pl*] it attaches a segment to the *N* node that is marked [+*Affix*, +*Pl*]. This transformation will turn Figure 7.3 into Figure 7.5.

This transformation will not apply to the second noun node in Figure 7.1 either, since that node is not [+*Pl*]. The phonological shape for the plural segment may be supplied either by the second lexical lookup or by another transformation. It is not clear which is better, so we shall not choose either, but rather assume that there is some process for getting the correct plural form of nouns.

After these transformations have applied and the second lexical lookup has occurred, the determiner and plural are represented by specific segments in the

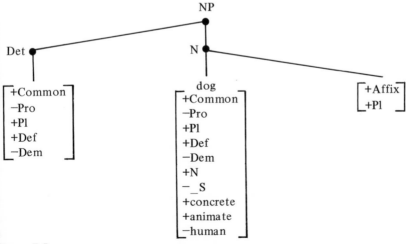

NP

Det

$$\begin{bmatrix} +\text{Common} \\ -\text{Pro} \\ +\text{Pl} \\ +\text{Def} \\ -\text{Dem} \end{bmatrix}$$

N

$$\begin{bmatrix} \text{dog} \\ +\text{Common} \\ -\text{Pro} \\ +\text{Pl} \\ +\text{Def} \\ -\text{Dem} \\ +\text{N} \\ -\_\text{S} \\ +\text{concrete} \\ +\text{animate} \\ -\text{human} \end{bmatrix}$$

$$\begin{bmatrix} +\text{Affix} \\ +\text{Pl} \end{bmatrix}$$

Figure 7.5

tree. But it is important to realize that the segment transformations have not added any meaning to the tree: The same information contained now by the new segments *Det* and *Affix* is present as features on the noun in deep structure. The transformations have merely changed that information into the surface form it has in English.

These segment transformations are applied after all the syntactic transformations. Thus, nouns will not be preceded by determiners when we discuss the syntactic transformations; instead, they will just be marked [+*Def*] or [-*Def*], both to indicate whether they are definite or indefinite and to remind us that had we but world enough and time, all of the segment features—those introduced by segment-structure rules and the inherent features—would be included. That they are not is a concession to brevity.

CHAPTER 8

Indirect-Object Switch

The second kind of transformation is the syntactic transformation. Unlike the segment transformations, these transformations differ from PS rules in an important way: PS rules operate on single symbols and rewrite them, but transformations apply to entire strings and rewrite one string as another string. Another characteristic of transformations will be clearer from the examples in Figure 8.1 and Sentences 8.1-8.4.

Sentence 8.1 The boy gave the girl the book.
Sentence 8.2 The boy gave the book to the girl.
Sentence 8.3 The boy sold the girl the book.
Sentence 8.4 The boy sold the book to the girl.

Figure 8.1 is the terminal string underlying all four sentences. Sentences 8.1 and 8.2 are closely related, as are Sentences 8.3 and 8.4. In Sentences 8.1 and 8.3,

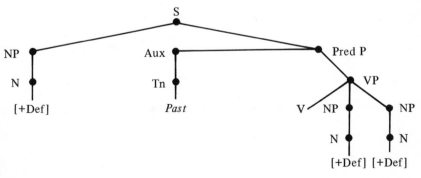

Figure 8.1

Exercises are on p. 196.

the indirect object is within the sentence, while in Sentences 8.2 and 8.4 it has been moved to the end and a preposition (*to* or *for*) inserted before it. Sentences 8.1 and 8.2 mean exactly the same thing, as do Sentences 8.3 and 8.4, so they should be derived from the same deep structure. Given the deep structures for Sentences 8.1 and 8.3 shown in Figures 8.2 and 8.3, we can formulate a transformation that will accomplish this. Starting with Figure 8.2, we can put it through the transformation:

$$\text{boy} + past + \text{give} + \text{girl} + \text{book} \Rightarrow \text{boy} + past + \text{give} + \text{book} + \text{to} + \text{girl}$$
$$[+Def] \qquad\qquad [+Def][+Def] \quad [+Def] \qquad\qquad\qquad [+Def] \qquad [+Def]$$

(Another device to save space is to represent just the linear order of elements in the string, without including the tree. The + is the concatenation symbol.) Ignoring for the moment the problem of turning *past* + *give* into *gave*, we can

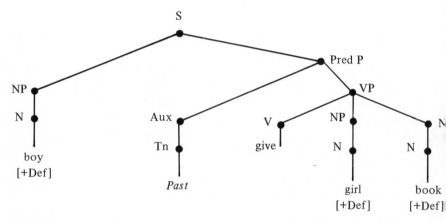

Figure 8.2

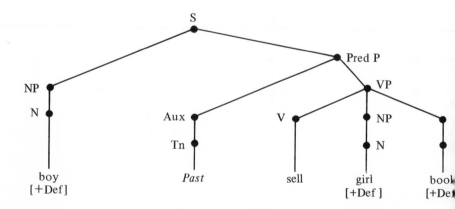

Figure 8.3

see that if we apply this transformation to Figure 8.1, we shall end up with the structure *The boy gave the book to the girl.* If we choose not to apply the transformation, we shall get *The boy gave the girl the book.* Likewise, to account for Sentences 8.3 and 8.4, we can set up a transformation that does the same thing:

$$\text{boy} + past + \text{sell} + \text{girl} + \text{book} \Rightarrow \text{boy} + past + \text{sell} + \text{book} + \text{to} + \text{girl}$$
$$[+Def] \qquad\qquad [+Def]\ [+Def]\ [+Def] \qquad\qquad [+Def] \qquad [+Def]$$

If we put Figure 8.3 through this transformation, the result will be Sentence 8.4; if we do not, the result will be Sentence 8.3.

But notice that we have two transformations that do exactly the same thing—they both take an indirect object from before the direct object and move it after the direct object, inserting a preposition before it. The reason we had to posit two different transformations is that we stated the transformation in terms of lexical items—and for the deep structure to meet the structural index, there would have to be as many different indirect-object transformations as there are different deep structures. Clearly, this is wrong. For one thing, it is uneconomical to have many transformations doing the same thing—a violation of the simplicity criterion we adopted for the grammar. For another, it does not square with what we feel about indirect objects—we know that indirect objects can be switched around no matter what words are used in those objects (as long as the direct object is not a pronoun, in which case the indirect object *must* be moved to the end in American English).

In short, we have been too specific when we want to be as general as possible. The most general formulation of the **indirect-object switch transformation** (*IO Switch*) would be something like this: Any indirect object can optionally be moved to the end of the sentence, with a preposition (*to, for*) inserted before it. This will account for both our examples. To state it formally:

IO Switch (opt)

$$NP_1 + Aux + V + NP_2 + NP_3 \Rightarrow NP_1 + Aux + V + NP_3 + \begin{Bmatrix} to \\ for \end{Bmatrix} + NP_2$$

This says, in symbolic notation, just what we have said above in words. But notice that we have a difficulty—we must be able to analyze our DS and see whether it fits the structural description—that is, we must know (in addition to the words) what the words are in terms of the *is a* relation. Consider Figure 8.4. To apply the *IO Switch*, we have to know that *girl* is a *NP*, that *book* is a *NP*, and that they appear in the correct order. The second major difference between phrase-structure and transformational rules, then, is that transformational rules are dependent on the structure of the string to which they apply (they are *structure dependent*), while PS rules are not—they apply whenever the symbol to the left of the arrow appears, no matter how that symbol relates to other symbols. To put it another way, a PS rule changes one symbol into another symbol or string of symbols; a transformational rule changes one structure into another structure.

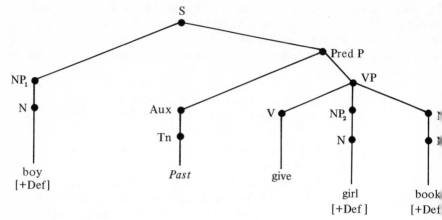

Figure 8.4

To state transformations with the most generality, then, we shall state them not in terms of the lexical items in the deep structure, but in terms of the structures containing those lexical items. There is another shorthand way to increase generality. Look at the *IO Switch* rule again:

IO Switch (opt)

$$NP_1 + Aux + V + NP_2 + NP_3 \Rightarrow NP_1 + Aux + V + NP_3 + \begin{Bmatrix} to \\ for \end{Bmatrix} + NP_2$$

The only parts of the string affected by this rule are NP_2 and NP_3—we do not really care what the subject *NP* is or what the auxiliary is. This can be indicated by using a **dummy symbol** (capital X and Y are usually used):

IO Switch (opt)

$$X + V + NP_1 + NP_2 \Rightarrow X + V + NP_2 + \begin{Bmatrix} to \\ for \end{Bmatrix} + NP_1$$

This states that the only part of the string we are interested in is the verb phrase—everything that precedes the verb is unchanged, no matter what it is. But the verb is also unchanged, so why do we include it in the structural index? Because we want to be sure that only real indirect objects get switched—that is, only two *NP*s immediately following a *V*. This ensures that two *NP*s immediately following each other elsewhere (if that situation should arise because of some transformations) do not get switched around. Figure 8.5 is the DS tree for Sentence 8.4, indicating how it is analyzed to meet the structural index of the *IO Switch*, and Figure 8.6 is a tree showing the results of the transformation. (Notice that we have abbreviated the deep structure to save time and space: The specifications left out—for example, *N* and *Tn*—would be included in a full derivation, but are omitted because they do not matter for the purposes of the present illustration.) One nasty matter: Figure 8.6 has an altogether new node, *PP*, dominating *to +NP*. It is not clear how that is to be represented in the

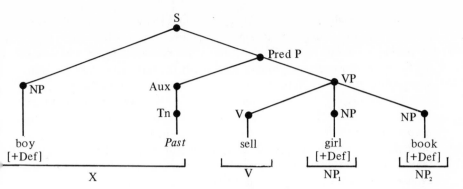

Figure 8.5

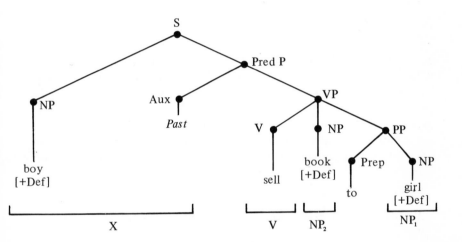

Figure 8.6

transformation, although it is clearly necessary. One device we might use is the distinction between + and -. When a transformation adds something, we will put a + between what is added and its sister nodes. In general, then, in the statement of transformations, + represents sister nodes, - represents nodes that are not sisters. When we are citing strings as examples, we shall use + as the general concatenation symbol.

Consider the following examples:

Sentence 8.5a Sam bought Sally a coat.
Sentence 8.5b Sam bought a coat for Sally.
Sentence 8.6a Sam saved Sally a seat.
Sentence 8.6b Sam saved a seat for Sally.

If these are actually indirect-object constructions (they may be **benefactive**—one person doing something for the benefit of another), we have the slight difficulty of stating explicitly when *to* is chosen as the preposition and when *for*. This matter is an idiosyncratic syntactic fact about the verb—*give* and *sell* require *to*, *buy* requires *for*—and will thus be included in the lexical entry for the verb.

Before we discuss the various transformations, there is one important transformation to look at. This is the tense-incorporation transformation. Recall that in deep structure the tense always precedes the verb, and if markers for aspect are present, they precede it as well. A transformation is needed that combines the tense (or marker for participles) with a following verb. In addition, there is agreement between the subject and the verb to be accounted for:

Sentence 8.7a John + *Pres* + see + girl
$$[+Def]$$
Sentence 8.7b Boys + *Pres* + see + girl
$$[+Def] \qquad [+Def]$$
Sentence 8.7c John + *Past* + *have* + *en* + *be* + *ing* + sleep

In Sentence 8.7a, the transformation must combine *Pres* and *see* and make it agree with the singular subject to give *sees*. In Sentence 8.7b, *Pres* and *see* must be combined and made to agree with the plural subject to give *see*. In Sentence 8.7c, *Past* and *have* are combined and made to agree with *John* to give *had*, *en* (the marker for the past participle) is combined with the following verb *be* to give the past participle of *be, been,* and *ing* (the marker for the present participle) combines with the following verb *sleep* to give *sleeping*. Since many verbs are strong (or irregular), this process may take some spelling out, but it is conceptually quite simple and we shall use a shorthand **affix-incorporation transformation**:

Affix Incorp (oblig)

$X - Af - Vb - Y \Rightarrow X - Vb + Af - Y$, where $Af = Tn, - ing, - en$, and $Vb = $ *have, be, M, V*

This does not say very much except that an affix combines with the *following* verbal item. We shall assume that matters of agreement and getting the correct form for past tense or past participles of verbs are taken care of by this transformation.

CHAPTER 9

Passive

Although passive sentences are quite common, our phrase-structure rules do not account for them. Consider the following sentences:

Sentence 9.1 John saw Mary.
Sentence 9.2 Mary was seen by John.
Sentence 9.3 Sam ate the cake.
Sentence 9.4 The cake was eaten by Sam.
Sentence 9.5 The boy raises horses.
Sentence 9.6 Horses are raised by the boy.

The odd-numbered sentences are **active** sentences. The even ones are the corresponding **passives**. They mean the same thing (within our limits on this term) and share lexical items, so we would like to derive them from the same underlying structures. Furthermore, we feel that the active sentences are somehow more basic—that they are closer to the deep structure than the passives. The deep structures for Sentences 9.1, 9.3, and 9.5 are as follows:

Sentence 9.1a John + *Past* + see + Mary
Sentence 9.3a Sam + *Past* + eat + cake
$\qquad\qquad\qquad\qquad$ [+*Def*]
Sentence 9.5a boy + *Pres* + raise + horse
$\qquad\quad$ [+*Def*] $\qquad\qquad\qquad$ [+*Pl*]

If we put these deep structures through the affix-incorporation transformation, we get Sentences 9.1, 9.3, and 9.5. What we need is a transformation, the **Passive**, that will transform Sentences 9.1a, 9.3a, and 9.5a into intermediate structures that will become Sentences 9.2, 9.4, and 9.6 after affix incorporation. If we undo the affix incorporation on Sentences 9.2, 9.4, and 9.6, we get

Exercises are on p. 196.

Sentence 9.2a Mary + *Past* + *be* + *en* + see + by + John
Sentence 9.4a cake + *Past* + *be* + *en* + eat + by + Sam
       [+*Def*]
Sentence 9.6a Horse + *Pres* + *be* + *en* + raise + by + boy
       [+*Pl*]   [+*Def*]

What we want the passive to do, then, is turn Sentence 9.1a into 9.2a, Sentence 9.3a into 9.4a, and Sentence 9.5a into 9.6a. If we compare these, we notice the following differences:

1. In Sentences 9.2a, 9.4a, and 9.6a, the direct object *NP* of Sentences 9.1a, 9.3a, and 9.5a occurs first.
2. In Sentences 9.2a, 9.4a, and 9.6a, the subject *NP* of Sentences 9.1a, 9.3a, and 9.5a occurs last, preceded by *by*.
3. In Sentences 9.2a, 9.4a, and 9.6a, *be* + *en* occurs between the tense and what comes next in Sentences 9.1a, 9.3a, and 9.5a.

As a first approximation, then, we propose:

Passive (opt)
$$NP_1 - Tn - V - NP_2 \Rightarrow NP_2 - Tn + be + en - V - by + NP_1$$

This states that the passive transformation does three things: (1) It takes the subject *NP* and puts it at the end and adds *by* before it. (2) It takes the *NP* after the *V* and puts it at the front. (3) It adds *be* + *en* between the *Tn* and the *V*. As you can see, this transformation will apply to Sentences 9.1a, 9.3a, and 9.5a to turn them into Sentences 9.2a, 9.4a, and 9.6a, and when these go through affix incorporation, we shall get Sentences 9.2, 9.4, and 9.6.

We have thus accounted for the fact that actives and the corresponding passives have the same meaning by deriving them from the same deep structure. And we have accounted for the fact that the actives seem somehow more basic by making the corresponding passives go through one more transformation—the *Passive*—than the actives do. The Passive transformation is optional, to account for the fact that we have both actives and passives—if the transformation were obligatory, all the strings meeting the structural index would have to go through it, and we would not be able to derive Sentences 9.1, 9.3, and 9.5.

But things are a little too simple: We have not accounted yet for the following correspondences:

Sentence 9.7a John will cook the dinner.
Sentence 9.7b The dinner will be cooked by John.
Sentence 9.8a John has seen the horses.
Sentence 9.8b The horses have been seen by John.
Sentence 9.9a John is cooking dinnner.
Sentence 9.9b Dinner is being cooked by John.

In each of these cases, there is another part to the auxiliary besides tense: In Sentence 9.7, a modal is present; in Sentence 9.8, the perfect; and in Sentence

9.9, the progressive. Our transformation must be modified to allow for this, and examination of the above examples, together with Sentence 9.10, indicates that we merely have to replace *Tn* in the *Passive* by *Aux*:

Sentence 9.10a John might have been dating Sally.
Sentence 9.10b Sally might have been being dated by John.

In Sentence 9.10b, *dated* is a past participle, and the *be* that is added by the *Passive* is a present participle, exactly the result if *be* + *en* is added after the whole auxiliary. In abbreviated form (without indications of structure), the passive will turn 9.11, the deep structure for both Sentences 9.10a and 9.10b, into 9.12, the underlying structure for Sentence 9.10b.

Sentence 9.11 John + *Past* + may + *have* + *en* + *be* + *ing* + date + Sally
Sentence 9.12 Sally + *Past* + may + *have* + *en* + *be* + *ing* + *be* + *en* + date + by + John

Putting 9.11 through affix incorporation will yield Sentence 9.10a; putting 9.12 through affix incorporation will give Sentence 9.10b.

Consider now:

Sentence 9.13a Obviously, John dated Sally.
Sentence 9.13b Obviously, Sally was dated by John.
Sentence 9.14a John gave the book to Sally.
Sentence 9.14b The book was given to Sally by John.

Sentence 9.13 shows that if anything comes before the subject *NP* in the deep structure (in this case, the sentence modifier *obviously*), it comes before the surface subject as well. Sentence 9.14 shows that the agent *NP*, when moved to the end of the sentence, moves to the very end. Thus, a more exact statement of the *Passive* is as follows:

Passive (opt)

$$X - NP_1 - Aux - V + NP_2 - Y \Rightarrow X - NP_2 - Aux + be + en - V - Y - by + NP_2$$

In our examples, *obviously* is *X*, and *to Sally* is *Y*.

Returning to Sentences 9.5 and 9.6, we can see that in Sentence 9.5, the verb agrees with the singular subject *boy*, but that in Sentence 9.6, it agrees with the plural *horses*. In the deep structure, *boy* is the subject for both, but the *Passive* produces a new subject (the **surface subject**) in Sentence 9.6. Agreement occurs between the surface subject and the verb, not between the deep-structure subject and the verb. We can ensure that this will happen in our grammar if we apply affix incorporation only after most of the other transformations have been applied, thus assuring that we do not produce agreement with the wrong subject.

Another problem arises with the middle verbs (see p. 152), those transitive verbs that do not passivize:

Sentence 9.15a   John has a car.
Sentence 9.15b   *A car is had by John.
Sentence 9.16a   John weighs two hundred pounds.
Sentence 9.16b   *Two hundred pounds is weighed by John.

The deep structures for Sentences 9.15a and 9.16a both meet the structural description for *Passive*, so how do we prevent the *Passive* from applying and thus producing the ungrammatical Sentences 9.15b and 9.16b? Remember that lexical entries contain information on syntactic idiosyncrasies; specifically, the entries for *have* and *weigh* will contain the information that they do not undergo the passive transformation, in some notation such as [-*Passive*]. For a transformation to apply, then, its structural description must be met, and there must be no item in the string that is marked negatively for that transformation. If the structural description is met but some item is marked negatively, as in Sentences 9.15 and 9.16, the transformation cannot apply.
Consider now:

Sentence 9.17   John gave Sally a book.
Sentence 9.18   Sally was given a book by John.
Sentence 9.19   John gave a book to Sally.
Sentence 9.20   A book was given to Sally by John.

These sentences are synonymous and presumably come from the same deep structure. Sentences 9.17 and 9.18 are an active sentence and its passive counterpart in just the sense we have been discussing. Likewise, Sentences 9.19 and 9.20 seem to be related by the *Passive*. The only difference, then, is that the four have different transformational histories. The deep structure for all is given in Figure 9.1. All are derived by means of these transformations:

Sentence 9.17: *Affix*
Sentence 9.18: *Passive, Affix*
Sentence 9.19: *IO Switch, Affix*
Sentence 9.20: *IO Switch, Passive, Affix*

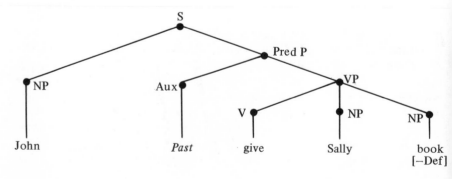

Figure 9.1

We can see that *IO Switch* has to be ordered before *Passive* to get these results; if *Passive* came first, we could derive only Sentences 9.17, 9.18, and 9.19. Sentence 9.20 could not be produced, since after *Passive* the structure would be as in Figure 9.2. This does not meet the structural index for *IO Switch* (the *V* is not followed by two *NP*s, but by a *NP* and a *PP*), and thus *IO Switch* can never apply. Similarly, *Passive* takes the *NP* immediately following the *V* and fronts it. But if *Passive* applies before *IO Switch*, there will never be a stage before *Passive* has applied when the *NP book* comes immediately after the *V*. Some transforma-

$$[-Def]$$

tions, then, must be ordered with respect to each other. There are two sets for the correct order: Incorrect ordering will result either in (1) grammatical sentences that cannot be produced (as in the present example) or (2) ungrammatical sentences that can be produced (if, for instance, we applied *Affix* before *Passive*, then we might get incorrect subject-verb agreement—see discussion of Sentences 9.5 and 9.6).

Consider next:

Sentence 9.21a John was killed.
Sentence 9.22a Sally was seen.
Sentence 9.23a The dinner was prepared.

These sentences seem to be strange passives: They have, before the affix transformation, the sequence *be + en* (*John + Past + be + en + kill, Sally + Past + be + en + see, dinner + Past + be + en + prepare*), which arises only as the

$$[+Def]$$

result of the passive transformation, but they are lacking the final agent phrase (*by + NP*). If we consider meaning, we see that they are related to active sentences with "dummy" agents—subject *NP*s that supply no information except that there is an agent. So we might suggest that their active counterparts would be

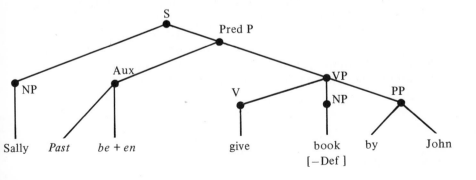

Figure 9.2

Sentence 9.21b $\begin{Bmatrix} \text{Somebody} \\ \text{Something} \end{Bmatrix}$ killed John.

Sentence 9.22b Somebody saw Sally.

Sentence 9.23b Somebody prepared the dinner.

(In Sentence 9.21b, the subject could be either a person or an object, to account for the choice of either *somebody* or *something*.) Working from this general intuition, we see that the underlying deep structures (abbreviated, that is, without structure) would be

Sentence 9.21c $\begin{Bmatrix} \text{Somebody} \\ \text{Something} \end{Bmatrix}$ + *Past* + kill + John

Sentence 9.22c Somebody + *Past* + see + Sally

Sentence 9.23c Somebody + *Past* + prepare + dinner

[+*Def*]

If we put these deep structures through the *Passive,* we get

Sentence 9.21d John + *Past* + be + en + kill + by + $\begin{Bmatrix} \text{somebody} \\ \text{something} \end{Bmatrix}$

Sentence 9.22d Sally + *Past* + be + en + see + by + somebody

Sentence 9.23d dinner + *Past* + be + en + prepare + by + somebody

[+*Def*]

Putting Sentences 9.21d, 9.22d, and 9.23d through the affix transformation will produce perfectly grammatical sentences. However, we can also delete the agent phrases to produce the Sentences 9.21a, 9.22a, and 9.23a. The transformation:

Agent Delete (opt)

$$X - be + en - Y - \text{by} + \text{some}\begin{Bmatrix} \text{body} \\ \text{thing} \end{Bmatrix} \Rightarrow X - be + en - Y$$

The transformation simply deletes the agent phrase in a passive *if* the agent is a dummy *somebody* or *something.* Notice that the only things specified in the structural index are the *be + en* and the agent phrase; this is to ensure that the *by + NP* actually is the result of the *Passive* (the *be + en* sequence, being produced only by the passive, ensures that) and not a prepositional phrase of place or time, as in *The house stands by the stream.* Since *Agent Delete* has to follow *Passive,* it must also follow *IO Switch*; although there is no evidence that it must precede *Affix,* we shall assume that it does.

CHAPTER 10

Questions

There are many ways of asking a question in English: *Is John here? Where is John? John is here?* (with rising intonation) *John is here, isn't he? John isn't here, is he?* We shall treat only the first two types, called *yes-no questions* (because they demand an answer of either *yes* or *no*) and *wh-* questions (because they begin with an interrogative pronoun or adverb such as *who, what, when, where, why,* or *how*). Consider the following sentences:

Sentence 10.1a John is here.
Sentence 10.1b Is John here?
Sentence 10.2a John will leave.
Sentence 10.2b Will John leave?
Sentence 10.3a John has gone.
Sentence 10.3b Has John gone?
Sentence 10.4a John is going.
Sentence 10.4b Is John going?
Sentence 10.5a John might have gone.
Sentence 10.5b Might John have gone?
Sentence 10.6a John has a car.
Sentence 10.6b Has John a car?
Sentence 10.6c Does John have a car?
Sentence 10.7a John went home.
Sentence 10.7b Did John go home?
Sentence 10.8a John reads books.
Sentence 10.8b Does John read books?

In each case, the "b" sentence is the question corresponding to the "a" sentence, and in each case the question can be fully answered by a simple *yes* or *no* (although it can also be answered by a fuller form). From Sentences 10.1-10.4, it appears that the yes-no question is formed by fronting the auxiliary; Sentence

Exercises are on p. 196.

10.5 shows, however, that when the auxiliary contains more than one item besides the tense, it is only the first element that is fronted. Sentences 10.7 and 10.8 indicate that when the tense is the only element in the auxiliary, a form of *do* (not present in the deep structure) appears at the front of the question. Sentences 10.1, 10.3, 10.4, and 10.6 bring up another problem: A form of *be*, whether it is part of the auxiliary, as in Sentence 10.4, or part of the verb phrase, as in Sentence 10.1, is fronted if it immediately follows the tense: Sentence 10.3 indicates that *have* is fronted if it is part of the auxiliary. If Sentence 10.6b is grammatical, then *have* functions just like *be*: It is fronted when it immediately follows the tense, whether it is part of the auxiliary or part of the verb phrase. If Sentence 10.6b is not grammatical (this is a question of dialect), then *have* as part of the verb phrase functions just like any other verb—like *go* and *read* in Sentences 10.7 and 10.8. Since Sentence 10.6b sounds a bit odd in American English (although it would be normal in some dialects of British English), we shall assume it is ungrammatical and account only for Sentence 10.6c, although it would in fact be easier to consider Sentence 10.6b fully grammatical.

The yes-no question transformation, then, has to take the tense and first element of the auxiliary and move them to the front of the string:

Q Yes-No

$NP - Tn \ (Aux_1 \ ) - X \Rightarrow Tn \ (Aux_1 \ ) - NP - X$, where $Aux_1 = M$; *be;* or *have* dominated by *Aux*

This transformation will clearly produce the correct result for Sentences 10.1-10.6. But there is a difficulty: If we make the transformation optional, like *IO Switch, Passive,* and *Agent Delete,* there is no way to tell from the deep structure whether the sentence will be a question (that is, go through the question transformation) or not. This is embarrassing, because the deep structure is supposed to represent fully the meaning of the sentence, and there is obviously a good deal of difference between a question and a statement. So we need some way of ensuring that *only* those sentences that are interpreted as questions by the semantic component actually go through the question transformation. There is a simple and elegant way of doing this: We include a *marker* in the deep structure of questions. This marker will serve two functions: It will represent for the semantic component that the deep structure underlies a question, and it will ensure that only those sentences containing that marker will go through the question transformation. (This is accomplished by making the question transformation obligatory, and allowing it to apply only to strings containing the question marker.) Thus, only those strings interpreted by the semantic component as questions will have the form of questions. The simplest marker to use is a *Wh-* element, derived through the sentence-modifier element of the PS rules. Thus, the yes-no question transformation would be:

Yes-No (oblig)

$Wh\text{-} \ - \ NP \ - \ Tn \ (Aux_1) \ - \ X \ \Rightarrow \ Tn\text{-}(Aux_1) \ - \ NP \ - \ X, \ Aux_1 \ = M; \ be; \ have$
dominated by Aux

This states that any string containing a *Wh-* marker must go through the yes-no transformation, and that the transformation fronts the tense and the first following element, if that element is either a modal, *be* (from any source), or *have* (the marker for the perfect). This accounts nicely for Sentences 10.1-10.6, although one should notice that in Sentence 10.5b, only the *first element* of the auxiliary following tense is fronted, in accordance with the structural change of the transformation.

But what about Sentences 10.7 and 10.8? According to the transformation we have so far, only the tense will be fronted in these, since there is no following form of *be, have,* or modal to be fronted with it. Thus, starting from deep structures such as 10.7c and 10.8c, the intermediate structures after the yes-no transformation will be 10.7d and 10.8d.

Sentence 10.7c $Wh\text{-} + \text{John} + Past + \text{go} + \text{home}$
Sentence 10.7d $Past + \text{John} + \text{go} + \text{home}$
Sentence 10.8c $Wh\text{-} + \text{John} + Pres + \text{read} + \text{book}$
                                                    $[+Pl]$
Sentence 10.8d $Pres + \text{John} + \text{read} + \text{book}$
                                                    $[+Pl]$

Notice that the tense of *do* in Sentences 10.7b and 10.8b is the tense that is already at the front of the strings in 10.7d and 10.8d. All we have to do, apparently, is insert a *do* immediately after the tense; then when *Affix Incorporation* applies, the tense will incorporate with the following *do* to produce the correct form. This transformation, called either **do insertion** or **do support**, is stated as follows:

Do Insert (oblig)

$$X - Tn - Y \Rightarrow X - Tn + \text{do} - Y, \text{ where } Y \neq \begin{Bmatrix} M \\ \text{have} \\ \text{be} \\ V \end{Bmatrix} + Z$$

This states that whenever a tense is followed immediately by something *other than* a modal, *have, be,* or a verb, *do* is inserted (Z is another dummy symbol). In the cases of Sentences 10.7d and 10.8d, *Tn* is followed by *N*, so *do* will be inserted immediately after the tense, and the later application of *Affix Incorporation* will combine the tense and *do* to give the correct forms.

Clearly, *Do Insertion* must follow the yes-no transformation, since the yes-no transformation provides the necessity for it. But how is the yes-no transformation ordered in relation to *Passive*? Consider:

Sentence 10.9a   John read the book.
Sentence 10.9b   Did John read the book?
Sentence 10.10a   The book was read by John.
Sentence 10.10b   Was the book read by John?
Sentence 10.11   *Did the book be read by John?

Sentence 10.10a is the passive counterpart of Sentence 10.9a; and it seems that the "b" sentences are the yes-no questions corresponding to the "a" sentences. In Sentence 10.10b, the element fronted is *Tn* + *be*. But this *be* is inserted by the passive transformation; there is no *be* in the deep structure of Sentence 10.9a or Sentence 10.10a to be fronted. Thus, the *Passive* must apply first to supply the *be*. The (abbreviated) derivation for Sentence 10.10b would thus be

Wh- + John + *Past* + read + book ⇒ (*Passive*)
$$[+Def]$$
Wh- + book + *Past* + *be* + *en* + read + by + John ⇒ (*Yes-No*)
$$[+Def]$$
Past + *be* + book + *en* + read + by + John ⇒ (*Affix*)
$$[+Def]$$
Was the book read by John?

If, on the other hand, we try to apply *Yes-No* **before** *Passive,* we get nowhere:

Wh- + John + *Past* + read + book ⇒ (*Yes-No*)
$$[+Def]$$
Past + John + read + book
$$[+Def]$$

This will not go through the *Passive* at all, since it does not meet the structural description for the *Passive,* which requires the auxiliary (in this case, *Past*) to follow the subject *NP.*

The second type of question to be discussed is the *wh-* question:

Sentence 10.12   What did John read?
Sentence 10.13   Who did John see?
Sentence 10.14   Where did John go?
Sentence 10.15   When will John go?
Sentence 10.16   How should John cook the fish?

These questions differ from yes-no questions in two ways: (1) They begin with an interrogative pronoun (*who, what*) or an interrogative adverb (*where, when, how,* respectively adverbs of place, time, manner) instead of a verbal element. (2) They require specific information as an answer rather than *yes* or *no.* Examining the sentences, we see that each begins with a question word which is followed by the tense, followed by either a modal (Sentences 10.15 and 10.16) or the *do* inserted by *Do Insert,* followed by the subject. The yes-no question ransformation already formulated will front the tense and following element, and the do-insertion transformation will insert a *do* in the correct place. All we have to do is ensure that the *wh-* word is put at the front of the sentence. This can be done quite simply:

Wh- *(oblig)*
$X - wh- - Y \Rightarrow wh- - X - Y$

This states that a *wh-* element is fronted, no matter where it occurs in the string. If we order this transformation after the *Yes-No*, we shall get the correct results. Figures 10.1-10.5 give complete derivations of Sentences 10.12-10.16, illustrating the PS source of the question words:

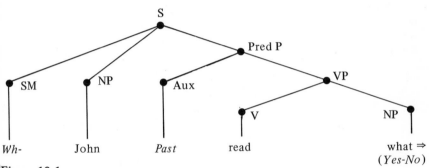

Figure 10.1

Past + John + read + what $\Rightarrow$ (*Wh-*)
What + *Past* + John + read $\Rightarrow$ (*Do Insert*)
What + *Past* + do + John + read $\Rightarrow$ (*Affix*)
What did John read?

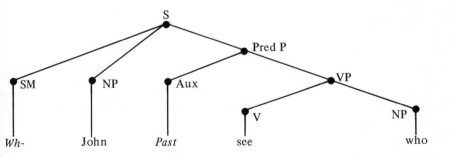

Figure 10.2

which proceeds the same as for Sentence 10.12.

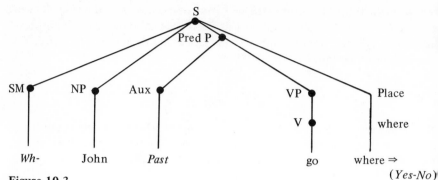

Figure 10.3

$Past$ + John + go + where ⇒ (Wh-)
Where + $Past$ + John + go ⇒ ($Do\ Insert$)
Where + $Past$ + do + John + go ⇒ ($Affix$)
Where did John go?

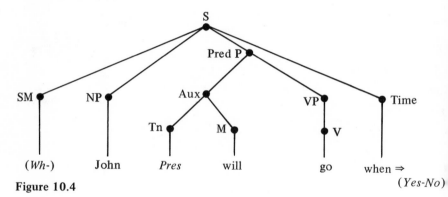

Figure 10.4

$Pres$ + will + John + go + when ⇒ (Wh-)
When + $Pres$ + will + John + go ⇒ ($Affix$)
When will John go?

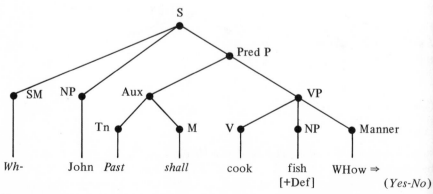

Figure 10.5

Past + shall + John + cook + fish + WHow ⇒ (*Wh-*)
                              [+*Def*]
WHow + *Past* + shall + John + cook + fish   ⇒ (*Affix*)
                              [+*Def*]
How should John cook the fish?

In Figure 10.5 we have represented *how* as *WHow,* just to show that it is a *wh-*element, and thus fronted by the *Wh-* transformation.

Now consider the following:

Sentence 10.17a Who saw John?

This begins with an interrogative pronoun, but shows no *Do Insertion,* even though there is no modal, *have,* or *be.* But if we put the presumed deep structure through the transformations we have, we get the correct result, as shown in Figure 10.6.

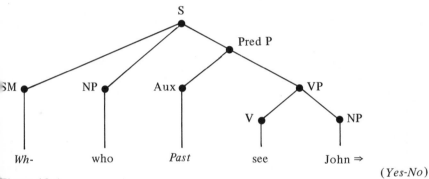

Figure 10.6

Past + who + see + John ⇒ (*Wh-*)
Who + *Past* + see + John ⇒ (*Affix*)
Who saw John?

When the wh- word functions as the subject of the sentence, the *Wh-* transformation undoes the effect of the yes-no transformation. Notice, however, that if *Do Insert* applies between *Yes-No* and *Wh-,* it will insert a *do* into this string, causing the ungrammatical

Sentence 10.17b *Who did see John?

(This is grammatical only with very heavy stress on *did*—an emphatic question, suggesting exasperation. This will be accounted for in Chapter 12.)

Questions and their answers are related in a very simple way: The answer substitutes lexical information for the *wh-* word in the question. A question beginning with *who* or *what* is thus answered by supplying a *NP,* one beginning with *when* by supplying an adverbial of time, and so on. The deep structures of questions and their answers differ only in that the answer has no initial question marker, and it has lexical information where the question has a *wh-* element (see Figures 10.7 and 10.8).

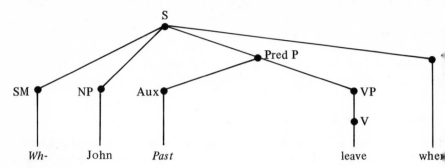

Figure 10.7

Sentence 10.18 When did John leave?

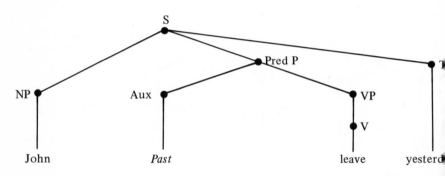

Figure 10.8

Sentence 10.19 John left yesterday.

From this relationship we can derive a useful diagnostic tool: Given a question, such as *When did John leave?*, formulate an answer such as *John left yesterday.* The function of the *wh-* word in the deep structure of the question will be exactly the same as the new word supplied by the answer. This device is especially useful in deciding which of the possible *NP* functions (subject, direct object, indirect object, and so on) a *who* or *what* fulfills:

Sentence 10.20a Who left yesterday?
Sentence 10.20b John left yesterday.
Sentence 10.21a What did John give Sally?
Sentence 10.21b John gave Sally a book.
Sentence 10.22a Who was seen by Sam?
Sentence 10.22b George was seen by Sam.

In the case of Sentence 10.20, the *who* is the DS subject; in Sentence 10.21, it is the DS direct object. In Sentence 10.22, it is the subject just before the question transformations have applied, but since Sentence 10.22b is a passive, we know that in DS the *who* is a direct object:

Sentence 10.22c *Wh-* + Sam + *Past* + see + who ⇒ (*Passive*)
     Wh- + who + *Past* + be + en + see + by + Sam ⇒ (*Yes-No*)
     Past + be + who + *en* + see + by + Sam ⇒ (*Wh-*)
     Who + *Past* + be + en + see + by + Sam ⇒ (*Affix*)
     Who was seen by Sam?

Sentences 10.21a and 10.21b raise an interesting point. Consider:

Sentence 10.23 Who did John give a book to?
Sentence 10.24 To whom did John give a book?
Sentence 10.25 *Who(m) did John give a book?

At least in our dialect, Sentence 10.25 would be ungrammatical, which suggests that an indirect object, to be questioned, must first go through the *IO Switch*. Just how this is to be stated is not clear, since the *IO Switch* is normally optional. Of course we can fix things up by stating that the *IO Switch* is obligatory if the *NP* immediately following the verb (that is, the indirect object) is a *wh-* element and optional otherwise, but that is not especially elegant.

Also we might notice that when a *wh-* element is the object of a preposition, the preposition may optionally be fronted with the *wh-* element—in Sentence 10.24 it is fronted (thus accounting for the *whom* in our dialect); in Sentence 10.23 it is not (and thus the *who*, since we get *whom* only immediately following a preposition).

Finally, we notice that in yes-no questions, the relationship mentioned above between the question and the answer holds, because in yes-no questions the constituent questioned is the sentence modifier, and these questions are answered by providing a lexical sentence modifier, such as *yes, no, certainly, probably,* and so on.

CHAPTER 11

Negatives

As with questions, there are many ways of expressing negation in English:

Sentence 11.1 Nobody saw anything.
Sentence 11.2 John saw nothing.
Sentence 11.3 John didn't see anything.
Sentence 11.4 John won't date Susan.
Sentence 11.5 Never will John date Susan.
Sentence 11.6 John has no morals.
Sentence 11.7 John doesn't have any morals.

Again we are going to limit our discussion to a restricted set of negatives: those in which *not* (or its contraction *n't*) appears, such as in Sentences 11.3, 11.4, and 11.7. Consider:

Sentence 11.8a John is a doctor.
Sentence 11.8b John is not a doctor.
Sentence 11.9a John will leave now.
Sentence 11.9b John will not leave now.
Sentence 11.10a John has gone home.
Sentence 11.10b John has not gone home.
Sentence 11.11a John has a car.
Sentence 11.11b John hasn't a car.
Sentence 11.11c John does not have a car.
Sentence 11.12a John is cooking shrimp.
Sentence 11.12b John is not cooking shrimp.
Sentence 11.13a John likes Susan.
Sentence 11.13b John does not like Susan.
Sentence 11.14a John read the book.
Sentence 11.14b John did not read the book.

Exercises are on p. 196.

The relation between the positive "a" sentences and their negative "b" counterparts is clear: The negative sentences have a *not* inserted after a modal (Sentence 11.9), after any form of *be* (Sentences 11.8, 11.12), or after the *have* that is immediately dominated by *Aux* (Sentence 11.10). If none of these elements occurs, the *not* is preceded by the proper form of *do*. Sentence 11.11 indicates that for negatives, as for questions, the "full verb" *have* (the one dominated by *VP*) functions like other full verbs rather than like the perfect marker *have* (the one dominated by *Aux*).[1] The *do* inserted in Sentences 11.13b and 11.14b will be taken care of by *Do Insertion,* so all we have to do is put the *not* in the correct place:

Neg (oblig)

$Neg - NP - Tn\ (Aux_1) - X \Rightarrow NP - Tn\ (Aux_1) + \text{not} - X, Aux_1 = M;\ be;\ have$
dominated by *Aux*

The *Neg* is a sentence modifier that serves a function similar to the sentence modifier *Wh-*: (1) It tells the semantic component that the deep structure is one for a negative, and (2) it ensures that the string goes through the negative transformation and thus has a *not* inserted in the correct place. Examples are given in Figures 11.1 and 11.2.

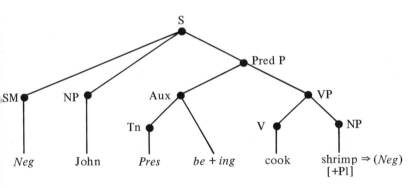

Figure 11.1

John + *Pres* + *be* + not + *ing* + cook + shrimp $\Rightarrow$ (*Affix*)
                                                    [+*Pl*]
John is not cooking shrimp.

---

[1] Like Sentence 10.6b, Sentence 11.11b is not grammatical in the American dialect, though in others, chiefly British, it may be. As with the questions, we will not account for it.

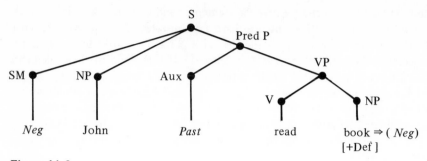

Figure 11.2

John + *Past* + not + read + book ⇒ (*Do Insert*)
　　　　[+*Def*]
John + *Past* + do + not + read + book ⇒ (*Affix*)
　　　　　　　　[+*Def*]
John did not read the book.

For statements this rule works perfectly well, but it is less satisfying for questions. Consider:

Sentence 11.15a John didn't go home.
Sentence 11.15b Didn't John go home?
Sentence 11.16a John won't leave now.
Sentence 11.16b Won't John leave now?

In negative questions, the negative *not* (or its contracted form) appears at the beginning of the sentence with the modal or a form of *do* (or the proper forms of *have* or *be*). The way we have stated the negative transformation, it must come before the yes-no transformation, since the latter transformation moves the tense to the beginning of the string and thus ensures that any string having gone through it will not meet the structural description for the negative transformation, which requires the tense to follow the subject *NP*. We have two choices: Either the yes-no transformation or the negative transformation must be altered. We can change the yes-no transformation thus:

Modified Yes-No

$Wh\text{-} - NP - Tn \ (Aux_1) \ (\text{not}) - X \Rightarrow Tn \ (Aux_1) \ (\text{not}) - NP - X$

This is to be interpreted that the yes-no transformation moves the tense to the front in any case; if either Aux_1 or *not* (or both) follows the tense, it (or both) is to be fronted also. This solution works, but it is messy: It involves complicating the question transformation. If we can change the negative transformation so that we get the correct results without complicating either it or the question transformation, we shall have a simpler, and thus preferable, solution. As it turns out, this is possible—in fact, a restatement of the negative transformation simplifies it. The only thing we have to notice is that in both negative statements and negative questions the *not* occurs in the same place—following the tense and Aux_1, no matter where these elements occur:

Neg (oblig)

$Neg - X - Tn \ (Aux_1) - Y \Rightarrow X - Tn \ (Aux_1) + \text{not} - Y; \ Aux_1 = M; \ be; \ have$
dominated by *Aux*

Neg can now be ordered after both the yes-no and *Wh-* question transformations. In the case of yes-no questions, X will be null (there will be nothing preceding the tense); in *wh-* questions, X will be the *wh-* word; in statements, X will be the subject *NP*. Examples are given in Figures 11.3 and 11.4.

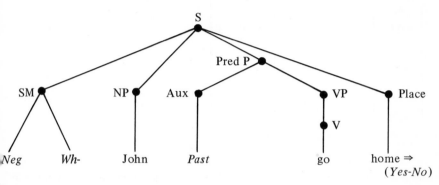

Figure 11.3

Neg + *Past* + John + go + home ⇒ (*Neg*)
Past + not + John + go + home ⇒ (*Do Insert*)
Past + do + not + John + go + home ⇒ (*Affix*)
Did not John go home?

Sentence 11.17 Who doesn't John like?

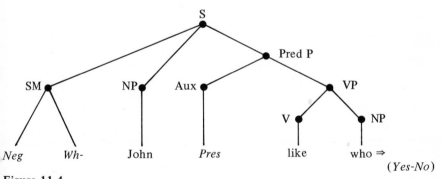

Figure 11.4

Neg + *Pres* + John + like + who ⇒ (*Wh-*)
Neg + who + *Pres* + John + like ⇒ (*Neg*)
Who + *Pres* + not + John + like ⇒ (*Do Insert*)
Who + *Pres* + do + not + John + like ⇒ (*Affix*)
Who does not John like?

Notice that after the affix transformation has applied, we have the uncontracted forms *did not* and *does not*. We can easily set up an optional contraction transformation to take care of these, ordered after the affix transformation:

Contraction (opt)

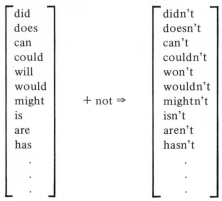

The square brackets are a device to indicate that whichever line is chosen on the left must also be chosen on the right. If the third line (*can*) is chosen in the left bracket, then the third line (*can't*) must be chosen on the right. The three dots at the bottom indicate that the list is incomplete.

CHAPTER 12

Emphatics

It is possible to emphasize any word in a sentence by putting extra-heavy stress on it:

Sentence 12.1 John is here.
Sentence 12.2 John is hére.
Sentence 12.3 John ís here.

The first sentence might be a reply to *Who is here?* The second might be a reply to *Where is John?* But the third sentence is somewhat different—in stressing *is,* it suggests that the entire sentence is being emphasized, as though it had already been stated that John is here but that the listener keeps assuming that it is not true that John is here. Thus, the sentence emphasis suggests exasperation. The distinction between the different emphatics parallels the distinction between different negations: It is possible to negate or emphasize a particular element in a sentence, or to emphasize or negate an entire sentence. As with the negatives, we will be interested only in whole-sentence emphasis.

Consider:

Sentence 12.4a John is here.
Sentence 12.4b John ís here.
Sentence 12.5a John will go home.
Sentence 12.5b John wíll go home.
Sentence 12.6a John has gone home.
Sentence 12.6b John hás gone home.
Sentence 12.7a John drove home.
Sentence 12.7b John díd drive home.
Sentence 12.7c John dróve home.
Sentence 12.8a John loves Lucy.
Sentence 12.8b John dóes love Lucy.

Exercises are on p. 196.

(There is some question as to whether Sentence 12.7c is the sentence emphatic counterpart of Sentence 12.7a—it more likely is element emphasis, stressing the fact that John *drove* instead of walking, running, flying, and so on. Sentence 12.7b seems more clearly to emphasize the entire sentence.) From an examination of these sentences, it appears that the stressed element is either a form of *be, have, do,* or a modal, and the similarity between this set and the one fronted in questions and immediately followed by *not* in negatives should make us suspect that we are dealing with the same set. As with negatives, apparently all we have to do is insert a marker after Tn (Aux_1). If there is an element of Aux_1, then it will receive the stress, as in Sentences 12.4b, 12.5b, and 12.6b; if there is not, the marker will trigger *Do Insert* (since the Tn will be followed by the emphatic marker rather than a verbal element) and the form of *do* will be stressed. And, as with the question and negative transformations, we shall add to the deep structure a sentence modifier that (1) tells the semantic component that the sentence is emphatic, and (2) ensures that it goes through the emphatic transformation.

Emphatic (oblig)

$Emph - X - Tn\ (Aux_1) - Y \Rightarrow X - Tn\ (Aux_1) + Emph - Y;\ Aux_1 = be;\ M;$
have dominated by Aux

After this transformation has applied, the strings underlying the "b" sentences will be

Sentence 12.4c John + *Pres* + be + *Emph* + here
Sentence 12.5c John + *Pres* + will + *Emph* + go + home
Sentence 12.6c John + *Pres* + *have* + *Emph* + *en* + go + home
Sentence 12.7d John + *Past* + *Emph* + drive + home
Sentence 12.8c John + *Pres* + *Emph* + love + Lucy

In Sentences 12.7d and 12.8c, *Do Insert* will apply to give

Sentence 12.7e John + *Past* + *do* + *Emph* + drive + home
Sentence 12.8d John + *Pres* + *do* + *Emph* + love + Lucy

What is now needed is a rule to convert this *Emph* into strong stress on the preceding word. This is most likely a phonological rule, part of the phonological component, which (among other things) assigns the proper stress to strings. In any case, we can show that it must come after the contraction rule:

Sentence 12.9a   John will nót go home.
Sentence 12.9b   John wón't go home.
Sentence 12.10a John did nót eat the steak.
Sentence 12.10b John dídn't eat the steak.

The "a" sentences indicate that if *not* is present, it is heavily stressed; but that if *not* has been contracted, then the word it contracts with is stressed. So we must know whether the contraction transformation has applied before we know where to put the stress.

To see how *Emph* and *Neg* are ordered, we try both ways. Presumably, Sentence 12.11b is derived from Sentence 12.11a:

Sentence 12.11a *Emph* + *Neg* + John + *Pres* + will + go + home
Sentence 12.11b John will nót go home.

If we first apply *Neg* and then *Emph* to Sentence 12.11a, we get

Emph + *Neg* + John + *Pres* + will + go + home ⇒ (*Neg*)
Emph + John + *Pres* + will + not + go + home ⇒ (*Emph*)
John + *Pres* + will + *Emph* + not + go + home

After *Affix* and stress placement, this will yield

*John wíll not go home.

This sentence is grammatical, but it stresses the element *will,* rather than the whole sentence, and is therefore an example of element emphasis. However, if we apply *Emph* first, we get

Emph + *Neg* + John + *Pres* + will + go + home ⇒ (*Emph*)
Neg + John + *Pres* + will + *Emph* + go + home ⇒ (*Neg*)
John + *Pres* + will + not + *Emph* + go + home

And after *Affix* and stress placement, this will become

John will nót go home.

So *Emph* must be ordered *before Neg.* The same argument used to show that *Neg* follows the question transformations can also be used to show that *Emph* follows them.

Since it is not clear whether the emphatic stress placement transformation is part of the phonological component, we shall not state it formally. In any case, its effect is clear: It deletes the *Emph* marker and places heavy stress on the preceding word.

So far we have 13 transformations that apply to strings containing no internal occurrence of the *S* symbol. These transformations, called **single-base** or **singulary** transformations, in the order we have established, are as follows:

1. *Indirect-Object Switch (opt)*
2. *Passive (opt)*
3. *Agent Delete (opt)*
4. *Yes-No Question (oblig)*
5. *Wh- Question (oblig)*
6. *Emphatic (oblig)*
7. *Negative (oblig)*
8. *Do Insertion (oblig)*
9. *Affix Incorporation (oblig)*
10. *Determiner Segment (oblig)*
11. *Plural Segment (oblig)*
12. *Contraction (opt)*
13. *Emphatic Stress Placement (oblig)*

Exercises (Chapters 7–12)

1. Provide complete derivations for the following sentences. You should show the deep-structure tree for each, although you need not give all the selectional or inherent features for the lexical items, and you should show how each transformation changes the string to which it applies.

   a. John gave Jane a book.
   b. John gave a book to Jane.
   c. Jane was given a book by John.
   d. A book was given to Jane by John.
   e. Jane was given a book.
   f. A car was provided for the ambassador.
   g. The accident might have been seen by the spectators.
   h. Is John a doctor?
   i. Did John give a book to Jane?
   j. Was Jane given a book?
   k. Did John sign the register?
   l. Should Sally have left?
   m. Who kissed Sally?
   n. Who did Sally kiss?
   o. When did John give Sally the book?
   p. How did John take the news?
   q. Where did the accident occur?
   r. Who was fired?
   s. John did not leave.
   t. Sally should not have bought the corsage for John.
   u. Hasn't John finished dinner yet?
   v. Where wasn't John wanted?
   w. Sam has been studying hard.
   x. John will not date Sally.
   y. Who did see the accident?
   z. Why wasn't the prize given to John?

2. As can be seen from Sentence 1z, *Wh-* questions may begin with the *wh-* element *why*, which has not been accounted for in the grammar. How would you account for it?

3.* One kind of question we have not treated is the tag question:

   a. John is here, isn't he?
   b. John isn't here, is he?
   c. John likes steak, doesn't he?
   d. John won't go, will he?

*Exercises preceded by asterisks are more advanced and/or more theoretical than the others.

These questions contain a statement followed by a tag which is negative if the statement is positive and positive if the statement is negative. The tag further consists of a pronoun which refers back to the subject of the statement, and a form of *have, be, do,* or a modal. Can you formulate a transformation that will generate these tag questions? The pronoun might be tricky, but a glance ahead to Chapter 15 should help.

4.* We have not treated imperative sentences at all. Below are some examples:

    a. You go home!
    b. You be good!
    c. Go home!
    d. Be good!
    e. Do not go home!
    f. Do not be good!

The subject does not necessarily appear; if it does, it is *you.* There does not seem to be agreement between the subject and the verb, as Sentence 4b illustrates, because if there were agreement, the verb would be *are.* In negative imperatives the subject does not appear (cf. **You do not go home!*), but *do* does. Can you account for these imperatives?

5.* Actually, the account of imperatives given in Exercise 4 is oversimplified. Consider:

    a. You will go home!
    b. You will not go home!
    c. *Will go home!
    d. *Will not go home!

These seem to indicate that when the subject *you* is present, *will* may optionally occur in positive imperatives, and *will* is obligatory in negative imperatives; *will* cannot occur without *you,* as Sentences 5c and 5d indicate. Assuming that Sentences 5a and 5b are imperatives, as well as the sentences given under Exercise 4, how could you derive all of them?

CHAPTER 13

Restrictive Relative Clauses

We now turn to transformations that apply to strings containing within them a second (or third, and so on) occurrence of *S*. From the phrase-structure rules it is apparent that an internal *S* can only be dominated by *NP* (PS rule 3.5 is reproduced here):

PS 3.5 $NP \rightarrow \begin{Bmatrix} NP + S \\ N\ (S) \end{Bmatrix}$

When *NP* is expanded as *NP + S*, we may get a restrictive relative clause; when expanded as *N + S*, we have a noun phrase complement. When a sentence contains within itself another *S* dominated by a *NP*, the second sentence (often represented S_2) is called an **embedded sentence**. The top *S*, usually labeled S_1, is called the **matrix sentence**.

In English there are two kinds of relative clauses, restrictive and nonrestrictive. **Restrictive relative clauses** restrict the reference of the *NP* they follow; **nonrestrictive relative clauses** add more information. Consider

Sentence 13.1a Professors who like poetry are underpaid.
Sentence 13.1b Professors, who like poetry, are underpaid.

In Sentence 13.1a, a statement is being made only about that subclass of professors who like poetry—nothing is asserted about those professors (and one suspects there may be one or two lurking about) who do not like poetry. Sentence 13.1b, however, makes a different claim—it asserts that *all* professors are underpaid *and* that *all* professors like poetry.

In addition to this semantic difference between *R Rels* and *NR Rels* (the standard abbreviations for restrictive and nonrestrictive relative clauses), there

Exercises are on p. 224.

are syntactic differences. The most obvious is that *NR Rels* have pauses before and after them, pauses that are indicated in writing by the commas around them. Only a *NR Rel* can modify a proper noun (perhaps because a proper noun is already restricted in its reference to one specific entity, and so cannot be further restricted, which is the function of the *R Rel*):

Sentence 13.2a John, who likes poetry, is underpaid.
Sentence 13.2b *John who likes poetry is underpaid.

Finally, a *NR Rel* can only have the relative pronouns *who* (for humans) or *which* (for nonhumans), whereas *R Rels* allow *who* for humans, *which* for nonhumans, and *that* for either.

Sentence 13.3a John, who likes poetry, is underpaid.
Sentence 13.3b Paris, which is in France, is congested.
Sentence 13.3c *John, that likes poetry, is underpaid.
Sentence 13.3d *Paris, that is in France, is congested.
Sentence 13.4a Professors who like poetry are underpaid.
Sentence 13.4b Cities which are in France are congested.
Sentence 13.4c Professors that like poetry are underpaid.
Sentence 13.4d Cities that are in France are congested.

In this chapter we shall study only *R Rels; NR Rels* are treated in Chapter 16.

If we look at a *R Rel,* we see that it consists of two parts: a head noun phrase, and the restrictive clause itself:

Sentence 13.5 The boy who broke the window ran away.
Sentence 13.6 The window that the boy broke was large.

In Sentence 13.5, *The boy* is the head *NP*; in Sentence 13.6, *The window* is the head *NP*; *who broke the window* and *that the boy broke* are the restrictive clauses. Each relative clause begins with a relative pronoun (*who, which,* or *that*) that refers back to the head noun phrase. So, in Sentence 13.5 we know that the boy broke the window, although the sentence does not in fact say that explicitly, and in Sentence 13.6 we know that the boy broke the window, although again that is not explicitly stated. In both cases, the *NP* within the relative clause that is the same as the head *NP* has been replaced by a relative pronoun, which is then moved to the front of the relative clause. We account for the basic structure of the relative clause—a head *NP* followed by a sentence—by deriving it from the PS rule, $NP \rightarrow NP + S$. The particular appearance of the relative clause is produced by a number of transformations. Figures 13.1 and 13.2 are the deep structures for Sentences 13.5 and 13.6, respectively.

The head *NP* is identical to some *NP* within the embedded *S*; the *NP* in the embedded *S* may fulfill any function—subject (Sentence 13.5), direct object (Sentence 13.6), indirect object, or object of a preposition. Wherever the *NP* occurs, it is replaced by a relative pronoun (*who* if the *NP* is [+*human*] ; *which* if it is [-*human*] , and *that* in either case), and the pronoun is moved to the front of the embedded *S*. To state this in the most general way:

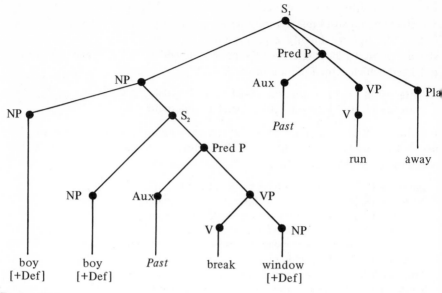

Figure 13.1

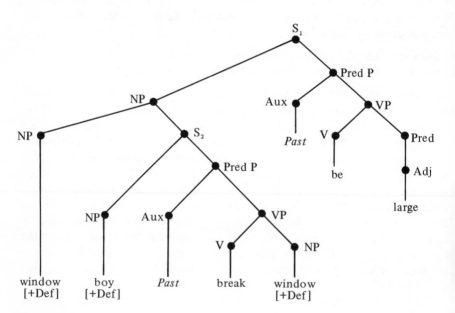

Figure 13.2

Rel Clause (oblig)

$$X - NP_1 - R + NP_2 + Q - Y \Rightarrow X - NP_1 - \begin{Bmatrix} who \\ which \\ that \end{Bmatrix} + R + Q - Y_1, \text{ where } R +$$

$NP_2 + Q$ *is a S* and $NP_1 = NP_2$

This transformation states just exactly what we have said: If a *NP* (which can occur anyplace in its own sentence) is followed by an embedded *S* in which a *NP* identical to it occurs someplace, then the *NP* in the embedded *S* is replaced by a relative pronoun and moved to the front of the embedded *S*, so that it immediately follows the *NP* in the matrix sentence. After the relative clause transformation has applied, Sentences 13.5 and 13.6 will have the structures shown in Figures 13.3 and 13.4, respectively. In Figure 13.3, the *NP* in the embedded *S* that is relativized is already at the front of its sentence, so it does not have to be moved; in Figure 13.4, the relativized *NP* is originally the direct object, so it must be moved to the front of the embedded *S*. If we put the structures in Figures 13.3 and 13.4 through the affix transformation, we shall get Sentences 13.5 and 13.6, respectively.

The following sentences illustrate that the head *NP* can fulfill any function in the matrix sentence—just as the *NP* in the embedded *S* can fulfill any function.

Sentence 13.7   I saw the boy who broke the window.
Sentence 13.8   I gave the book to the boy who broke the window.
Sentence 13.9   I was seen by the boy who broke the window.
Sentence 13.10 I saw the window that the boy broke.
Sentence 13.11 I saw the boy that the girl gave the book to.
Sentence 13.12 I saw the boy that the window was broken by.

In Sentence 13.7, the matrix *NP* is the direct object, in Sentence 13.8 it is the indirect object (and could have come right after the verb), in Sentence 13.9 it is the object of a preposition (although, of course, in deep structure it is the subject). In Sentence 13.7 the *NP* in the embedded *S* is the subject, in Sentence 13.10 it is the direct object, in Sentence 13.11 it is the indirect object, and in Sentence 13.12 it is the object of a preposition (although it is again the subject in deep structure). In the section on *Wh-* questions, we noticed that when the *wh-* word was preceded by a preposition, the preposition could be fronted with the *wh-* word. The same is true with *R Rels*—although if the preposition is fronted, *that* cannot be chosen as the relative pronoun:

Sentence 13.13a I saw the boy to whom the girl gave the book.
Sentence 13.13b *I saw the boy to that the girl gave the book.
Sentence 13.14a I saw the boy by whom the window was broken.
Sentence 13.14b *I saw the boy by that the window was broken.

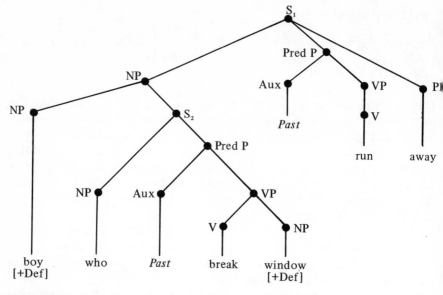

Figure 13.3

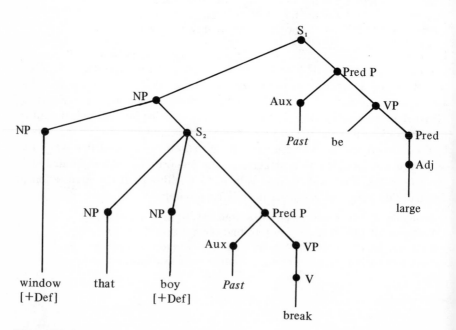

Figure 13.4

Sentences 13.13 and 13.14 indicate that the embedded S can undergo transformations that do not apply to the matrix (*IO Switch* in Sentence 13.13, *Passive* in Sentence 13.14). Similarly, Sentences 13.8 and 13.9 show that the matrix can undergo transformations that do not apply to the embedded S (*IO Switch* in Sentence 13.8, *Passive* in Sentence 13.9). Other combinations are obviously possible:

Sentence 13.15 I didn't see the boy that the window was broken by.
Sentence 13.16 Did you see the boy who won't eat fish?
Sentence 13.17 Was the boy who won't eat fish apprehended by the police?

In Sentence 13.15, the embedded S has gone through *Passive* and the matrix through *Negative*; in Sentence 13.16, the embedded S has undergone *Negative* and the matrix *Yes-No question*; in Sentence 13.17 the matrix is a passive question, while the embedded S is negative. This suggests (see pp. 228-230 for further discussion and examples) the existence of a **transformational cycle** in which all the transformational rules, in their proper order, apply first to the most deeply embedded S, then all the rules apply to the next higher S, and so on, until the top S is reached. Thus, it is perfectly possible that in one cycle the negative will apply, but in the next cycle it will not. For convenience of reference, each time the transformational rules are applied it is called a **cycle**; to indicate what sentence the transformation rules are being applied to, each S in a deep-structure tree is numbered and the number of the S under consideration precedes the cycle. Thus, in the schematic diagram in Figure 13.5 (where triangles indicate that we are not interested in the internal structure of a constituent), all the transformational rules apply to S_2 on the S_2 cycle. There are thus as many complete runs through the transformational rules as there are S symbols, although of course not all the rules apply on each cycle, and in fact none may. Notice that the way we have stated it so far, the affix transformation would apply on the S_2 cycle, the S_3 cycle, and the S_1 cycle. Since it does the same thing on each cycle, this seems a bit wasteful, so we allow the affix (and contraction) transformation to apply only on the last cycle. It is then called a **final-cycle** (or **last-cyclic**) **rule**. (Actually, better reasons for doing this will be presented in Chapter 14.)

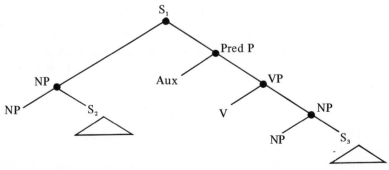

Figure 13.5

To return to our *R Rels,* consider:

Sentence 13.18a I saw the window that the boy broke.
Sentence 13.18b I saw the window the boy broke.
Sentence 13.19a I saw the boy that the window was broken by.
Sentence 13.19b I saw the boy the window was broken by.
Sentence 13.20a I saw the boy that the girl gave the book to.
Sentence 13.20b I saw the boy the girl gave the book to.

In each case, the "a" sentence represents the basic relative clause, while the "b" sentence, which means exactly the same thing and is equally grammatical, shows deletion of the relative pronoun. It is not always possible to delete the relative pronoun:

Sentence 13.21a I saw the boy who broke the window.
Sentence 13.21b *I saw the boy broke the window.
Sentence 13.22a I saw the girl who gave a book to the boy.
Sentence 13.22b *I saw the girl gave a book to the boy.

The difference between Sentences 13.21b and 13.22b, and Sentences 13.18b, 13.19b, and 13.20b can be stated in two ways. First, in Sentences 13.21b and 13.22b, the relative pronoun represents the subject of the embedded S; in Sentences 13.18b, 13.19b, and 13.20b, it performs some other function. Another way of saying this (remembering that the relative clause transformation fronts the relative pronoun, no matter where it was originally located) is that in Sentences 13.18a, 13.19a, and 13.20a the relative pronoun follows the head *NP and* precedes another *NP* in the embedded *S,* whereas in Sentences 13.21a and 13.22a the relative pronoun follows the head *NP* but *does not* immediately precede another *NP* in the embedded *S.* Thus, if the relative pronoun *immediately precedes* a *NP* in the embedded sentence, it can be deleted.

Rel Clause 2 (opt)

$$X - NP_1 - \begin{Bmatrix} who \\ which \\ that \end{Bmatrix} + NP_2 + R - Z \Rightarrow X - NP_1 - NP_2 + R - Z, \text{ where}$$

$$\begin{Bmatrix} who \\ which \\ that \end{Bmatrix} + NP_2 + R \text{ is a } S$$

Notice that this transformation is optional: Sentences 13.18a and 13.18b, 13.19a and 13.19b, 13.20a and 13.20b are equally grammatical. Obviously, this transformation must follow the relative clause transformation, since the structural index contains relative pronouns, which are introduced only by the relative clause transformation.

Now consider:

Sentence 13.23a The girl who was sitting on the grass was pretty.
Sentence 13.23b The girl sitting on the grass was pretty.
Sentence 13.24a The window that was broken by John was expensive.

Sentence 13.24b The window broken by John was expensive.
Sentence 13.25a The horse that was raced past the grandstand won the prize.
Sentence 13.25b The horse raced past the grandstand won the prize.

In each case, the "b" sentence means the same thing as the "a" sentence, and differs only in lacking the relative pronoun and an inflected form of *be*. The *be* can be from any source—the examples above show the *be* that is part of the progressive marker (Sentence 13.23) and the *be* introduced by the passive (Sentences 13.24, 13.25). We shall discuss the *be* introduced in the *VP* below. Our transformation, then, must optionally delete a relative pronoun, a tense, and *be*:

Rel Clause 3 (opt)

$$X - \left\{ \begin{array}{l} \text{who} \\ \text{which} \\ \text{that} \end{array} \right\} + Tn + \text{be} + R - Y \Rightarrow X - R - Y, \text{ where} \left\{ \begin{array}{l} \text{who} \\ \text{which} \\ \text{that} \end{array} \right\} + Tn + \text{be} + R$$

is a embedded *S*

Notice that we have to specify that the $\left\{ \begin{array}{l} \text{who} \\ \text{which} \\ \text{that} \end{array} \right\}$ + *Tn* + *be* occurs in a relative clause to block the possibility of deleting *who is* in *Who is here?*

Consider next:

Sentence 13.26a The girl who is pretty left town.
Sentence 13.26b *The girl pretty left town.
Sentence 13.26c The pretty girl left town.
Sentence 13.27a The dog which is ferocious bit John.
Sentence 13.27b *The dog ferocious bit John.
Sentence 13.27c The ferocious dog bit John.
Sentence 13.28a The boy who is intelligent won the prize.
Sentence 13.28b *The boy intelligent won the prize.
Sentence 13.28c The intelligent boy won the prize.

In each of these cases, we have a form of *be* dominated by *VP* (that is, introduced by the PS rule *VP → be + Pred*). In each case, also, the "a" sentence meets the structural description for *Rel Clause 3*. When the transformation is applied, however, the ungrammatical "b" strings result. What is needed is another transformation that moves an adjective immediately before the head noun:

Adj Fronting (oblig)

$$X - N - Adj - Y \Rightarrow X - Adj + N - Y$$

Applied to the results of *Rel Clause 3,* this will produce the grammatical "c" strings above; the transformation is obligatory because if its structural description is met but it does not apply, the result is ungrammatical (as the "b" strings above show).

If you glance back at the PS rules, you will notice that there is no provision in them for attributive adjectives (adjectives immediately preceding nouns, as *the tall boy, the vicious dog, the deciduous tree*) but only for predicate adjectives—those dominated by *VP*: attributive adjectives are derived from DS predicate adjectives. This accounts for the synonymy of the following phrases:

Sentence 13.29a   The girl who is tall
Sentence 13.29b   The tall girl
Sentence 13.30a   The tree which is deciduous
Sentence 13.30b   The deciduous tree

Unfortunately, things are not as clear-cut as this presentation has made them seem. There are some adjectives that can be only predicates, and some that are only attributive:

Sentence 13.31a   The ship is afire.
Sentence 13.31b   *The afire ship
Sentence 13.32a   *The reason is main
Sentence 13.32b   The main reason

In Sentence 13.31, *afire* is an adjective that can function only predicatively. We can block the derivation from Sentence 13.31a to Sentence 13.31b by including among the syntactic idiosyncrasies of *afire* (that is, in its lexical entry) the fact that it cannot undergo the *Rel Clause 3* transformation. In Sentence 13.31, *main* is an adjective that can be used only attributively. Since the reduction of relative clauses to attributive adjectives is normally optional, this presents a rather sticky situation. Several solutions are possible. These attributive adjectives could have represented among their syntactic idiosyncrasies that they must go through *Rel Clause 3* and *Adj Fronting* (that is, that the transformations are obligatory for them). Alternatively, we might build into the PS rules a small class of prenominal adjective modifiers. It is not clear which choice is better.

There are several other problems. Consider:

Sentence 13.33a   The boy who is here is unhappy.
Sentence 13.33b   The boy here is unhappy.
Sentence 13.33c   *The here boy is unhappy.
Sentence 13.34a   The boy who is a doctor is unhappy.
Sentence 13.34b   *The boy a doctor is unhappy.
Sentence 13.34c   *The a doctor boy is unhappy.

Remember that the PS rules expand *Pred* as either an adjective, an adverbial of place, or a noun phrase. We have seen that adjectives in reduced relative clauses are fronted. Sentence 13.33c suggests that adverbials are not fronted. But Sentences 13.34b and 13.34c suggest that predicate nominals cause trouble no matter what we do: Reducing the relative clause by *Rel Clause 3* leads to the ungrammatical Sentence 13.34b; fronting the *NP* after reduction (which helped with adjectives) leads to the ungrammatical Sentence 13.34c. Apparently, we have to ensure that relative clauses containing predicate nominals are not reduced. We can do this by adding restrictions to the *Rel Clause 3* transformation:

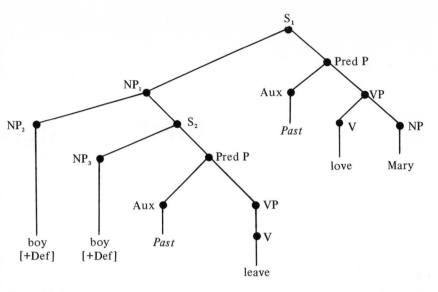

Figure 13.6

Rel Clause 3 (opt)

$$X - \begin{Bmatrix} \text{who} \\ \text{which} \\ \text{that} \end{Bmatrix} + Tn + \text{be} + R - Y \Rightarrow X - R - Y; \begin{Bmatrix} \text{who} \\ \text{which} \\ \text{that} \end{Bmatrix} + Tn + \text{be} + R \text{ is}$$

a embedded *S*, $R \neq NP$

By adding the restriction that R cannot be only an NP, we have blocked the transformation from applying to predicate nominals.

An important point about ordering: Consider Figure 13.6. On the S_2 cycle, we apply no transformations: The structural description for none of the singulary transformations is met, and the relative clause transformation requires that we look outside of S_2 to apply it—we have to know that a NP precedes S_2 that is the same as a NP within S_2. So the relative clause transformations apply only on the S_1 cycle, and they are ordered before the singulary transformations. After the various relative clause transformations, NP_1 will function, for the purposes of further singulary transformations, just like any other NP even though it dominates more than the others (has a richer internal structure). Thus, NP_1 can be moved by the *Passive*, and so on.

CHAPTER 14

Complementation

The PS rules introduce an embedded sentence in two different configurations: $NP \rightarrow NP + S$ and $NP \rightarrow N + S$. We have already seen that the first configuration leads to restrictive relative clauses. The second, which underlies the noun phrase complement, may lead to surface structures that appear very similar to *R Rels*:

Sentence 14.1 The argument that John presented is false.

Sentence 14.2 The argument that Columbus discovered America is false.

The first is a *R Rel*: *that* is a relative pronoun (and can be replaced by *which*) standing for the deep-structure object of the embedded *S*, *the argument*. The second is slightly different: *that* cannot be replaced by *which*, and represents no DS constituent of the embedded *S*, which still has its subject, verb, and object. The *that* in the second sentence is a **complementizer**, introduced by a transformation.

Now consider:

Sentence 14.3 That Columbus discovered America is false.

Sentence 14.4 It is false that Columbus discovered America.

Sentence 14.3 seems very similar to Sentence 14.2 except that it lacks the head *N argument*. Sentence 14.4 means the same thing as Sentence 14.3, so we would like to derive it from the same DS. We thus have to account for three things: (1) that a sentence can be embedded directly after a noun; (2) that the embedded sentence can occur with no noun preceding it (as in Sentence 14.3); and (3) that it is possible to move the embedded *S* to the end of the matrix *S*, as long as the pronoun *it* is left behind to mark its original DS position. The first is accounted for by the PS rule $NP \rightarrow N + S$: *argument* is *N*, and *Columbus discovered America* is *S*. The second and third are a little more difficult: the *S* seems to have no noun preceding it. But consider:

Sentence 14.2a The argument is false that Columbus discovered America.

Exercises are on p. 224.

Sentence 14.2a shows the same operation as Sentence 14.4—the embedded S is moved to the end of the matrix S, leaving the head N behind. If we assume that Sentences 14.3 and 14.4 are related in the same way as Sentences 14.2 and 14.2a, then in Sentence 14.3 there was a head noun *it* in the DS which has been subsequently deleted. When the embedded S is moved to the end of the matrix as in Sentence 14.4, the head noun *it* is left behind, exactly as in Sentence 14.2a. Thus, the deep structures for Sentences 14.2 and 14.3-14.4 will be as shown in Figures 14.1 and 14.2. The only DS difference between the two is that Figure 14.1 has a lexical head noun *argument* while Figure 14.2 has the pronoun *it*.

We now need two transformations: one to move the embedded S to the end of the matrix S, and one to delete *it* in case the embedded S is not so moved. The first is called **extraposition**:

Extraposition
$X - N + S - Y \Rightarrow X - N + Y + S$, where $N + S$ is a NP

Since both Sentences 14.2 and 14.2a, and Sentences 14.3 and 14.4 are grammatical, this transformation must be optional. Notice that the condition on the transformation prevents it from applying to the structures underlying R *Rels*, since in them the N preceding the S is immediately dominated by a NP that does not dominate the S. The difference in structures is shown in Figure 14.3. Extraposition will apply to Figure 14.1 to give the structure underlying Sentence 14.2a, and will apply to Figure 14.2 to give the structure underlying Sentence 14.4. Now we need a transformation to delete the *it* in Figure 14.2 in case extraposition has not applied, thus turning Figure 14.2 into the structure underlying Sentence 14.3. This is **it deletion**:

It Deletion
$X - it + S - Y \Rightarrow X - S - Y$, where it $+ S$ is a NP

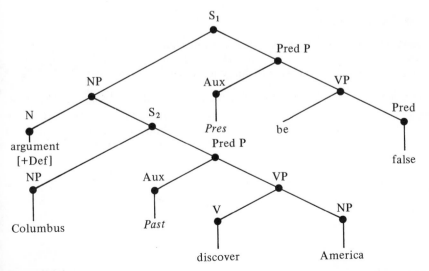

Figure 14.1

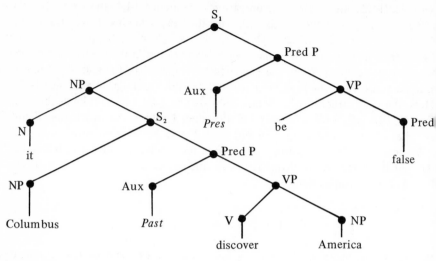

Figure 14.2

We have already seen that extraposition must be optional. In that case, *It Deletion* must be obligatory and follow *Extraposition*—that is, if an embedded *S* following an *it* is not extraposed (if the embedded *S* still follows *it*), then the *it* must be deleted.

Starting from the deep structures of Figures 14.1 and 14.2, we can now derive Sentences 14.2, 14.2a, 14.3, and 14.4. Putting Figure 14.1 through *Affix Incorporation* will give Sentence 14.2; putting it through *Extraposition* and *Affix Incorporation* will give Sentence 14.2a; putting Figure 14.2 through *It Deletion* and *Affix Incorporation* gives Sentence 14.3; and putting Figure 14.2 through *Extraposition* and *Affix Incorporation* gives Sentence 14.4.

We still have not specified the transformation that introduces *that* before the embedded *S*. Before we do so, consider:

Sentence 14.5 That John dates Mary bothers Martha.
Sentence 14.6 John's dating Mary bothers Martha.
Sentence 14.7 For John to date Mary bothers Martha.

These sentences seem to be synonymous, and since they all share lexical items, we would like to account for this by deriving all of them from one DS. Presumably the DS underlying Sentences 14.5-14.7 is as shown in Figure 14.4. The kind

Figure 14.3

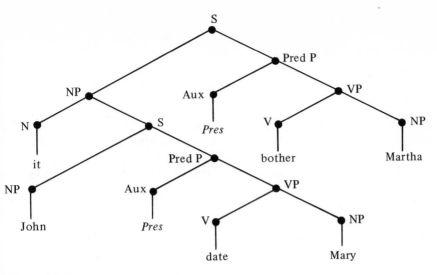

Figure 14.4

of complementizer exemplified in Sentence 14.5 is called the **clausal comple-mentizer**: It merely inserts *that* before the embedded *S*. In Sentence 14.6, we have the **gerundive complementizer**: It adds a possessive marker to the subject *NP* of the embedded *S*, and replaces the tense by the present participial marker *-ing*. The **infinitive complementizer**, in Sentence 14.7, adds *for* before the sub-ject *NP* of the embedded *S*, and replaces the tense with *to*.

The restrictions on these complementizers are a little more complicated than may appear at first:

Sentence 14.8a   That John will date Mary bothers Martha.
Sentence 14.8b   That John is dating Mary bothers Martha.
Sentence 14.8c   That John has dated Mary bothers Martha.
Sentence 14.9a   *John's willing date Mary bothers Martha.
Sentence 14.9b   *John's being dating Mary bothers Martha.
Sentence 14.9c   John's having dated Mary bothers Martha.
Sentence 14.10a *For John to will date Mary bothers Martha.
Sentence 14.10b For John to be dating Mary bothers Martha.
Sentence 14.10c For John to have dated Mary bothers Martha.

Sentences 14.8a-14.8c show that the clausal complementizer can apply no mat-ter what occurs in the auxiliary of the embedded *S*. Sentences 14.9a-14.9c indicate that the gerundive complementizer cannot apply if the auxiliary of the embedded *S* contains either a modal or the marker for the progressive. Sentences 14.7a-14.7c suggest that the infinitive complementizer cannot apply if the auxil-iary of the embedded *S* contains a modal. The three complementizer transforma-tions, with the restrictions, are as follows:

Clausal Comp

$X - \text{it} - NP + Pred\ P - Y \Rightarrow X - \text{it} - \text{that} + NP + Pred\ P - Y$

Gerundive Comp

X - it - NP - Tn (have + en) - $Y \Rightarrow X$ - it - NP + $Poss$ - ing (have + en) − Y, where $Y \neq be + ing + Z$

Infinitive Comp

X - it - NP - Tn + R - VP - $Y \Rightarrow X$ - it - for + NP - to + R - VP - Y, where $R \neq Modal + Z$

The restriction on the gerundive complementizer states that the NP Comp cannot be progressive; the one on the infinitive complementizer says that the rest of the *Aux* (R) cannot begin with a modal. Whether these transformations are optional or obligatory is a difficult question. In Sentences 14.5-14.7 one must apply, but which one is optional. In other circumstances, one may be required by a lexical item in the matrix sentence—either the head N (*fact,* for instance, allows either clausal or gerundive: *the fact that Sam left* and *the fact of Sam's leaving*; *premise* and most other lexical head nouns—*conjecture, inference, implication, conclusion, position, argument*—seem to allow only clausal)—or the predicate (*true* and *false* allow only clausal, *seems* and *appears* allow either clausal or infinitive, the latter with an extra twist to be discussed below). These restrictions will have to be listed among the syntactic idiosyncrasies of the lexical items in the lexicon. In general, though, we can ensure that at least one of the complementizer transformations applies by ordering them from the least to the most general, and making only the last obligatory. That way, if neither of the earlier complementizer transformations has applied, the last will have to; if one of the earlier ones has applied, the SI for later ones will not be met, so there will be no danger of them applying. The ordering, then, would be (1) *Gerundive (opt),* (2) *Infinitive (opt),* (3) *Clausal (oblig).*

Consider:

Sentence 14.11 It bothers Martha that John dates Mary.
Sentence 14.12 *It bothers Martha John's dating Mary.
Sentence 14.13 It bothers Martha for John to date Mary.

These are extraposed versions of Sentences 14.5-14.7. As can be seen, gerundives cannot in general be extraposed, although in some dialects they are grammatical with a pause (represented in writing by a comma) before the extraposed *S*.

However, even with infinitives and clausals there are restrictions:

Sentence 14.14a *That John likes Mary seems.
Sentence 14.14b It seems that John likes Mary.
Sentence 14.15a *For John to like Mary seems.
Sentence 14.15b *It seems for John to like Mary.
Sentence 14.16a *John's liking Mary seems.
Sentence 14.16b *It seems John's liking Mary.

With the matrix verb *seem,* we can use the clausal complementizer, but only with extraposition. The gerundive and infinitive complementizers are no good at all. However, consider:

Sentence 14.17 John seems to like Mary.

This seems to mean the same as Sentence 14.14b, and shows some similarity to the infinitive construction (in that it contains an infinitive). But there is no *it*; instead, the *it* has been replaced by the DS subject of the embedded *S*. Other examples underline the similarity:

Sentence 14.18   It happens that John likes Mary.
Sentence 14.19a   *It happens for John to like Mary.
Sentence 14.19b   John happens to like Mary.
Sentence 14.20   It is likely that John likes Mary.
Sentence 14.21a   *It is likely for John to like Mary.
Sentence 14.21b   John is likely to like Mary.

What apparently happens in these sentences is that, instead of extraposition, a similar process operates which replaces the *it* with the subject of the embedded *S*, attaches the rest of the *S* to the *VP* of the matrix *S* (this accounts for the fact that *happens to like Mary* is intuitively one *VP* rather than a *VP happens* followed by another constituent *to like Mary*, the result under extraposition), and the *for* is deleted when it comes directly before the *to*. The exact statement of all this in a transformation is a bit sticky, so we shall use a simplified version:

It Replacement

$X - it - for + NP + to + R - Y \Rightarrow X - NP - Y - for + to + R$, where *for* + *NP* + *to* + *R is a S*

This states that an embedded *S*, having gone through the infinitive complementizer (this is ensured by the *for* + *NP* + *to* sequence), is moved to the end of the matrix sentence, and the subject *NP* of the embedded *S* is substituted for *it* in the matrix. The *X* and *Y* indicate that the *NP* complement can occur anywhere in the matrix *S*, and *R* represents whatever follows *to* in the embedded *S*. There is no simple apparatus for representing that the embedded *S* is attached to the *VP* of the matrix rather than to the highest *S* (as with extraposition); we shall assume that this is done. The *for* is easily deleted:

For Deletion
$X - for + to - Y \Rightarrow X - to - Y$

For is not deleted as part of the it-replacement transformation to account for dialects in which *John wants for to go home* is grammatical—a point discussed below.

To derive Sentences 14.18 and 14.19b, then, we begin with the DS shown in Figure 14.5. For Sentence 14.18, we put the DS through the *Clausal Complementizer* and *Extraposition*, giving the structure in Figure 14.6. After the affix transformation, we get Sentence 14.18. For Sentence 14.19b, we put the structure in Figure 14.5 through the *Infinitive Complementizer, It Replacement,* and *For Deletion* to give the structure in 14.7. After *Affix Incorporation,* this becomes Sentence 14.19b.

Again, the application of these various transformations is dependent on lexical

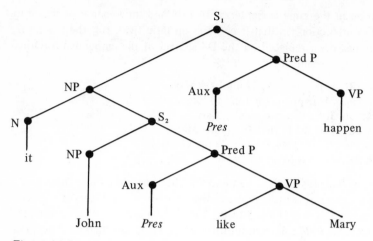

Figure 14.5

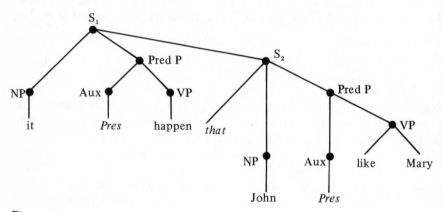

Figure 14.6

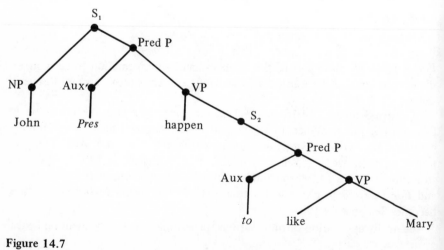

Figure 14.7

items in the matrix sentence. *True, false, possible, seem, appear, happen, sure, likely, certain* allow clausal complementizers; *possible, seem, appear, happen* require *Extraposition,* while it is optional with the others. The *Infinitive Complementizer* can occur with the above predicates except *true, false, possible* (*It is possible for John to like Mary* is different in DS from *It is possible that John likes Mary);* however, if the *Infinitive* is chosen, then *It Replacement* is obligatory.

A small group of verbs, such as *begin, continue, start, stop* allow *Infinitive* or *Gerundive* and *It Replacement:*

Sentence 14.22   *It began that John likes Mary.
Sentence 14.23a   *It began for John to like Mary.
Sentence 14.23b   John began to like Mary.
Sentence 14.23c   *It began John's liking Mary.
Sentence 14.23d   John began liking Mary.

However, for a large group of verbs, *It Replacement* is not allowed: *bother, surprise, outrage, humiliate,* and so on:

Sentence 14.24a   That John likes Mary surprises Martha.
Sentence 14.24b   It surprises Martha that John likes Mary.
Sentence 14.25a   For John to like Mary surprises Martha.
Sentence 14.25b   It surprises Martha for John to like Mary.
Sentence 14.25c   *John surprises Martha to like Mary.

So far we have been concerned with *NP* complements in subject position in the matrix sentence. But they can also appear in object position:

Sentence 14.26   John knew that Sarah liked bagels.
Sentence 14.27   John wanted (for) Sarah to go home.
Sentence 14.28   John believed that Sarah hated Sally.

There are a number of different classes of verbs that impose different restrictions on the embedded sentence. As before, these restrictions are idiosyncratic, and must be entered in the lexical entries of the verbs involved. Apparently, the restrictions deal with two aspects of the embedded sentence: (1) what complementizers are permitted, and (2) what restrictions are placed on the subject *NP* of the embedded *S* if infinitival or gerundival complementizers are chosen.

On the one hand, we find many verbs that allow the *Clausal Complementizer:* Sentences 14.26 and 14.28, and the following:

Sentence 14.29   John dreamed that Sally loved Sam.
Sentence 14.30   John remembered that Sally loved Sam.
Sentence 14.31   John denied that Sally loved Sam.
Sentence 14.32   John admitted that Sally loved Sam.

Other verbs in this class include *forget, believe, think, suspect.* In a few cases we find verbs that allow a direct object followed by an embedded clausal complement:

Sentence 14.33   John persuaded me that Sally loved Jim.
Sentence 14.34   Sam reminded me that Nancy liked bagels.

The sentences with clausal complementizers are relatively simple, since nothing further can be done with them, except perhaps to delete the *that* in some instances (see Sentences 14.26, 14.28, 14.29; the others sound worse without *that*, at least to us).

A smaller group of verbs allows the *Gerundive Complementizer*:

Sentence 14.35 Sam remembered Jim's eating the steak.
Sentence 14.36 Eva was aware of Edward's dating Sally.
Sentence 14.37 John admitted Sam's desiring more money.
Sentence 14.38 John preferred Sally's cooking the dinner.

Most interesting, however, are the verbs and adjectives that allow infinitival complements as their objects. We can delimit four such classes.

Class I

Sentence 14.39 John wanted (for) Sally to go.
Sentence 14.40 John wanted to go.
Sentence 14.41 John was eager for Sally to go.
Sentence 14.42 John was eager to go.

Sentences 14.39 and 14.41 are straightforward examples of infinitival complements in object position, differing only in that *eager* requires that *For Deletion* not apply (a syntactic idiosyncrasy) while *want*, in many dialects, imposes no such restriction. Sentences 14.40 and 14.42 seem to be similar but lack the subject *NP* in the embedded *S*. Clearly, the meaning of these sentences is that John wanted John himself to go, and that John was eager for John himself to go. It appears, then, that the subject of the embedded *S* is deleted in some circumstances if it is identical with the subject of the matrix *S*. This is accomplished by the **Equi-NP Deletion** transformation:

Equi-NP *Deletion*   *[handwritten: more general rule applies to both sub + object of higher matrix]*

$X - NP_1 - Y - \text{it} + \text{for} + NP_2 + \text{to} + R - Z \Rightarrow X - NP_1 - Y + \text{it} + \text{for} + \text{to} + R - Z$, where $\text{for} + NP_2 + \text{to} + R$ *is a S and* $NP_1 = NP_2$

This states that the subject *NP* of an infinitive complement is deleted under identity with an *NP* earlier in the matrix *S*. We shall not make it more explicit since, as will appear below, the *NP* in the matrix *S* may be either the subject or the direct object. Sentences 14.39 and 14.40 would be derived from the deep structure shown in Figure 14.8. If Figure 14.8 (with *Sally* the subject of S_2) is put through (1) *Infinitive Complementizer*, (2) *It Deletion*, (3) *For Deletion*, and (4) *Affix Incorporation*, Sentence 14.39 will result. Putting Figure 14.8 (with *John* as subject of S_2) through (1) *Infinitive Complementizer*, (2) *Equi-NP Deletion*, (3) *It Deletion*, (4) *For Deletion*, and (5) *Affix Incorporation* will result in Sentence 14.40. Other verbs that require *Equi-NP Deletion* if the subject of the complement is the same as their own subject but allow other subjects in the complement are *expect, intend, prefer, anxious, willing, demand,*

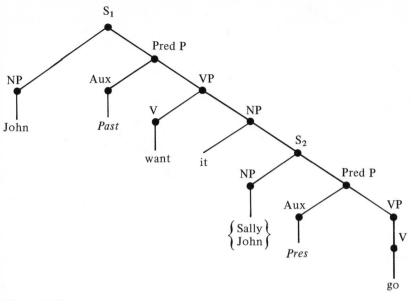

Figure 14.8

and *hope*. Again, notice the idiosyncratic behavior with relation to the deletion of *for: intend, anxious, willing, demand* require the *for* when the equi-*NP* deletion has not applied (that is, *For Deletion* cannot apply); *prefer* allows *for* but does not require it; and *expect* does not allow it. Most likely, the deletion of *for* is a dialectal matter—different dialects will differ on what verbs allow or prohibit the *for;* the restrictions have been stated for one dialect only.

Class II. Consider now:

> **Sentence 14.43a** John hesitated to go.
> **Sentence 14.43b** *John hesitated for Sam to go.
> **Sentence 14.44a** John pretended to drink the potion.
> **Sentence 14.44b** *John pretended for Sam to drink the potion.

There is a somewhat smaller class of verbs that allows an infinitive complement as direct object only if the subject of the embedded *S* is identical to the subject of the matrix *S*. Of course, *Equi-NP Deletion* is also required. The deep structure of Sentence 14.43a is shown in Figure 14.9. After *Infinitive Complement, Equi-NP Deletion, It Deletion, For Deletion,* and *Affix Incorporation,* this will become Sentence 14.43a. Notice again that the requirement that the subject of an embedded infinitival complement be the same as its own subject is an idiosyncrasy of these verbs, and as such will have to be represented in the lexical entry. Other verbs in this class are *refuse, condescend, decline, endeavor, fail,* and *manage*. The difference between the first two classes is simple: Class I allows

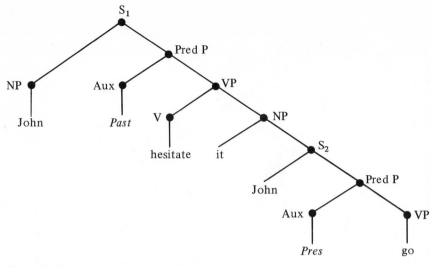

Figure 14.9

infinitival complements with any subject, whereas Class II allows infinitival complements only if their subject is the same as that of the main verb. In both classes, *Equi-NP Deletion* applies when the two subjects are the same.

Class III.   Consider the following:

Sentence 14.45a *George considers to be talented.
Sentence 14.45b George considers himself (to be) talented.
Sentence 14.45c George considers Sally (to be) talented.
Sentence 14.46a *Sam named (to be) president.
Sentence 14.46b Sam named himself (to be) president.
Sentence 14.46c Sam named Sally (to be) president.

From these sentences, we see that a group of verbs allow the subject of the embedded infinitival complement to be either the same as or different from its own subject. The difference between this class and Class I is that whereas in Class I the subject of the infinitival was deleted by *Equi-NP Deletion,* here the subject is retained and reflexivized. This raises a problem, since *Reflexivization* usually applies only within one simplex *S* (see Chapter 15), and the *NP* reflexivized is in a different *S* in the deep structure (Figure 14.10). For *George* in S_2 to be reflexivized by *George* in S_1, it must be raised into S_1. But we already have a transformation that does just that: *It Replacement.* If we allow that to apply (after *Infinitive Complementizer*) to the structure in Figure 14.10, the result will be the structure in Figure 14.11. *Reflexivization* can now apply to Figure 14.11, changing the second occurrence of *George* within the same simplex into the proper reflexive pronoun. After *For Deletion* and *Affix Incorporation,* the result will be Sentence 14.45b. Notice that in these constructions there is a further optional deletion of *to be* that may apply.

Now that we have a derivation to get Sentence 14.45b from the structure in

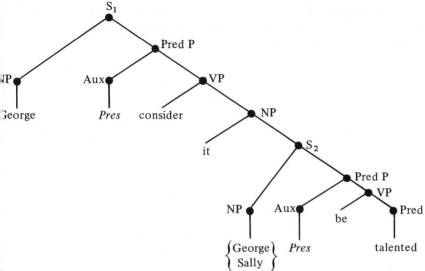

Figure 14.10

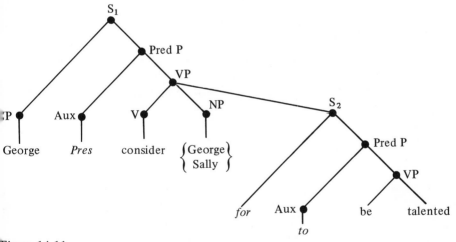

Figure 14.11

Figure 14.10, we must ask whether the same transformations will produce Sentence 14.45c. They will, since *It Replacement* will move *Sally* into the top sentence in Figure 14.11. However, a derivation from the structure in Figure 14.10 through *Infinitival Complementizer, It Deletion,* and another type of *For Deletion* would produce the same results. Why should the first derivation be preferred to the second? For one thing, if we put Sentence 14.45c through exactly the same transformations as Sentence 14.45b, we shall simplify the list of lexical idiosyncrasies for *consider:* We shall have to state only that with the infinitival complementizer it requires *It Replacement.* For another, certain other sentences are nicely handled in this way:

Sentence 14.47a Sally is considered (to be) talented by George.
Sentence 14.47b *For Sally (to be) talented is considered by George.
Sentence 14.48a Sally was named (to be) president by Sam.
Sentence 14.48b *For Sally to be president was named by George.

If we put the structure in Figure 14.10 through *Infinitival Complementizer* and *It Deletion,* we get the structure in Figure 14.12. The passives in Sentence 14.47 and 14.48 indicate that before the *Passive* applies, the *NP Sally* must immediately follow the *V.* However, in Figure 14.12, the *NP Sally* does not immediately follow the verb, and the *NP* that does—*for Sally to be talented*—cannot be fronted by the *Passive,* as indicated by the ungrammatical "b" sentences. The other derivation (through *It Replacement*) would result in the structure of Figure 14.11 just prior to the *Passive*—and Figure 14.11 contains just the right *NP* to be fronted by the *Passive* to give Sentence 14.47a. So there are two reasons for preferring the derivation through *It Replacement*: one based on considerations of simplicity and one based on syntactic behavior. The verbs in Class III include *suppose, think, believe, consider, suspect, understand, presume, conclude.*

Class IV. Compare the following two sentences:

Sentence 14.49a Sally expected John to kiss Susan.
Sentence 14.50a Sally persuaded John to kiss Susan.

Although they look as though they are both examples of the processes described under classes I and III above, they are in fact slightly different. The difference shows up under passivization of the embedded sentence:

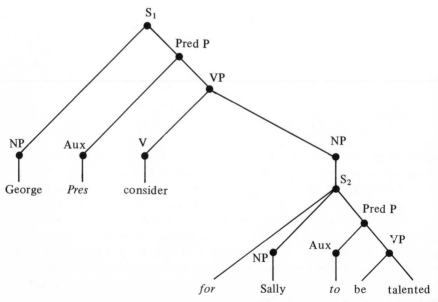

Figure 14.12

Sentence 14.49b Sally expected Susan to be kissed by John.
Sentence 14.50b Sally persuaded Susan to be kissed by John.

Sentences 14.49a and 14.49b are **cognitively synonymous**: If one is true, so is the other. However, Sentences 14.50a and 14.50b are not cognitively synonymous: Sally can persuade John to kiss Susan without necessarily persuading Susan to be kissed. There must thus be a deep-structure difference between Sentences 14.50a and 14.50b. A bit of reflection suggests what the difference should be: In Sentence 14.50a, Sally persuades John to do something—that is, to kiss Susan—while in Sentence 14.50b, Sally persuades Susan to do something—that is, to allow herself to be kissed by John. It appears, then, that these sentences have a direct object after the verb in addition to the embedded *S*. We can derive Sentence 14.50a from the deep structure in Figure 14.13. If we put this through *Infinitival Complementizer, Equi-NP Deletion* (using the closest *NP*—in this case the direct object *NP* of S_1, *John*), *It Deletion, For Deletion,* and *Affix Incorporation,* we shall get Sentence 14.50a. To derive Sentence 14.50b, we begin with the structure in Figure 14.14. First we put S_2 through the *Passive,* then *Infinitival Complementizer, Equi-NP Deletion* (again using the closest *NP,* in this case *Susan*), *It Deletion, For Deletion,* and *Affix Incorporation.* This leads to Sentence 14.50b. The difference in meaning between Sentences 14.50a and 14.50b is thus captured by a difference in deep structure: For Sentence 14.50a the direct object of *persuade* is *John,* for Sentence 14.50b it is *Susan.*

Other verbs requiring a direct object as well as an embedded *S* are *require, remind, convince, compel, bribe, cause, encourage, force, impel, order, warn, make,* and so on.

To summarize the four separate types of relation between the matrix verb and an embedded infinitival complement:

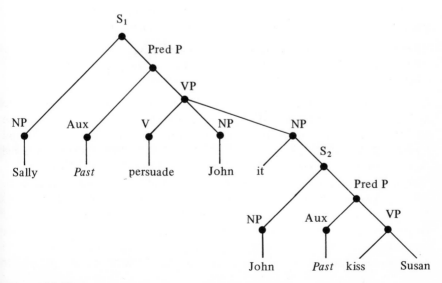

Figure 14.13

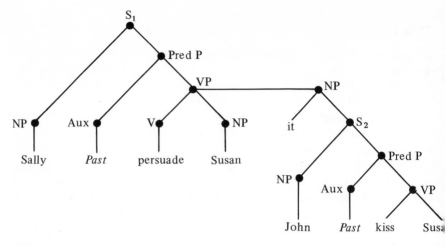

Figure 14.14

I. The subject of the embedded *S* may or may not be the same as the subject of the matrix *S*; if it is, it is deleted by *Equi-NP Deletion*.

II. The subject of the embedded *S* must be the same as the subject of the matrix *S* and must be deleted by *Equi-NP Deletion*.

III. The subject of the embedded *S* may or may not be the same as the subject of the matrix; *It Replacement* applies, and (if the subject of the embedded *S* and the matrix *S* were the same) subsequent reflexivization.

IV. The subject of the embedded *S* (after the transformations on its cycle have applied to it) must be the same as the direct object of the matrix *S*; *Equi-NP Deletion* applies.

Complements are a very difficult topic: There are many idiosyncrasies involved and many difficulties we have not faced. For one example, consider:

Sentence 14.51 John remembered that he kissed Susan.
Sentence 14.52 John remembered kissing Susan.
Sentence 14.53 John remembered to kiss Susan.

According to our discussion, all three would be derived from the deep structure in Figure 14.15: Sentence 14.51 by way of *Clausal Complementizer,* Sentence 14.52 by *Gerundive* and *Equi-NP Deletion*, and Sentence 14.53 by *Infinitive* and *Equi-NP Deletion*. But Sentences 14.51-14.53 clearly do not mean the same thing, so presumably our analysis must be modified to reflect this difference.

In this discussion we have introduced a number of transformations relating to *NP* complements: the three complementizer transformations, *Equi-NP Deletion, It Replacement, Extraposition, It Deletion, For Deletion,* and an optional and unspecified deletion of *to be*. How are they ordered with respect to the other transformations? We have seen under Class III that *It Replacement* must precede passivization, and since the complementizer transformations must precede *It*

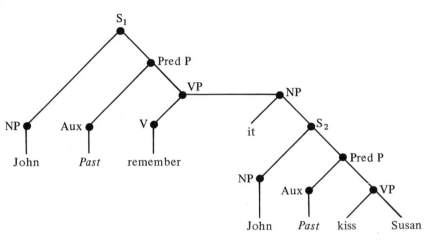

Figure 14.15

Replacement, they too must precede passivization. Similarly, *Equi-NP Deletion* precedes passivization.

The ordering of *Extraposition* and *It Deletion* presents more problems. Consider:

Sentence 14.54a   That Sally loves Sam surprises John.
Sentence 14.54b   It surprises Sam that Sally loves John.
Sentence 14.55a   *John is surprised by that Sally loves Sam.
Sentence 14.55b   John is surprised by it that Sally loves Sam.
Sentence 14.56a   *Does that Sally loves Sam surprise John?
Sentence 14.56b   Does it surprise John that Sally loves John?

Sentences 14.54a and 14.54b show *It Deletion* and *Extraposition*, respectively. Sentence 14.55a suggests that *It Deletion* cannot precede passivization, while Sentence 14.55b suggests that if the *Passive* has been applied, then *It Deletion* must not. Sentence 14.56a shows that *It Deletion* cannot precede the yes-no question transformation, and Sentence 14.56b indicates that *Extraposition* must apply in questions. The easiest way to account for these phenomena is to order *Extraposition* and *It Deletion* after both the question and passive transformations, and to ensure that they apply or do not apply in the proper circumstances. We shall do this, without specifying exactly the circumstances under which they can apply, and assume that both *Extraposition* and *It Deletion* immediately precede *For Deletion,* which immediately precedes *Affix Incorporation.* The ordering we have so far is then:

1. Relative Clause
2. Relative Clause 2
3. Relative Clause 3
4. Adjective Fronting
5. Gerundive Complement

6. Infinitive Complement
7. Clausal Complement
8. It Replacement
9. Equi-*NP* Deletion
10. Indirect-Object Switch
11. Passive
12. Agent Deletion
13. Yes-No Question
14. *Wh-* Question
15. Emphatic
16. Negative
17. Do Insertion
18. Extraposition
19. It Deletion
20. For Deletion
21. Affix Incorporation
22. Segment Transformations
23. Contraction
24. Emphatic Stress Placement

Exercises (Chapters 13, 14)

1. Provide derivations for the following sentences:

   a. The boy who stole the book went home.
   b. Sally gave the book to the boy who enjoys poetry.
   c. The girl who was given the prize was happy.
   d. John didn't like the girl that Sam was dating.
   e. John broke the window that was replaced yesterday.
   f. The window that Sam didn't break was broken by June.
   g. Did John sell the car that wouldn't run?
   h. Did John eat the steak Sam had left?
   i. Sam read the book John recommended.
   j. The book on the table was given to Sally.
   k. John told the story to the girl standing in the corner.
   l. John avoided the men accused by the police.
   m. The tall girl encouraged the disheartened salesman.
   n. The brown table wasn't sold last year.
   o. Why won't John tell his ribald stories?
   p. Sam ogled the pretty girl in the miniskirt.

2. On pp. 205-206 we discussed adjectives that could be used only attributively, as *main,* and those that occurred only in the predicate, as *alive.* Provide more examples of each type.

3. Provide derivations for the following sentences:

    a. John doesn't believe the proposition that Columbus discovered America.

    b. The belief that toads cause warts is widespread.

    c. It annoyed John that Sam ate the steak.

    d. For John to hit Susan is an outrage.

    e. John's passing the course is a surprise.

    f. It is likely that John will fail.

    g. John is likely to fail.

    h. Sally seems to be ill.

    i. John seems to doubt that Sam will pay the debt.

    j. Sam heard that Sally was leaving.

    k. Sam wanted to pass the test.

    l. John preferred Sally to go.

    m. Bill hoped that Sam would sell the car.

    n. John refused to vacate the apartment.

    o. Sam managed to pay the check.

    p. Bill considers John a fool.

    q. John believes himself to be talented.

    r. The class elected Sam president.

    s. John named himself dictator.

    t. Bill persuaded John to pay the bill.

    u. Sally was expected to pass the test.

    v. The professor was encouraged to postpone the test.

    w. Mary made Sam see a psychoanalyst.

    x. Bill convinced Sally that Sam was a bore.

    y. Sam was ordered to be examined by Dr. Jones.

    z. Is it true that John was forced to resign by Mary?

4. We discussed (pp. 213-215) the adjectives and verbs that allow *NP* complements as their subjects. Can you find others? Do they allow *Extraposition* or *It Replacement*? Require them?

5. In discussing *NP* complements as direct objects, we distinguished four classes of verbs which imposed different restrictions on the embedded sentences. For your dialect, are all the verbs given as examples in the proper class? Can you provide more examples of verbs that belong in these classes?

6.* It was claimed above (p. 223) that *It Deletion* cannot occur in questions or passives. While this is generally true, it is not true in all cases. Can you specify the conditions under which *It Deletion* can apply? How can one ensure that *It Deletion* does not apply under the wrong circumstances?

7.* Although we have not treated embedded questions at all, they seem rather similar to *NP* complements. Consider:

---

*Exercises preceded by asterisks are more advanced and/or more theoretical than the others.

a. John wonders whether Bill went.
b. John wonders where Bill went.
c. John wonders when Bill went.
d. John wonders how Bill went.
e. John wonders why Bill went.

After several verbs, notably *wonder, ask, question,* and *inquire,* embedded sentences similar to questions occur. In these a *wh-* word is fronted, and if there is no *wh-* word, *whether* or *if* occurs. There is, however, no fronting of the *Aux* (at least in our dialect). How could you account for this in transformational terms?

CHAPTER 15

Pronominalization

At the outset of our discussion of pronouns, we must distinguish two different kinds of pronouns:

Sentence 15.1 John said that he was sick.
Sentence 15.2 He said that John was sick.

In Sentence 15.1, *he* may refer either to John or to somebody not mentioned by name, while in Sentence 15.2, *He* can refer only to somebody other than John. Thus, Sentence 15.1 is ambiguous in a way that Sentence 15.2 is not; to account for the ambiguity, we shall have to provide it with two different deep structures.

When a pronoun refers back to a noun already mentioned in the sentence (or conversation), it is called **anaphoric**. When the pronoun does not refer back to a noun, we shall call it a **deep-structure pronoun**. In Sentence 15.1, *he* may be either anaphoric or DS; in Sentence 15.2, *He* can only be DS. Deep-structure pronouns, as the name implies, will be present in DS as pronouns, while anaphoric pronouns will not be present in DS at all: instead, the noun to which they refer will be present, and a pronominalization transformation will convert the noun to the proper pronoun. The ambiguity of Sentence 15.1 will thus be accounted for by deriving it from either 15.3 or 15.4:

Sentence 15.3 John + *Past* + say + it + John + *Past* + be + sick
Sentence 15.4 John + *Past* + say + it + he + *Past* + be + sick

A special class of anaphoric pronouns is called **reflexives**: These are *myself, yourself, herself, himself, itself, ourselves, yourselves,* and *themselves.* Consider:

Sentence 15.5a I hurt myself.
Sentence 15.5b *I hurt I.
Sentence 15.5c I hurt him.
Sentence 15.6a John hurt himself.

Exercises are on p. 243.

Sentence 15.6b *John$_1$ hurt John$_1$.
Sentence 15.6c John hurt them.

The "a" sentences show that when the same noun occurs twice in a simple sentence, the second occurrence must be a reflexive; the "b" sentences show that the noun cannot be repeated (Sentence 15.6b is ungrammatical if both occurrences of *John* refer to the same person, but grammatical if two different people are referred to); the "c" sentences indicate that any other pronoun can occur.

Sentence 15.7 I gave myself a present.
Sentence 15.8 John devoted himself to bridge.

From Sentences 15.7 and 15.8, we can see that the second occurrence of the *NP* can perform any function: here, indirect and direct object. The transformation would be as follows:

Reflexive (oblig)

$X - NP_1 - Y - NP_2 - Z \Rightarrow Z - NP_1 - Y - NP_2 - Z$, where $NP_1 = NP_2$, NP_1;
$[+Refl]$

NP_2 dominated by same S

That is, the obligatory reflexive transformation adds to the second occurrence of a *NP* in a simple sentence the feature $[+Refl]$. On the second lexical lookup (see p. 163), the proper reflexive pronoun will be substituted for the DS noun. Remember, the DS noun will be fully specified for number, gender, and so on, so it will be fairly easy to ensure that the proper reflexive is selected.

Now consider:

Sentence 15.9a *John thought that himself was handsome.
Sentence 15.9b John thought himself (to be) handsome.
Sentence 15.10 John intended to defend himself.
Sentence 15.11 John convinced himself to defend himself.

Sentence 15.9a illustrates that both occurrences of the *NP* must be in the same simple sentence for *Reflexivization;* here they are not, so *Reflexivization* produces an ungrammatical sentence. Since *Reflexivization* has occurred in Sentence 15.9b, the subject of the embedded sentence must have been moved into the matrix sentence before *Reflexivization* has applied. As we have seen, this is accomplished by *It Replacement.* Now consider Sentence 15.10. The DS must be as shown in Figure 15.1, where the subscripts on *John* indicate that they all refer to the same person. To get the correct result, *Reflexivization* must first apply in S_2 to give the structure shown in Figure 15.2. Now, on the S_1 cycle *Infinitive Complementizer, Equi-NP Deletion, It Deletion, For Deletion,* and *Affix Incoporation* apply to give Sentence 15.10.

For Sentence 15.11, we have the deep structure shown in Figure 15.3. On the S_2 cycle, *Reflexivization* applies. On the S_1 cycle, we have *Infinitive Complemen-*

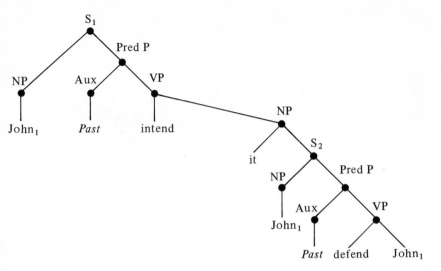

Figure 15.1

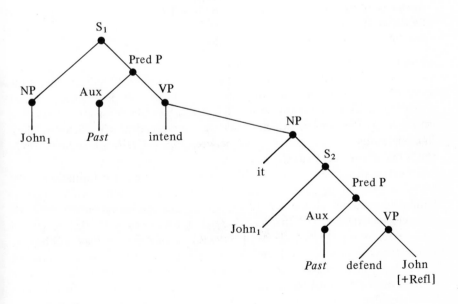

Figure 15.2

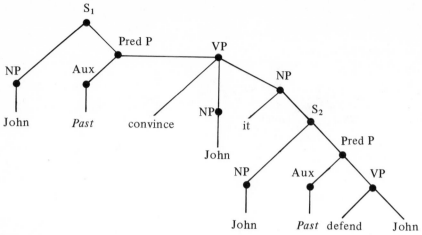

Figure 15.3

tizer, *Equi-NP Deletion, Reflexivization, It Deletion, For Deletion,* and *Affix Incorporation.* Since *Reflexivization* must apply in two different places in the derivation, we conclude that it is a cyclic rule, following *Equi-NP Deletion* and *It Replacement.*

Sentence 15.12a John gave himself a present.
Sentence 15.12b John gave a present to himself.
Sentence 15.13a *John sold Sally himself.
Sentence 15.13b John sold himself to Sally.

Assuming that Sentence 15.12b is grammatical, we see that a reflexivized indirect object can undergo IO switch. The sentences in 15.13 indicate that if the direct object is a reflexive (actually, any pronoun) then the indirect object must be switched. This restriction on *IO Switch* will be easiest to state if we know, before *IO Switch* applies, which *NP*s are pronouns and which reflexives. Thus, *Reflexivization* is apparently ordered between *Equi-NP Deletion* and *IO Switch,* and is one of the cyclic rules.

Reflexives occur only as the result of the reflexivization transformation: They are never present in deep structure. Pronouns, on the other hand, may be. Without considering all the details, we can see that the lexical entries for *I* and *you* will include +*N*, [+*Common*], [+*Pro*], [-*Pl*], [+*human*]; that *he* will be +*N*, [+*Common*], [+*Pro*], [-*Pl*], [+*human*], [+*masc*]; that *they* will be +*N*, [+*Common*], [+*Pro*], [+*Pl*]; and so on. These lexical items may be inserted into the proper terminal strings by the lexical insertion rule: For *they* to be inserted into a terminal string, for instance, the string would have to contain a noun specified [+*Common*], [+*Pro*], [+*Pl*] by the segment-structure rules.

More interesting are the anaphoric pronouns, which are produced by the operation of pronominalization rather than being present in deep structure. Consider:

Sentence 15.14a John$_1$ said that Sally loved him$_1$.
Sentence 15.14b *John$_1$ said that Sally loved John$_1$.
Sentence 15.14c *He$_1$ said that Sally loved John$_1$.
Sentence 15.15a John$_1$ said that Bill thought that Sally loved him$_1$.
Sentence 15.15b John said that Bill$_1$ thought that Sally loved him$_1$.

The subscripts indicate that the two nouns with the same subscript are taken
to refer to the same entity: Sentences 15.14b and 15.14c are both ungrammatical if the two nouns have the same reference, although of course Sentence
15.14b is grammatical if *John* refers to two different people, and Sentence
15.14c is impeccable with no referential identity intended. It seems, then, that a
NP pronominalizes a coreferential *NP* to its right. The sentences in 15.15 suggest
that this is operative no matter how far apart the coreferential *NP*s are: In
Sentence 15.15a, they are two sentences apart, as shown in Figure 15.4. The
deep structure for Sentence 15.15b would be exactly the same as that in Figure
15.4 except that the second occurrence of *John* would be replaced by *Bill*. In
general, then, when there are two coreferential *NP*s in one *S,* one of two things
happens to the rightmost *NP*: If the two *NP*s are in the same simple sentence, it
becomes a reflexive; if not, it becomes a pronoun. This is called **forward pronominalization**, and the *NP* to which the pronoun refers back is called the
antecedent.

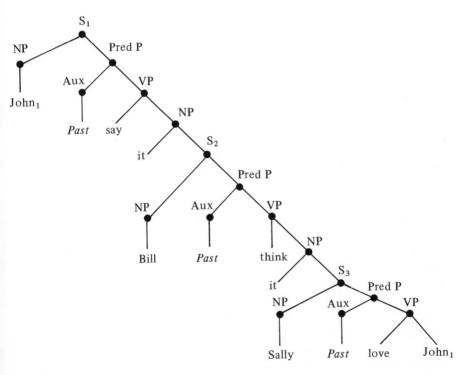

Figure 15.4

Consider, however,

Sentence 15.16a That Sally loves John$_1$ surprises him$_1$.
Sentence 15.16b That Sally loves him$_1$ surprises John$_1$.
Sentence 15.17a The boy who hates John$_1$ hit him$_1$.
Sentence 15.17b The boy who hates him$_1$ hit John$_1$.

In the "a" sentences we have forward pronominalization, but in the "b" sentences the pronominalization is **backward**: The pronoun precedes its antecedent. This is strange, since Sentence 15.14c was ungrammatical just because the pronoun preceded the antecedent. However, in Sentences 15.16b and 15.17b, we notice that the pronoun is in an embedded sentence—a *NP* complement in Sentence 15.16b and a restrictive relative clause in Sentence 15.17b. Apparently, backward pronominalization can occur if the *NP* being pronominalized is in a lower sentence than its antecedent.

But now consider:

Sentence 15.18a The girl who loved John$_1$ hit the boy who hated him$_1$.
Sentence 15.18b The girl who loved him$_1$ hit the boy who hated John$_1$.
Sentence 15.19a The girl who loved John$_1$ thought he$_1$ was handsome.
Sentence 15.19b The girl who loved him$_1$ thought John$_1$ was handsome.

In the "a" sentences, forward pronominalization has again taken place. In the "b" sentences, backward pronominalization has occurred even though the antecedent *NP* is not in a higher sentence that the pronominalized *NP*: They are both in embedded sentences. And the antecedent can be in a more deeply embedded sentence than the pronoun:

Sentence 15.20 The girl who hated him$_1$ forced Sam to say that John$_1$ was a troglodyte.

Summing up: Forward pronominalization can always occur, and backward pronominalization can occur except when the antecedent *NP* occurs in a sentence that is embedded in the sentence containing the pronominalized *NP*. Although the environment is clear, it is difficult to state it transformationally without introducing more transformational machinery, so we shall not.

The pronominalization transformation adds the feature [+*Pro*] to the pronominalized noun. In the second lexical lookup, the proper pronoun is substituted for the DS noun: The pronoun must be the same as the *NP* in terms of plurality, gender, humanness (*he, she* for [+*human*], *it* for [−*human*]), and person. This latter brings up an interesting point: Although pronouns are traditionally spoken of as first person (*I, we*), second person (*you*), and third person (*he, she, it, they*), nouns are always third person, as can be seen from subject-verb agreement in the present singular:

Sentence 15.21a I go.
Sentence 15.21b You go.
Sentence 15.21c He (she, it) goes.
Sentence 15.21d The man goes.

Sentence 15.21e   The woman goes.
Sentence 15.21f   The dog goes.

The only anaphoric pronouns are third-person pronouns: First- and second-person pronouns must be deep structure, since there are no *NP*s for which they can substitute. In the lexicon, we can then mark each [*-Pro*] noun as third person by a redundancy rule, and thus ensure that only third-person pronouns are produced by pronominalization.

CHAPTER 16

Conjunction

So far we have been considering simple sentences; we now turn to compound sentences. Of the many kinds of coordinate and subordinate constructions, we shall treat only one in detail: sentences conjoined by *and*.

It seems that any two sentences can be conjoined by *and* as long as they are the same type of sentence—both questions, both statements, both imperatives:

Sentence 16.1 John arrived and Jane left.
Sentence 16.2 Did John arrive and will Jane leave?
Sentence 16.3 Go home and shut the window!
Sentence 16.4 *John arrived and will Jane leave?
Sentence 16.5 *Did John arrive and go home!

Further, any number of sentences can be conjoined:

Sentence 16.6 John arrived and Jane left and Sam laughed and Sally wept. . . .

We need some source for these conjoined sentences. The simplest one is a PS rule:

$S \rightarrow$ and $+ S*$

This is called a **rule schema**, because it represents an infinite number of rules: The asterisk after the S on the right-hand side indicates that any number of Ss can be chosen. Each of these will then be expanded by the PS rules. A rule is now needed that distributes *and* correctly, that is, that puts it between each two Ss rather than just once at the beginning.

Conjunction Distribution (oblig)

and $+ S_1 + S_2 + \ldots + S_n \Rightarrow S_1 +$ and $+ S_2 +$ and $\ldots$ and $+ S_n$, where $S_1 \ldots$ are S_n are all of the same type

Exercises are on p. 243.

The transformation simply puts *and* between each two sentences, as long as they are of the same type. It is not clear what "of the same type" means exactly, so the specification is left rather vague. If several sentences are conjoined, it is possible to delete all but the last *and,* the others being replaced by pauses (indicated in writing by commas). It is not clear how to represent a pause, so we shall just use a comma.

And Reduction (opt)

S_1 + and + S_2 + ... + and + S_n ⇒ S_1, S_2, ... + and + S_n

We choose *and* for study because various reductions are possible when the two conjuncts thus joined have identical constituents. Consider first what happens when the conjoined *S*s have identical predicate phrases.

Sentence 16.7a   John left and Mary left.
Sentence 16.7b   John left and Mary did too.
Sentence 16.8a   John has left and Mary has left.
Sentence 16.8b   John has left and Mary has too.
Sentence 16.9a   John will leave and Mary will leave.
Sentence 16.9b   John will leave and Mary will too.
Sentence 16.10a John has been reading and Mary has been reading.
Sentence 16.10b John has been reading and Mary has been too.
Sentence 16.10c John has been reading and Mary has too.
Sentence 16.11a John should leave and Mary has left.
Sentence 16.11b *John should leave and Mary has too.

Sentences 16.7-16.10 indicate that when conjuncts have identical *Pred P* constituents, the *VP* of the second conjunct can be deleted. Sentence 16.11 indicates that this may not be possible when the *Aux* constituents are not also identical. (Again, speakers of different dialects may disagree about the grammaticality of some sentences.) The *too,* which is necessary in the "b" sentences, may also optionally appear in the "a" sentences. Finally, Sentence 16.10c suggests that when the *Aux* in the second conjunct contains more than tense plus one other element, the rest of them can be deleted.

We shall need a series of transformations to account for these results. First, we optionally add *too*:

Too Addition (opt)

NP_1 + *Pred* P_1 ‒ and ‒ NP_2 + *Pred* P_2 ⇒ NP_1 + *Pred* P_1‒ and ‒ NP_2 + *Pred* P_2 + too, where *Pred* P_1 = *Pred* P_2

Then we delete the second *VP* in those sentences to which *too* has already been added (thus ensuring that *Pred* P_1 = *Pred* P_2):

Equi-VP Deletion (opt)

NP_1 + Aux_1 + VP_1 ‒ and ‒ NP_2 + Aux_2 + VP_2 + too ⇒ NP_1 + Aux_1 + VP_1 ‒ and ‒ NP_2 + Aux_2 + too

Finally, we delete additional elements in Aux_2:

Aux Reduction (opt)

$X - NP - Tn (Aux_1) + Y - too \Rightarrow X - NP - Tn (Aux_1) - too$, where Tn $(Aux_1) + Y$ *is a Aux; Aux_1 = Modal; be; have* dominated by Aux

Notice that here we do not have to specify anything that precedes the second conjunct: The preceding transformations have ensured that the necessary constituents are identical.

These transformations will produce correct results except in two cases. The first is Sentence 16.10b: *Aux Reduction,* as we have stated it, deletes all but the first element after the tense, but in Sentence 16.10b the seond element, *be,* is also retained. This suggests that instead of *Aux Reduction* we need a transformation that peels away successive layers of equal *Aux* elements, starting at the right. Applied once, this would produce Sentence 16.10b; applied twice, it would give Sentence 16.10c.

Unfortunately, this solution has a problem. Consider:

Sentence 16.12a John is being difficult and Mary is being difficult.
Sentence 16.12b John is being difficult and Mary is too.
Sentence 16.13a John is being examined by Sam and Mary is being examined by Sam.
Sentence 16.13b *John is being examined by Sam and Mary is being too.
Sentence 16.13c John is being examined by Sam and Mary is too.

The deep structure for Sentence 16.12 would presumably be as shown in Figure 16.1. After *Conjunction Distribution, Too Addition, Equi-VP Deletion,* and *Aux Reduction,* we shall get Sentence 16.12b: Here *be* is part of the *VP* and thus deleted. However, in Sentence 16.13b, *being* must also be deleted, even though it is part of the auxiliary: After *Conjunction Distribution* and *Passive* in S_2 and S_3, the underlying structure for Sentence 16.13 will be as shown in Figure 16.2. Apparently, this *being* in the auxiliary must be obligatorily deleted (that is, *Aux* reduction must apply). But if we allow a transformation to peel off successive layers from the right, there is no way of ensuring this. So we shall stick with *Aux Reduction,* noting that it (like so many other things) is not entirely adequate.

There is another method of reducing conjuncts that have identical *Pred P* constituents:

Sentence 16.14a John left and Mary left.
Sentence 16.14b John left and so did Mary.
Sentence 16.15a John will leave and Mary will leave.
Sentence 16.15b John will leave and so will Mary.
Sentence 16.16a John has been reading and Mary has been reading.
Sentence 16.16b *John has been reading and so has Mary been.
Sentence 16.16c John has been reading and so has Mary.

When two conjuncts have identical *Pred P* constituents, the *VP* of the second can be deleted if the tense and Aux_1 of the second are fronted and preceded by *so.*

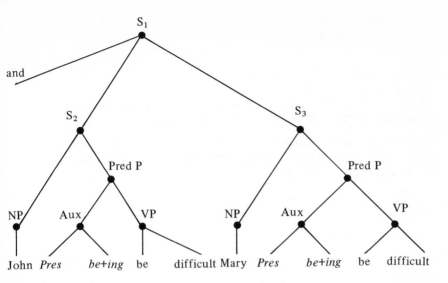

Figure 16.1

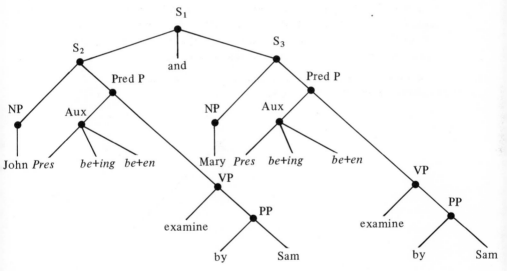

Figure 16.2

The other elements of the second auxiliary are deleted, as can be seen from Sentence 16.16b. The fronting operation involves the same elements as the *Yes-No Question,* so the transformation would be something like the following:

So Reduction (opt)

$NP_1 - Tn_1 \, (Aux_1) + X - VP_1 - \text{and} - NP_2 - Tn_2 \, (Aux_1) + X - VP_2 \Rightarrow NP_1 - Tn \, (Aux_1) + X - VP_1 - \text{and} - \text{so} + Tn_2 \, (Aux_1) - NP_2,$ where $VP_1 = VP_2,$ $Tn_1 = Tn_2,$ and $Aux_1 = Modal; \, be; \, have,$ dominated by Aux

The statement is a bit messy, but it does the job.

There is a third method for reducing conjuncts having identical *Pred P* constituents:

Sentence 16.17a John left and Mary left.
Sentence 16.17b John and Mary left.
Sentence 16.18a John has been reading and Mary has been reading.
Sentence 16.18b John and Mary have been reading.

When the *Pred P* constituents are identical, the subject *NP* of the second conjunct can be conjoined to the subject *NP* of the first conjunct, and the rest of the second conjunct deleted:

VP Conjunction Reduction (opt)

NP_1 + *Pred* P_1 - and - NP_2 + *Pred* P_2 $\Rightarrow$ NP_1 + and + NP_2 - *Pred* P_1, where *Pred* P_1 = *Pred* P_2

This straightforward operation will change the structure in Figure 16.3 into the structure in Figure 16.4. But notice that there is an ambiguity in Sentences 16.17b and 16.18b that has not been accounted for: Sentence 16.17b can mean that John and Mary left either *together* or *separately*, Sentence 16.18b that John and Mary are reading *together* or *separately*. In addition, there are some sentences that would appear to be derived by this process, except that the underlying conjoined sentences would be ungrammatical:

Sentence 16.19a *John is similar and Mary is similar.
Sentence 16.19b John and Mary are similar.

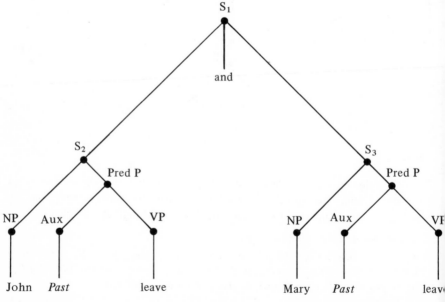

Figure 16.3

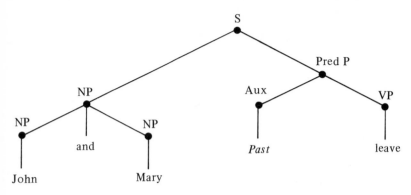

Figure 16.4

Sentence 16.19b cannot be derived from Sentence 16.19a because Sentence 16.19a is ungrammatical, and, since our *VP Conjunction Reduction* is optional, we cannot ensure that the structure underlying Sentence 16.19a will always be transformed into that underlying Sentence 16.19b. Further, Sentence 16.19b seems to mean the same as Sentences 16.19c and 16.19d:

Sentence 16.19c John is similar to Mary.
Sentence 16.19d Mary is similar to John.

Sentences 16.19c and 16.19d are examples of **symmetric predicates**: predicates in which, if $NP_1 - X - NP_2$ is true, so are $NP_2 - X - NP_1$ and NP_1 *and* $NP_2 - X$, where X represents the predicate (other examples of symmetric predicates are *marry, fight, debate, argue,* and so on). It is not clear whether Sentence 16.19b, 16.19c, or 16.19d is closer to the basic structure of these sentences, but we shall assume that Sentence 16.19b is, since whatever arguments can be presented for the priority of Sentence 16.19c can also be used for Sentence 16.19d. We must then distinguish two different kinds of conjunction: **derived conjunction**, the type we have been discussing so far, and **phrasal conjunction**, which occurs when two constituents are conjoined in deep structure. Thus, Sentence 16.17b can also be derived from the structure in Figure 16.5. This structure will be produced by a PS rule of the type $NP \rightarrow$ and $+NP^*$, exactly paralleling the rule schema for S. Similarly, we shall extend the conjunction distribution transformation to apply to NPs. The ambiguity of Sentence 16.17b is thus accounted for: If it is derived from Figure 16.3, the semantic interpretation will be that of two actions; if Sentence 16.17b is derived from Figure 16.5, the interpretation will be that there is only one action but two participants.

Thus, sentences such as 16.17b and 16.18b can be derived from two deep structures, and are consequently ambiguous; symmetric predicates, on the other hand, can be derived only from phrasal conjunction and so are unambiguous. Since being a symmetric predicate is a syntactic idiosyncrasy, these lexical items will have the fact that they require plural or conjoined subjects represented in their lexical entries.

The reductions we have treated so far apply to conjuncts with identical *Aux*

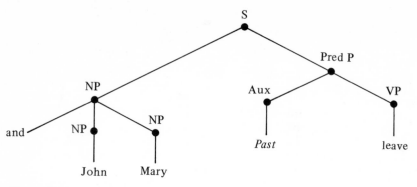

Figure 16.5

and *VP* constituents. If the subject *NP*s of two conjuncts are identical, other reductions can be applied.

Sentence 16.20a　*John left and John called Susan.
Sentence 16.20b　John left and he called Susan.
Sentence 16.20c　John left and called Susan.
Sentence 16.21a　*John has left and John is going home.
Sentence 16.21b　John has left and he is going home.
Sentence 16.21c　John has left and is going home.
Sentence 16.22a　*John is going home and John has left.
Sentence 16.22b　?John is going home and he has left.
Sentence 16.22c　?John is going home and has left.

The "a" sentences are suspect if both occurrences of *John* refer to the same person; normally, pronominalization would apply, as in the "b" sentences. The "c" sentences exhibit deletion of the subject *NP* of the second conjunct. All the sentences in 16.22 are odd, perhaps because the progression of tenses is strange; in any case, the "a" sentence is odder than the others (a question mark before a sentence indicates that the authors are doubtful about its grammaticality). We can state the *NP* reduction thus:

NP Conjunction Reduction (opt)

$NP_1 - X - \text{and} - NP_2 - Y \Rightarrow NP_1 - X + \text{and} + Y$, where $NP_1 = NP_2$

Notice that further specification is really necessary here to avoid sentences such as 16.22, but we shall not specify it. The transformation is optional—either it or pronominalization can apply.

If two conjuncts have an identical *NP*, even though it performs different functions in each, other reductions are possible:

Sentence 16.23a　John is tall and he is handsome.
Sentence 16.23b　John, and he is handsome, is tall.
Sentence 16.23c　John, who is handsome, is tall.

Sentence 16.24a John left and Sam saw him.
Sentence 16.24b John, and Sam saw him, left.
Sentence 16.24c John, who Sam saw, left.
Sentence 16.25a Sally loves John and Sam gave him a book.
Sentence 16.25b Sally loves John, and Sam gave him a book.
Sentence 16.25c Sally loves John, who Sam gave a book to.

Here the "a" sentences represent the simple conjunction with pronominalization. In the "b" sentences, the second conjunct has been inserted into the first after the *NP* that appears in both. The "c" sentences contain nonrestrictive relative clauses. The operation to produce the "b" sentences is the following:

NP Conjunction Insertion (opt)

$X - NP_1 - Y - and - R + NP_2 + Z \Rightarrow X - NP_1 - and - R + NP_2 + Z - Y,$
where $NP_1 = NP_2$ and $R + NP_2 + Z$ *is a S*

This will transform Figure 16.6 into Figure 16.7. It is not clear that this is the structure we actually want (in particular, the attachment of *and* seems counterintuitive), but we shall accept it for the time being.

To produce nonrestrictive relative clauses, we can either turn structures like Figure 16.7 into them, or operate instead on deep structures—that is, the nonrestrictive relative clause transformation can operate in addition to *NP Conjunction Insertion* or instead of it. Suppose we take the former possibility. Then the transformation must simply delete the *and,* turn the identical *NP* in the (now) embedded *S* into a relative pronoun (*who* for [*+human*] *NP*s, *which* for [*−human*] *NP*s) and front the relative pronoun:

NR Rel Clause (opt)

$X - NP_1 - and - R + NP_2 + Z - Y \Rightarrow X - NP_1 - \begin{Bmatrix} who \\ which \end{Bmatrix} + R + Z - Y,$ where
$NP_1 = NP_2$ and $R + NP_2 + Z$ *is a S*

If we put Figure 16.7 through this transformation, we shall have Figure 16.8. For *NR Rels* this structure makes sense: It is different enough from that of *R Rels* to account for the difference in intonation (the pause before and after the *NR Rel*). This is presumptive evidence that the structure of Figure 16.7 is not too far wrong, though the *and* is still annoying.

Remember that several reductions of restrictive relative clauses were possible. These do not seem to be possible for nonrestrictive relative clauses:

Sentence 16.26a John, who is handsome, is tall.
Sentence 16.26b ?Handsome John is tall.
Sentence 16.27a John, who is lying on the grass, is handsome.
Sentence 16.27b ?John, lying on the grass, is handsome.
Sentence 16.28a John, who Sam saw, is handsome.
Sentence 16.28b *John, Sam saw, is handsome.

Sentence 16.28b is clearly out; about Sentences 16.26b and 16.27b we are less certain. The adjective *handsome* in Sentence 16.26b seems more part of the

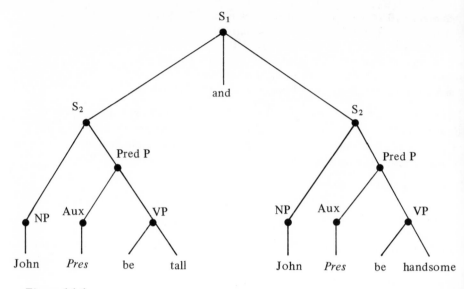

Figure 16.6

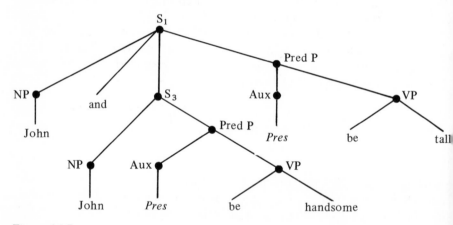

Figure 16.7

proper noun than modifying. Sentence 16.27b might be grammatical in some dialects. If Sentence 16.26b is grammatical, then a sentence such as 16.29,

Sentence 16.29 The tall boy is handsome.

must be ambiguous, since the adjective *tall* could be derived either from a sentence conjunction and a nonrestrictive relative clause or from an embedded sentence through the restrictive relative clause transformations. Sentence 16.29 does not seem ambiguous to us, although again our judgments are not firm.

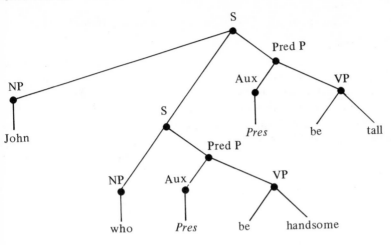

Figure 16.8

Exercises (Chapters 15, 16)

1. Derive the following sentences. Remember that if a sentence is ambiguous, as some with pronouns may be, then two or more derivations must be provided for it.

    a. Sam claimed that he had left.
    b. He claimed that Sam had left.
    c. Judy consoled herself.
    d. John persuaded himself to defend himself.
    e. John expected Sally to see her.
    f. The house he bought occupied John completely.
    g. The suggestion that he might be insane bothered Sam.
    h. Sally disappointed the boy who loved her.
    i. John thinks Sally is pretty and Sam does too.
    j. Jim is reading a novel and so is Sally.
    k. John and Jane went to the dance.
    l. John and Jane are married.
    m. Sam ate and ran.
    n. Sam, who is brilliant, failed the exam.
    o. The committee appointed Sam, who declined the honor.
    p. The boy, who was learning Greek, tutored the girl failing Latin.

2. On p. 239, symmetric predicates were discussed and a few examples were provided. What other symmetric predicates exist in your dialect?

3. In discussing the various reductions possible when the predicate phrases of two conjuncts are identical, we claimed that the two sentences must be

"of the same type" (p. 234). Can you state more formally what this restriction is?

4.* To account for the ambiguity of *John and Jim played cards* and sentences like it, we distinguished between phrasal and derived conjunction (pp. 238-239). That is, we claimed that such sentences could be derived either from deep-structure conjoined sentences or from deep-structure conjoined *NP*s. Are there any examples that suggest that a similar mechanism is necessary in *NP* reduction, for example, sentences that must be derived from deep-structure conjoined *VP*s rather than deep-structure conjoined sentences?

5.* All the discussion of conjunction reduction treated positive conjuncts. What happens when one or both conjuncts are negative? Consider

    a.   Sally went and John didn't go.
    b. *Sally went and John didn't go too.
    c. *Sally went and John didn't too.
    d. ?Sally went and John didn't.
    e.   Sally went but John didn't.
    f. *Sally went and so didn't John.
    g.   Sally didn't go and John didn't go.
    h.   Sally didn't go and John didn't go either.
    i.   Sally didn't go and John didn't either.
    j.   Sally didn't go and neither did John.

What changes must be made in the conjunction-reduction transformation to account for these and similar examples of negatives?

6.* Our discussion of conjunction has treated only coordination, and only one conjunction—*and*—in detail. However, a complete grammar must also account for subordination. How can this be done? (Note that most of the subordinate clauses we have not discussed will be adverbials of one type or another.)

7.* The *Equi-VP Deletion* rule (p. 235) deletes a *VP* in the second conjunct when it is identical to the *VP* in the first conjunct. But, as stated, this operation might leave an *affix* at the end of the *Aux* of the second conjunct: in Sentence 16.8b the structure after *Equi-VP Deletion* would presumably be *John + Pres + have + en + leave + and + Mary + Pres + have + en + too.* How can we ensure that there are no affixes without verbs to incorporate with left over?

---

*Exercises preceded by asterisks are more advanced and/or more theoretical than the others.

CHAPTER 17

Review of Phrase-Structure Rules and Transformations

During the discussion of lexical insertion and the transformational component, we have suggested revisions in the original phrase-structure rules—rewriting lexical categories as dummy symbols to facilitate lexical insertion, distinguishing between lexical sentence modifiers and those that trigger the question, negative, and emphatic transformations, adding rule schemas to account for conjoined sentences and noun phrases. Here it would be a good idea to spell out our revised phrase-structure rules:

PS 17.1 $S \rightarrow \begin{Bmatrix} and + S* \\ (SM) \, NP + Pred \, P \, (Place) \, (Time) \end{Bmatrix}$

PS 17.2 $Pred \, P \rightarrow Aux + VP$

PS 17.3 $Aux \rightarrow Tn \, (M) \, (have + en) \, (be + ing)$

PS 17.4 $VP \rightarrow \begin{Bmatrix} be + Pred \\ V \, (NP) \, (NP) \, (Manner) \end{Bmatrix}$

PS 17.5 $Pred \rightarrow \begin{Bmatrix} Adj \\ NP \\ Place \end{Bmatrix}$

PS 17.6 $NP \rightarrow \begin{Bmatrix} and + NP* \\ NP + S \\ N \, (S) \end{Bmatrix}$

PS 17.7 $Tn \rightarrow \begin{Bmatrix} Past \\ Pres \end{Bmatrix}$

PS 17.8 $SM \rightarrow (Neg) \, (Emph) \, (\begin{Bmatrix} WH \\ SM_{lex} \end{Bmatrix})$

PS 17.9 $N \rightarrow [\pm Common]$

PS 17.10 $[+Common] \rightarrow [\pm Pro, \pm Pl]$

PS 17.11 $[-Pro] \rightarrow [\pm Def]$

PS 17.12 $[+Def] \rightarrow [\pm Dem]$

PS 17.13 $[+Dem] \rightarrow [\pm Near]$

PS 17.14 $M \rightarrow \Delta$

PS 17.15 $V \rightarrow \Delta$

PS 17.16 $Adj \rightarrow \Delta$
PS 17.17 $N \rightarrow \Delta$
PS 17.18 $SM_{lex} \rightarrow \Delta$

The strange appearance of PS 17.8 accounts for the fact that lexical sentence modifiers (*probably, yes, no, certainly*) occur in negative and emphatic statements but not in questions. And notice that the adverbs of place, time and manner are not further categorized: Since an adverbial can be either a single lexical item or a prepositional phrase, and a prepositional phrase can be an adverbial of either place, time, or manner, the relation between the function and the form is somewhat complex, and we have not tried to sort it out, either in the grammar itself or here.

Since the last time we reviewed the transformations (at the end of Chapter 14, P. 223), we have added several new ones: the pronominalization and conjunction transformations. Following is a list of all the transformations in order:

1. Conjunction Distribution (for both Ss and NPs)
2. And Reduction
3. Too Addition
4. Equi-VP Deletion
5. Aux Reduction
6. So Reduction
7. VP Conjunction Reduction
8. NP Conjunction Reduction
9. NP Conjunction Insertion
10. Nonrestrictive Relative Clause
11. Restrictive Relative Clause 1
12. Restrictive Relative Clause 2
13. Restrictive Relative Clause 3
14. Adjective Fronting
15. Gerundive Complement
16. Infinitive Complement
17. Clausal Complement
18. It Replacement
19. Equi-NP Deletion
20. Reflexivization
21. Indirect-Object Switch
22. Passive
23. Agent Deletion
24. Yes-No Question
25. *Wh*- Question
26. Emphatic
27. Negative
28. Extraposition
29. It Deletion
30. Do Insertion
31. For Deletion
32. Affix Incorporation

33. Determiner Segment
34. Plural Segment
35. Contraction
36. Emphatic Stress Placement

After the phrase-structure rules comes lexical insertion; after the transformations comes the second lexical lookup. The semantic component operates on the deep structure; the phonological component operates on the surface structure (the structure after the second lexical lookup).

CHAPTER 18

Complete Derivation

So far we have been sketching in what a transformational grammar might look like, and in so doing we have often neglected the details of a derivation to illustrate the points under discussion. To correct a false impression about the process of deriving a sentence that the fragmentary discussion might have fostered, we now present a complete derivation, beginning with the terminal string

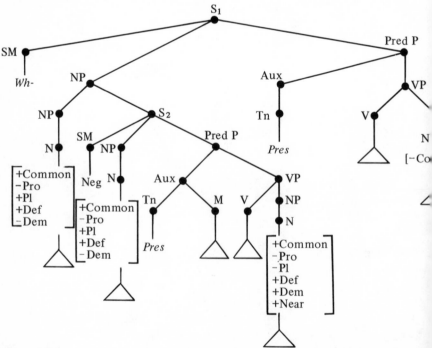

Figure 18.1

shown in Figure 18.1. Each lexical category is represented by the dummy symbol Δ, as discussed in the section on lexical insertion, and each *N* has been further specified by the segment-structure rules. This terminal string underlies many sentences, depending on the lexical items we choose to substitute for the dummy symbols. Let us choose one:

Sentence 18.1 Is John outraged by the students who won't defy this aaministration?

After the process of lexical insertion, we shall have the structure shown in Figure 18.2. This is the deep structure for *Is John outraged by the students who won't defy this administration?* The lexical items are fully specified: For the nouns, the features above the dashed lines are those added by phrase-structure rules, those below the lines are inherent features listed in the lexicon. For the verbs, −*Obj Del* in both indicates that they must be followed by objects (**John defies* or **Sam outrages* would be ungrammatical); [+[+*animate*] _] for *defy* indicates that it requires an animate subject (**The tree defies John* is ungrammatical, although note another *defy*, presumably with a separate lexical entry, which allows abstract subjects: *This phenomenon defies explanation*), while [+_[+*human*]] for *outrage* shows that the direct object of *outrage* must be

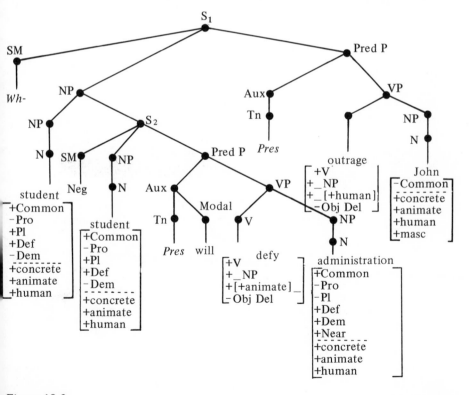

Figure 18.2

human. Rather than copying all the lexical information in each step, we shall just copy the word; when we reach the segment transformations at the end of the derivation, however, we shall need that information, so we shall represent it again there.

First we look at S_2 to see whether any transformations apply to it. S_2 has the *SM Neg,* indicating that it must go through the negative transformation. After *Neg,* then, we have the structure shown in Figure 18.3. No further transformations apply to S_2 (remember that *Affix Incorporation,* the segment transformations, and *Contraction* apply only on the last cycle), so we consider S_1. First we apply the relative clause transformation to get the structure shown in Figure 18.4.

Next we apply the *Passive* to Figure 18.4 to get Figure 18.5.

Now, since S_1 begins with the *SM Wh-,* we put it through the yes-no question transformation (Figure 18.6).

Next we apply *Affix Incorporation,* and in preparation for the segment transformations to follow, again give all the specifications for the relevant lexical items (Figure 18.7).

The full specifications for the verbs have not been supplied because nothing further is done with them. However, both *student* and *administration* are marked [+*Def,*], indicating that a segment transformation will apply. After it, we have the structure shown in Figure 18.8.

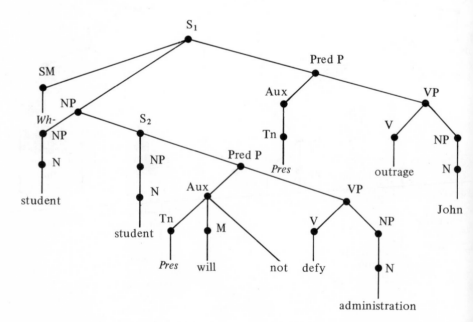

Figure 18.3

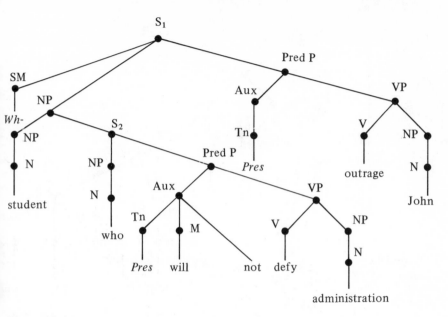

Figure 18.4

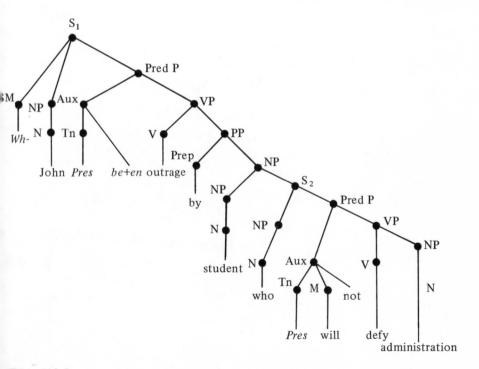

Figure 18.5

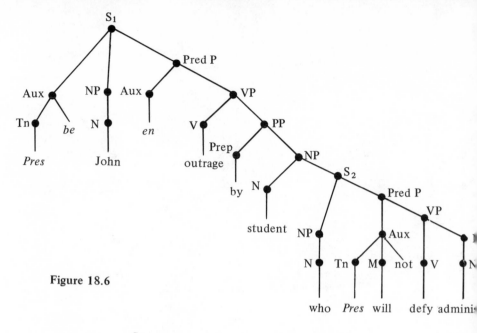

Figure 18.6

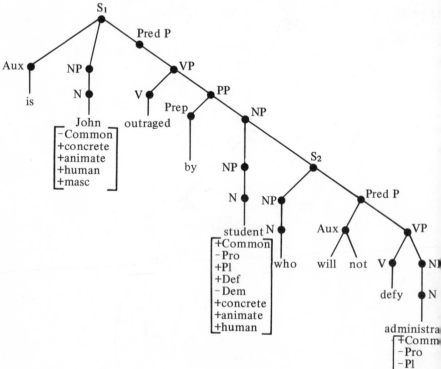

Figure 18.7

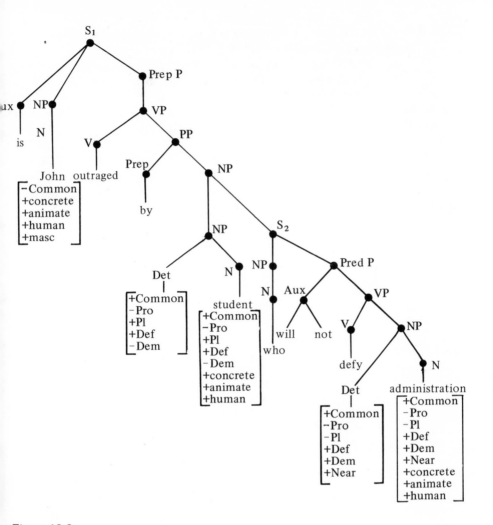

Figure 18.8

253

Now the second segment transformation, the one that supplies the plural affix, will apply to *student,* since it is marked [+*Pl*] (Figure 18.9).

The second lexical lookup will now occur: Segments that have been created by the segment transformations will have items substituted for them. *The* will substitute for [+*Det,* +*Def,* -*Dem*] and *this* for [+*Det,* -*Pl,* +*Def,* +*Dem,* +*Near*]. At this point, we can drop the lexical specifications: Since all the major transformations have applied and the lexicon has been consulted a second time, they serve no further function (Figure 18.10).

There are only two things left to do: first, *student* and [+*Affix,* +*Pl*] must be combined to give the plural of *student, students*; second, the contraction transformation must combine *will* and *not* into *won't.* After these, we have the surface structure shown in Figure 18.11.

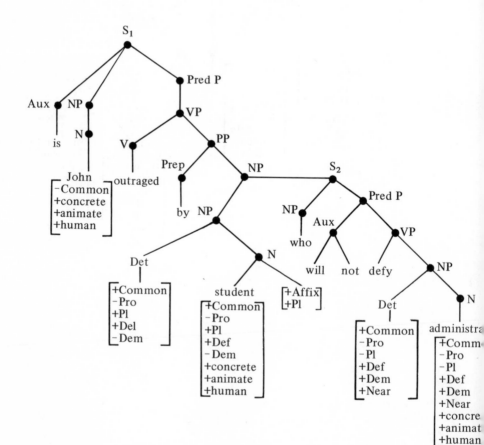

Figure 18.9

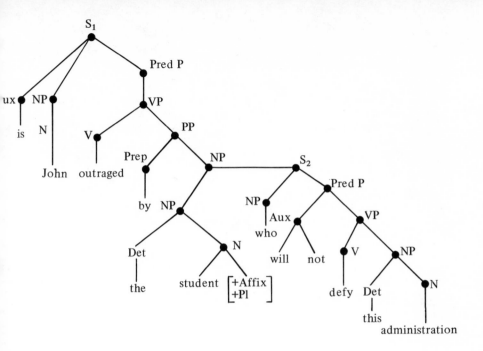

Figure 18.10

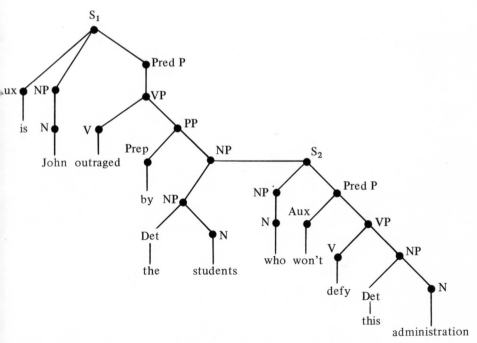

Figure 18.11

The Generative
Semanticist Argument

If the change discussed on pp. 111-120 was the only one made by the generative semanticists, there might still be disagreement between them and the interpretive semanticists, although the issue would not be particularly crucial. But, in fact, the generative semanticists proposed additional changes which are a natural development of the first change and which do, in their opinion, make the issue crucial. We can look briefly at two of these suggested changes.

First, the generative semanticists recognized that the rules of symbolic logic were not fully adequate to a description of natural language, since these rules were never intended to describe the process of subordination. As McCawley puts it, "Symbolic logic has largely been used as a device for representing the content of mathematics. [But] 'subordination' relates to an important way in which the sentences of natural languages differ from the propositions involved in mathematics."[1] Whereas *propositions* (an n-place predicate plus an argument for each n place) represent the content of mathematics, the representation of semantic content in a natural language requires not only a proposition but also a set of noun phrases "which provide the material used in identifying the indices of the 'proposition,' [see Figure 1],"[2]

The "indices" to which McCawley refers are represented by x_1 and x_2 in Figure 1. The "proposition" obviously resembles the simple trees of the *Aspects* model (Figure 2). Here again, it may seem that this proposed change from the standard model is not particularly drastic (although we must notice that insertion involves "indices" as well as lexical items). But the extent of the change becomes more obvious as, following McCawley's example, we develop it further.

Sentence 1 John said that he had seen the woman who lives at 219 Main Street.

[1] James D. McCawley, "Where Do Noun Phrases Come From?" p. 173 (see Bibliography). In other words, the logic rules that apply to mathematics are a subset of a larger group of rules that would apply to both natural languages and mathematics.
[2] McCawley, "Where Do Noun Phrases Come From?" pp. 173–174.

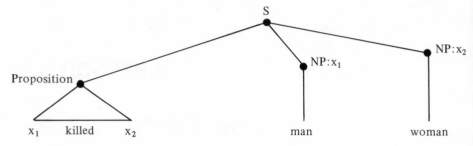

Figure 1 Semantic representation (reproduced by permission of the publisher, with the title added, from "Where Do Noun Phrases Come From?" by James D. McCawley, published in *Readings in English Transformational Grammar,* edited by Roderick Jacobs and Peter Rosenbaum. Copyright © 1970 by Roderick Jacobs and Peter S. Rosenbaum. Published by Xerox College Publishing. All rights reserved)

A sentence such as this is ambiguous. It is appropriate "either when John said something such as *I saw the woman who lives at 219 Main Street* or when John has said something such as *I saw Mary Wilson* and the speaker is describing Mary Wilson as *the woman who lives at 219 Main Street.*"[3]

In the first of the two possible interpretations (where John actually used the clause *who lives at 219 Main Street*), the clause is an embedded sentence that is part of the proposition itself, as indicated in Figure 3. In the second case (where the speaker—but *not* John—said *the woman who lives at 219 Main Street*), the clause is *not* part of the fundamental proposition. McCawley represents this structure as indicated in Figure 4.

Given the trees in these two figures, we can apply transformations to substitute the noun phrases for their respective indices in the propositions. Notice, in particular, that the trees that would be produced by these transformations would resemble the deep-structure trees of standard theory. Thus, the generative semanticists claim that their "propositional trees" actually underlie the deep-structure trees of standard theory, and if this claim is true, then the standard level of deep structure would—in fact—be artificial.

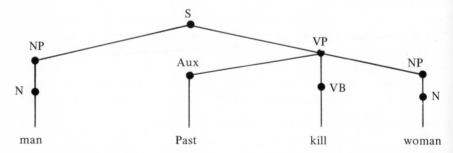

Figure 2 The standard representation

[3] Sentence 1 and this quotation are from McCawley, "Where Do Noun Phrases Come From?" pp. 174–175.

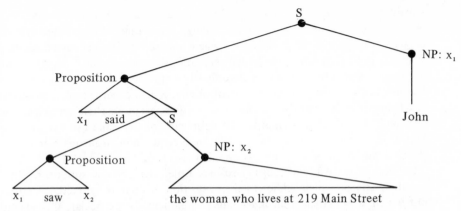

Figure 3 First reading of Sentence 1 (reproduced by permission of the publisher, with title added, from "Where Do Noun Phrases Come From?" by James D. McCawley; rest of credit same as for Figure 1)

McCawley's general conclusion is a succinct statement of the position held by many generative semanticists:

These considerations suggest that there is no natural breaking point between a "syntactic component" and a "semantic component" of a grammar such as the level of "deep structure" was envisioned to be in [*Aspects*] and imply that the burden of proof should be on those who assert that such a breaking point exists.[4]

A key element in McCawley's argument (as well as in those of other generative

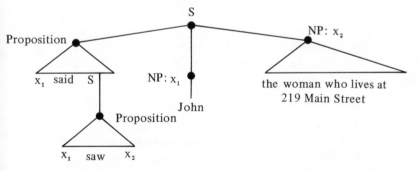

Figure 4 Second reading of Sentence 1 (reproduced by permission of the publisher, with title added, from "Where Do Noun Phrases Come From?" by James D. McCawley; rest of credit same as for Figure 1)

[4] "Where Do Noun Phrases Come From?" pp. 171–172. McCawley provides many additional examples in support of his position. Those that relate to pronominalization are particularly interesting. McCawley's basic argument has been expanded and tightened in several later publications. See, among others, "Interpretive Semantics Meets Frankenstein," the full citation for which is given in the Bibliography.

semanticists) is that no "natural" line can be drawn between syntax and semantics. (And it is for this reason, among others, that we have listed syntactic/semantic features in a single set when representing lexical items; see, for example, p. 95). In other words, the generative semanticists claim that there are *no* purely syntactic features of words—that, in fact, all so-called syntactic features actually have semantic content. Again, if this claim is true, it would be an argument in favor of the generative semanticist position. The claim is a strong one, and the question is empirical. If opponents of the claim can demonstrate that at least one "purely syntactic" feature is required in an adequate grammar, then this argument of the generative semanticists would be destroyed.

But the generative semanticists also have other arguments in support of their position, one of which relates to their rejection of "purely syntactic" features but which is nonetheless an independent argument. In particular, this second argument (which, we can note, gives the name to the "school") concerns the nature of the lexicon.

In standard theory, the lexicon consists of a finite number of lexical items, each defined by a set of phonological and syntactic/semantic features. These items can be inserted into any tree that conforms to the selectional restrictions which are part of the definition of the lexical item. In effect, each of these items is discrete. Although many items have features (for example, *male*) that also help define other items, there is no formal way—in the lexicon of standard theory—of indicating how various items are interrelated.

The generative semanticists believe that such an organization misses many possible generalizations about interrelationships among apparently quite different words, and, moreover, that these are generalizations which a normal speaker recognizes. The generative semanticists would, in effect, use transformations to derive many words that are phonologically unrelated (that is, they would derive "words" in the process of applying transformations that develop a deep semantic structure into a surface structure). By way of illustration, we can consider an example that has been used by McCawley, Postal, and others. For our purposes, however, we shall adapt the example so it relates to the sentence presented in Figure 1, which we can repeat as

Sentence 2 The man killed the woman.

The "standard representation" of this sentence is given in Figure 2.

First, consider the surface verb: *kill*. In the standard lexicon, this verb might be marked for the following semantic features (among others):

alive,　since that which is not alive cannot be killed.

cause,　since the act of killing is caused by an agent; contrast *die*, which may or may not be caused by an agent.

become,　since the act of killing involves a transition from one state ("being alive") to another state ("being dead").

In effect, the generative semanticists treat these "features" as separate "deep verbs." Moreover, they also classify tense and negation as "deep verbs." That is, many of the items that are classed as syntactic/semantic features in standard theory are, in generative semantics, treated as verbs. (In keeping with the practice of most generative semanticists, we shall use capital letters to represent these "deep verbs" on a propositional tree.)

The generative semanticists also believe that there are only three nonterminal categories: *S, NP,* and *V,* and, moreover, that these three categories correspond (approximately) to the three "form categories" of symbolic logic:

> *S* corresponds to the use of "sentence" in the terms "closed sentence" (= "proposition") and "open sentence" (= "propositional function"), *V* to "predicate" (taken as including "operator"), and *NP* to "argument."[5]

(Because of the close correspondence of these terms, they are sometimes used interchangeably on propositional trees.)

Figure 1, then, is actually a simplification of a deep propositional tree. For our purposes, we can represent this deeper tree as shown in Figure 5. In effect, this tree indicates that Sentence 2 consists of a proposition and two noun phrases which identify the indices of the proposition (that is, the noun phrases identify x_1 and x_2). The proposition, in turn, consists of a two-place predicate and two arguments, one for each place in the predicate. In the tree, the *V* node under "Proposition" represents the predicate, the two *NP* nodes represent the two arguments. In this sentence, the predicate is the "deep verb," *cause*; the first

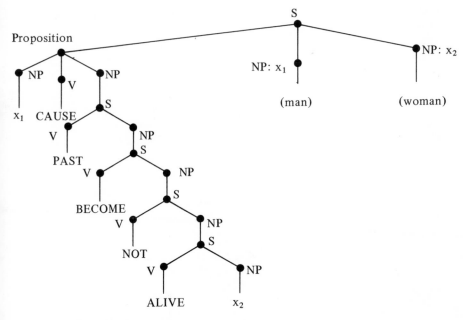

Figure 5   Deep semantic representation of Sentence 2

[5] McCawley, "Interpretive Semantics Meets Frankenstein," p. 292.

argument is an index, x_1; and the second argument is a sentence. (That is, the left-most *NP* of the proposition is rewritten as x_1; the *V* is rewritten as *cause*; and the right-most *NP* is rewritten as *S*.) This *S* expands to a series of propositional functions, each containing a one-place predicate (represented by a *V* node) and an argument (represented by a *NP* node). The argument of the "lowest" propositional function is an index: x_2. Through a series of transformations (known as **predicate raising**) we shall eventually produce a tree like the one shown in Figure 6. This tree indicates how "semantic pairings" (for example, *cause, past, become, not, alive*) are generated *on a tree* by transformations. Only after all these "predicates" are grouped together under the domination of a single predicate (that is, the highest *V* node) do we turn to something like a lexicon, and we do so only for the purpose of determining how to "pronounce"—or to "spell"—this set of predicates in English. Thus, in many cases the predicates of the generative semanticists are similar to the syntactic/semantic features of the standard theory.

Presumably, very similar trees could be constructed for any language. That is, the categorical rules are presumably identical for all languages. Moreover, all languages (presumably) have predicates that correspond to the English forms: *cause, past, become,* and so on. Thus, we could "speak" Sentence 2 in other languages if their lexicons contained entries corresponding to the semantic data represented in the predicate of Figure 5. (Naturally, we would also need to know the words for *man* and *woman,* which we have ignored in this example, and moreover, we would need to know the transformations that would arrange the words in an acceptable order.)

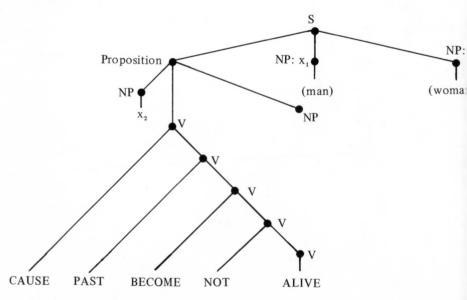

Figure 6 Tree after predicate-raising transformations

Notice also that we can easily expand Figures 5 and 6 so they would represent structures that underlie phonologically distinct verbs:

Sentence 3 The man murdered the woman.
Sentence 4 The man assassinated the woman.
Sentence 5 The man drowned the woman.

and so on. The derivation of these sentences would require only that we insert additional semantic information (that is, additional predicates) into the underlying structures given in Figures 5 and 6.

In sum, in the generative semantics model, the sets of semantic features are generated directly on the tree itself; in the interpretive semantics model, full sets of lexical items are inserted onto a tree and then combined ("interpreted") by projection rules. The result of each model—a pairing of sound and meaning—is the same, but the organization of the grammar that describes this pairing is (in the opinion of some linguists) significantly different for the two cases.

Morphemes

The word **morpheme** is derived from the Greek word *morphē*, which means "form." Morphemes are certainly a part of the formal—or syntactic—structure of language. Yet is is difficult to give a notional definition of the term. Linguists have debated a definition for more than 30 years, and they are still a long way from agreement. For our purposes, however, we can resort to an illustrative—rather than notional—definition. In particular, we can present several examples of English morphemes, and on the basis of these examples the reader can construct his own "working definition" of the term.

We know that languages are generally made up of individual words, which grammarians classify under the headings of "parts of speech." But not all parts of speech are complete words. In English, and in most other languages, there are in fact some parts of speech that are not complete words but that nonetheless occur again and again throughout the language. For example, there are many common affixes (that is, prefixes and suffixes) in English:

un- pre- re- -ly -ness -ish

In addition, there is a small class of suffixes known as **inflectional endings**; the following are the most important:

-s, -es   indicating plurality in most nouns
-'s, -s'   indicating the genitive case in most nouns
-s, -es   indicating the third person singular, present tense of most verbs
-ed   indicating either the past tense or the past participle of many verbs
-ing   indicating the gerund or present participle forms of verbs
-er, -est indicating, respectively, the comparative and superlative degrees of many adjectives.

All these affixes belong to a large class of items known as morphemes. In writing, linguists sometimes enclose morphemes within braces:

$\{un\text{-}\}$ $\{pre\text{-}\}$ $\{\text{-}ly\}$ $\{\text{-}ness\}$ $\{\text{-}s\}$ $\{\text{-}ed\}$

But the category of morphemes contains other things in addition to affixes. As we have just noted, there is an {-s} morpheme on many nouns in English, which serves the syntactic function of indicating plurality. Yet the feature of plurality may also be indicated in other ways; for example, by an -es (as in *dresses*), by an -en (as in *oxen*), by changing the vowel in the middle of the word (as in the change from *man* to *men*), and sometimes by nothing at all (as in *sheep*, which can be either singular or plural).

In order to have a convenient means of discussing these various ways of indicating plurality, many linguists use the term **plural morpheme** which, by definition, is the element that, when added to the singular form of a noun, changes that noun into the plural form, whatever it may be.

And there are other morphemes similar to the plural morpheme. For example, in discussing verbs, linguists sometimes speak of the **past participle morpheme**, which is the element that, when added to the base form of the verb, produces the past participle form, whatever it may be. With regular verbs, the past participle morpheme takes the form of an -ed added to the verb base. If we add the past participle morpheme to the regular verb *walk*, we produce *walked*. If, on the other hand, we add the past participle morpheme to such irregular verbs as *eat* and *drive*, then we produce the forms *eaten* and *driven*. And if we add the past participle morpheme to verbs such as *sing* and *swim*, then we produce *sung* and *swum*.

The following symbols have sometimes been used by linguists to indicate various morphemes:

$\{Z_1\}$ the **agreement morpheme**, which is generally indicated by the inflectional ending -s on the third-person singular, present tense, of verbs (the subscript "1" differentiates this morpheme from the one that indicates plurality in nouns)

$\{-en\}$ the **past participle morpheme**

$\{Past\}$ the **past tense morpheme**

$\{-ing\}$ the **present participle morpheme**

$\{Z_2\}$ the **plural morpheme**

$\{Z_3\}$ the **genitive morpheme**

These, then, are generalized morphemes. It is sometimes useful, however, to indicate the particular form that any generalized morpheme may take in a given instance. For example, the plural morpheme $\{Z_2\}$ may take any of the following forms in a particular word:

$\{-s\}$ $\{-es\}$ $\{-en\}$ $-\emptyset$

(The $\emptyset$ is called a **zero morph**.) These varieties of the plural morpheme are known technically as **allomorphs**.

But morphemes are more than affixes. In fact, every word in English contains at least one morpheme. That is, individual words such as *boy* and *walk* are morphemes, and suffixes such as -s and -ed are also morphemes. A word such as *boys*, therefore, contains *two* morphemes: {*boy*}, which can also stand alone and is therefore called a **free morpheme**; and $\{-s\}$, which must be joined to a word and is therefore called a **bound morpheme**. In a word such as *walked*, there are also two morphemes: $\{walk\}$, a free morpheme; and $\{-ed\}$, a bound morpheme. And in a word such as *childishly*, there are three morphemes: $\{child\}$, a free morpheme; $\{-ish-\}$, a bound morpheme; and $\{-ly\}$, another bound morpheme.

We can sum up these initial illustrations by looking at a word that contains five morphemes: *ungentlemanliness*. The following morphemes are included:

1. The negative prefix morpheme $\{un-\}$, a bound morpheme
2. a free morpheme $\{gentle\}$
3. a second free morpheme $\{man\}$
4. a second bound morpheme $\{-li-\}$, which is an allomorph of the morpheme $\{-ly\}$
5. a third bound morpheme $\{-ness\}$, which can be called a **nominalization morpheme**

Finally, we must note that not all morphemes are indicated by particular sounds or varieties of spelling. We have, in fact, already noted the existence of a zero morph, which is an allomorph of $\{Z_2\}$ and occurs with such words as *sheep* and *moose*. But there are also other kinds of morphemes that are not indicated in a sentence by variations in spelling. There is a difference, for example, between the following sentences:

Sentence 1a John has eaten the snails.
Sentence 1b John *has* eaten the snails.

The second sentence is more emphatic, and we indicate this difference—in print—with italics and—in speech—by a combination of heavy accent and rising inflection on the auxiliary verb. We can also say that the second sentence contains the **emphatic morpheme** (sometimes also called the **affirmative morpheme**). The morpheme is indicated symbolically by $\{Emph\}$.

The **interrogative morpheme** is similar to the emphatic morpheme, since it is not always indicated in a sentence by a variation in spelling and sometimes not even by a variation in word order. Thus, we can have the question:

Sentence 2a Has John eaten the snails?

which is called a yes/no question because it requires a "yes" or "no" answer. But we can also have a variant of the yes/no question, called an echo question, by taking a simple statement and making the voice rise at the end:

Sentence 2b John has eaten the snails?

And we can ask what linguists call a tag question:

Sentence 2c John has eaten the snails, hasn't he?

The symbolic representation of each of these questions contains an interrogative morpheme, generally represented by $\{Q\}$.

We may sum up the major points concerning morphemes both by way of review and for convenience of reference:

1. Morphemes are regularly recurring features of English.
2. Every word contains at least one morpheme and may contain several.
3. There are two kinds of morphemes: bound and free.[1]
4. A basic morpheme, such as the plural morpheme, may be represented in spelling or pronunciation in more than one way; these variant ways are called allomorphs of the basic morpheme.

[1] Not all English words contain a free morpheme. Some, like *conceive, deceive, perceive,* and *receive,* are made up of two bound morphemes.

Bibliography

The bibliography, selective as it is, is in two parts. Part 1 includes some standard, nontransformational works on grammar and English grammar. Part 2 comprises recent work in transformational grammar, especially those items referred to in the text. Although some of these articles and books are quite technical, the reader who has mastered this book should be able to understand them. Especially important items are prefixed with an asterisk.

Readers interested in current disputes in transformational grammar and allied fields will want to consult the important periodicals—*Foundations of Language, Journal of Linguistics, Language,* and *Linguistic Inquiry*—and, for a complete review of work through 1968, Stockwell (1969).

1 Nontransformational Studies

*Bloomfield, Leonard. 1933. *Language.* New York: Holt, Rinehart and Winston.
Cook, Walter A., S.J. 1969. *Introduction to Tagmemic Analysis.* New York: Holt, Rinehart and Winston.
Curme, George Oliver. 1931. *Syntax.* Boston: D. C. Heath.
Curme, George Oliver. 1935. *Parts of Speech and Accidence.* Boston: D. C. Heath.
Francis, W. Nelson. 1958. *The Structure of American English.* New York: Ronald Press.
Fries, Charles Carpenter. 1940. *American English.* New York: Appleton-Century-Crofts.
*Fries, Charles Carpenter. 1952. *The Structure of English.* New York: Harcourt Brace Jovanovich.
Garvin, Paul O., ed. 1964. *A Prague School Reader on Esthetics, Literary Structure, and Style.* Washington, D.C.: Georgetown University Press.
Gleason, H. A., Jr. 1965. *Linguistics and English Grammar.* New York: Holt, Rinehart and Winston.

Hamp, Eric P., Fred W. Householder, and Robert P. Austerlitz, eds. 1966. *Readings in Linguistics II.* Chicago: University of Chicago Press.

Havránek, Bohuslav. 1964. "The Functional Differentiation of the Standard Language." In Garvin (1964, pp. 3-16).

Hill, Archibald A. 1958. *Introduction to Linguistic Structures.* New York: Harcourt Brace Jovanovich.

Jespersen, Otto. 1909-1949. *A Modern English Grammar on Historical Principles,* 7 vols. Copenhagen: Einar Munksgaard.

Long, R. B. 1961. *The Sentence and Its Parts.* Chicago: University of Chicago Press.

Mukařovský, Jan. 1964. "Standard Language and Poetic Language." In Garvin (1964, pp. 17-30). Also in Freeman (1970, pp. 40-56).

Pike, Kenneth L. 1967. *Language in Relation to a Unified Theory of the Structure of Human Behavior.* The Hague: Mouton.

Roberts, Paul. 1956. *Patterns of English.* New York: Harcourt Brace Jovanovich.

*Sapir, Edward. 1921. *Language: An Introduction to the Study of Speech.* New York: Harcourt Brace Jovanovich.

*Saussure, Ferdinand de. 1959. *Course in General Linguistics,* trans. by Wade Baskin. New York: Philosophical Library.

Sledd, James. 1959. *A Short Introduction to English Grammar.* Chicago: Scott, Foresman.

Sweet, Henry. 1891, 1898. *A New English Grammar,* Part I, 1891; Part II, 1898. London: Clarendon Press.

*Trager, George L., and Henry Lee Smith, Jr. 1951. *An Outline of English Structure.* (Identical with *Studies in Linguistics: Occasional Papers 3*).

Whitehall, Harold. 1956. *Structural Essentials of English.* New York: Harcourt Brace Jovanovich.

*Whorf, Benjamin Lee. 1956. *Language, Thought, and Reality,* John B. Carroll, ed. Cambridge, Mass.: M.I.T. Press.

Zandvoort, R. W. 1957. *A Handbook of English Grammar.* London: Longmans, Green.

2 Transformational Studies

Akmajiian, Adrian. 1970. "On Deriving Cleft Sentences from Pseudo-Cleft Sentences." *Linguistic Inquiry* 1:149-168.

Anderson, John. 1968. "On the Status of Lexical Formatives." *Foundations of Language* 4:308-318.

Anastasiow, Nicholas. 1971. *Oral Language: Expression of Thought.* Newark, Del: The International Reading Association.

Bach, Emmon. 1964. *An Introduction to Transformational Grammars.* New York: Holt, Rinehart and Winston.

Bach, Emmon. 1967. *"Have* and *Be* in English Syntax." *Language* 43:462-485.

Bach, Emmon. 1968. "Nouns and Noun-Phrases." In Bach and Harms (1968, pp. 90-122).

Bach, Emmon, and Robert T. Harms, eds. 1968. *Universals in Linguistic Theory.* New York: Holt, Rinehart and Winston.

Blake, Frank. 1930. "A Semantic Analysis of Case." *Curme Volume of Linguistic Studies* (identical with *Language Monograph* No. 7), James Taft, Hatfield, Werner Leopold, and A. J. Friedrich Ziegelschmid, eds. Baltimore: Waverly Press, pp. 34–49.

Cassidy, Frederick G. 1937. "'Case' in Modern English." *Language* 13:240–245.

*Chomsky, Noam. 1957. *Syntactic Structures.* The Hague: Mouton.

Chomsky, Noam. 1962. "The Logical Basis of Linguistic Theory." *Proceedings of the Ninth International Congress of Linguists,* Horace G. Lunt, ed. The Hague: Mouton.

Chomsky, Noam. 1964. "Current Issues in Linguistic Theory." In Fodor and Katz (1964, pp. 50–118).

*Chomsky, Noam. 1965. *Aspects of the Theory of Syntax* Cambridge, Mass.: M.I.T. Press.

Chomsky, Noam. 1966. *Cartesian Linguistics.* New York: Harper & Row.

Chomsky, Noam. 1967. "The Formal Nature of Language." In *Biological Foundations of Language,* E. H. Lenneberg, ed. New York: Wiley, pp. 397–442.

*Chomsky, Noam. 1968. "Remarks on Nominalization." In Jacobs and Rosenbaum (1970, pp. 184–222).

*Chomsky, Noam. 1969. "Deep Structure, Surface Structure, and Semantic Interpretation." In Jakobovits and Steinberg (1971, pp. 183–216).

Chomsky, Noam. 1971. *Problems of Knowledge and Freedom.* New York: Pantheon.

Chomsky, Noam, and Morris Halle. 1968. *The Sound Pattern of English.* New York: Harper & Row.

Dougherty, Ray. 1969. "An Interpretive Theory of Pronominal Reference." *Foundations of Language* 5:488–519.

Fillmore, Charles J. 1963. "The Position of Embedding Transformations in a Grammar." *Word* 19:208–231.

Fillmore, Charles J. 1966. "Deictic Categories in the Semantics of 'Come'." *Foundations of Language* 2:219–227.

Fillmore, Charles J. 1967. "On the Syntax of Preverbs." *Glossa* 1:91–125.

*Fillmore, Charles J. 1968. "The Case for Case." In Bach and Harms (1968, pp. 1–90).

Fillmore, Charles J., and D. Terence Langendoen, eds. 1971. *Studies in Linguistic Semantics.* New York: Holt, Rinehart and Winston.

Fodor, J., and M. Garrett. 1967. "Some Reflections on Competence and Performance." *Psycholinguistics Papers,* J. Lyons and R. J. Wales, eds. Edinburgh: Edinburgh University Press, pp. 135–154.

*Fodor, Jerry, and Jerrold J. Katz, eds. 1964. *The Structure of Language.* Englewood Cliffs, N.J.: Prentice-Hall.

Fraser, Bruce. 1970. "Idioms Within a Transformational Grammar." *Foundations of Language* 6:22–42.

*Freeman, Donald C., ed. 1970. *Linguistics and Literary Style.* New York: Holt, Rinehart and Winston.

Garcia, E., 1967. "Auxiliaries and the Criterion of Simplicity." *Language* 43: 853–870.

Gleitman, Lila. 1965. "Coordinating Conjunctions in English." *Language* 51: 260–293. Reprinted in Reibel and Schane (1969, pp. 80–112).

Gruber, Jeffrey. 1967. "Topicalization in Child Language." *Foundations of Language* 3:37–65.

Halle, Morris. 1962. "Phonology in Generative Grammar." *Word* 18:54–72. Reprinted in Fodor and Katz (1964, pp. 324–333).

Halliday, Michael A. K. 1966. "Some Notes on 'Deep' Grammar." *Journal of Linguistics* 2:55–67.

Hancock, R. 1960. "Presuppositions." *The Philosophical Quarterly* 10:73–78.

Hockett, Charles. 1968. *The State of the Art.* The Hague: Mouton.

Jackendorf, Ray S. 1969. "An Interpretive Theory of Negation." *Foundations of Language* 5:218–241.

Jacobs, Roderick A., and Peter S. Rosenbaum. 1968. *English Transformational Grammar.* Lexington, Mass.: Xerox College Publishing.

*Jacobs, Roderick, and Peter Rosenbaum, eds. 1970. *Readings in English Transformational Grammar.* Lexington, Mass.: Xerox College Publishing.

Jakobovits, Leon A., and Danny D. Steinberg, eds. 1971. *Semantics.* Cambridge: Cambridge University Press.

Katz, Jerrold J. 1964. "Analyticity and Contradiction in Natural Language." In Fodor and Katz (1964, pp. 519–543).

Katz, Jerrold J. 1966. *The Philosophy of Language.* New York: Harper & Row.

Katz, Jerrold J. 1970, "Interpretative Semantics vs. Generative Semantics." *Foundations of Language* 6:220–59.

Katz, Jerrold J. 1972. *Semantic Theory.* New York: Harper & Row.

*Katz, Jerrold J., and Jerry Fodor. 1963. "The Structure of a Semantic Theory." *Language* 39: 170–210. Reprinted in Fodor and Katz (1964, pp. 479–518).

*Katz, Jerrold J., and Paul M. Postal. 1964. *An Integrated Theory of Linguistic Descriptions.* Cambridge, Mass.: M.I.T. Press.

Kiparsky, Paul. 1968. "Tense and Mood in Indo-European Syntax." *Foundations of Language* 4:30–57.

Klima, Edward S. "Negation in English." In Fodor and Katz (1964, pp. 246–323).

Koutsoudas, Andreas. 1966. *Writing Transformational Grammars.* New York: McGraw-Hill.

Kuhn, Thomas S. 1970. *The Structure of Scientific Revolutions,* 2nd ed. Chicago: University of Chicago Press.

Labov, William. 1963. "The Social Motivation of a Sound Change." *Word* 19:273–309.

Labov, William. 1965. "On the Mechanism of Linguistic Change." *Report of the Sixteenth Annual Round Table Meeting on Linguistics and Language Studies* (identical with *Georgetown University Monograph Series on Languages and Linguistics* 18), Charles W. Kreidler, ed. Washington, D.C.: Georgetown University Press, pp. 91–114.

Labov, William. 1970. *The Study of Nonstandard English.* Urbana, Ill.: National Council of Teachers of English.

Lakoff, George. 1968. "Instrumental Adverbs and the Concept of Deep Structure." *Foundations of Language* 4:4–29.

*Lakoff, George. 1969. "On Generative Semantics." In Jakobovits and Steinberg (1971, pp. 232–296).

Lakoff, George. 1970. *Irregularity in Syntax.* New York: Holt, Rinehart and Winston.

Lakoff, Robin. 1969. "Some Reasons Why There Can't Be Any *Some-Any* Rule." *Language* 45:608–615.

Langendoen, D. Terence. 1969. *The Study of Syntax.* New York: Holt, Rinehart and Winston.

Lees, Robert B. 1960. *A Grammar of English Nominalizations.* Indiana University Research Center in Anthropology, Folklore, and Linguistics, Publication 12 (identical with *International Journal of American Linguistics,* XXVI, No. 3, Part II). Bloomington, Ind.

Lees, Robert B. 1962. "Discussion." *Report on the Eleventh Annual Round Table Meeting on Linguistics and Language Studies,* Bernard Choseed, ed. Washington, D.C.: Georgetown University Press.

Lees, Robert B., and Edward Klima. 1963. "Rules for English Pronominalization," *Language* 39:17–29.

McCawley, James D. 1968a. "Concerning the Base Component of a Transformational Grammar." *Foundations of Language* 4:243–269.

*McCawley, James D. 1968b. "The Role of Semantics in Grammar." In Bach and Harms (1968, pp. 125–169).

McCawley, James D. 1968c. "Where Do Noun Phrases Come From?" In Jacobs and Rosenbaum (1970, pp. 166–183).

McCawley, James D. 1970. "English as a VSO Language." *Language* 46:286–299.

McCawley, James D. 1971a. "Interpretive Semantics Meets Frankenstein." *Foundations of Language* 7:285–96.

McCawley, James D. 1971b. "Tense and Time Reference in English." In Fillmore and Langendoen (1971, pp. 97–113).

McNeill, David. 1966. "Developmental Psycholinguistics." *The Genesis of Language,* Frank Smith and George A. Miller, eds. Cambridge, Mass.: M.I.T. Press, pp. 15–84.

Montague, Richard. 1969. "Presupposing." *The Philosophical Quarterly* 19: 98–110.

Partee, Barbara H. 1970. "Negation, Conjunction and Quantifiers: Syntax vs. Semantics." *Foundations of Language* 6:153–165.

Perlmutter, David, and John R. Ross. 1970. "Relative Clauses with Split Antecedents." *Linguistic Inquiry* 1:350.

Postal, Paul M. 1966a. "On So-Called 'Pronouns' in English." *Report of the Seventeenth Annual Round Table Meeting on Linguistics and Language Studies* (identical with *Georgetown University Monograph Series on Languages and Linguistics* 19), Francis P. Dinneen, S.J., ed. Washington, D.C., pp. 177–206. Also in Reibel and Schane (1969, pp. 201–24).

Postal, Paul M. 1966b. "A Note on 'Understood Transitively'." *International Journal of American Linguistics* 32.1:90–93.

Postal, Paul M. 1971. *Cross-Over Phenomena.* New York: Holt, Rinehart and Winston.

*Reibel, David A., and Sanford A. Schane, eds. 1969. *Modern Studies in English*. Englewood Cliffs, N.J. Prentice-Hall.

Rosenbaum, Peter. 1967. *The Grammar of English Predicate Complement Constructions*. Cambridge, Mass.: M.I.T. Press.

Ross, John R. 1967a. "On the Cyclic Nature of English Pronominalization." *To Honor Roman Jakobson*, III, 1669–1682. The Hague: Mouton.

Ross, John R. 1967b. "Auxiliaries as Main Verbs." In *The Structure and Psychology of Language,* Thomas G. Bever and William Weksel, eds. New York: Holt, Rinehart and Winston.

Ross, John R. 1969. "Adjectives as Noun Phrases." In Reibel and Schane (1969, pp. 352–360).

Searle, John. 1969. *Speech Acts.* Cambridge: Cambridge University Press.

Sebeok, Thomas, Ed. 1966. *Current Trends in Linguistics,* Vol. III. The Hague: Mouton.

Smith, Carlota S. 1964. "Determiners and Relative Clauses in a Generative Grammar of English." *Language* 40:37–52.

*Stockwell, Robert et al. 1969. *Integration of Transformational Theories on English Syntax.* Los Angeles: UCLA. (Reprinted in slightly condensed form as *The Major Syntactic Structures of English.* New York: Holt, Rinehart and Winston, 1973.)

Thorne, James P. 1966. "English Imperatives." *Journal of Linguistics* 2:69–78.

Weinreich, Uriel. 1966. "Explorations in Semantic Theory." In Sebeok (1966, pp. 395–477).

Ziff, Paul. 1965. "What an Adequate Grammar Can't Do." *Foundations of Language* 1:5–13.

Index